The Economics and Management of Small Business

Despite the seemingly relentless march of the multinationals, small businesses continue to thrive across the globe and form a vital part of all successful economies.

This book provides an international perspective on this important topic, and includes a wealth of data from a range of countries in the European Union, North America, East Asia and developing countries. The analysis of the historical role of small firms in economic development throughout the world demonstrates how small businesses contribute to the mobilisation and deployment of resources for growth and technical advance.

This book challenges much conventional thinking on the subject and contains examples from the over 40 countries in which the author has worked or studied. Students of small business and entrepreneurship will find Graham Bannock's accessible writing style to be very helpful in gaining a good understanding of this important field.

Graham Bannock is a consultant and co-author of the best-selling *Penguin Dictionary of Economics*.

The Economics and Management of Small Business

An international perspective

Graham Bannock

Routledge
Taylor & Francis Group

LONDON AND NEW YORK

First published 2005
by Routledge
2 Park Square, Milton Park, Abingdon, Oxon OX14 4RN

Simultaneously published in the USA and Canada
by Routledge
270 Madison Ave, New York, NY 10016

Routledge is an imprint of the Taylor & Francis Group

Typeset in Times New Roman by
BOOK NOW Ltd
Printed and bound in Great Britain by
The Cromwell Press, Trowbridge, Wiltshire

British Library Cataloguing in Publication Data
A catalogue record for this book is available from the British Library

Library of Congress Cataloging in Publication Data
A catalog record for this book has been requested

ISBN 0–415–33666–X (hbk)
ISBN 0–415–33667–8 (pbk)

Contents

Preface

This book is about the economics of small and medium-sized enterprises (SMEs); not only their micro-aspects but also their larger macroeconomic role, which has achieved little attention until quite recently. The word 'management' is included in the title because the author believes that it is impossible to understand small firms without appreciating the nature of the managerial imperatives, the constraints and motivations under which their business owners operate. It is not a guide to managing a small firm, nor is it about how entrepreneurship can be nurtured, though it should be of some value to those interested in these things. In particular, it should help more people to understand that the management of small firms is quite different in many respects from that of large firms.

Small business economics is, or should be, central to all business education and is an important element in undergraduate and postgraduate work in a wide range of social studies courses, from economics to sociology and even technology. The book provides an introduction to the economic literature and concepts in small business economics and policy, as far as possible in plain language.

The book is unusual in its field in that it is global in scope. This is because the author has learned that, although often different in degree, small business issues are of the same kind everywhere, from Texas to Tokyo to Timbuktu. It is not directly about the process of globalisation as such, but it does draw illustrations from many of the 40 countries in which the author has worked in his later career as an economic consultant. It is hoped that the findings in the book will be useful to policymakers concerned with small business in national governments and international institutions in both advanced and developing countries.

Small business is now a large field of study, and this book does not cover all aspects of it: for example, there is little about female or minority enterprise, co-operatives, networking, regional issues, supply chains, franchising and much else.

There are several themes running through the book, in addition to the distinctive nature of small business management and the global similarities in the key issues, which have already been mentioned. One is that despite much lip service, the economic and social role of small business has been underestimated: it is in fact central in all market economies. Another theme is that although good government is essential for the provision of an environment in which small firms can thrive, there are severe limitations on the effectiveness of most official support for small business, and indeed doubt about the necessity for it. Finally, the book has been written in the conviction that there are many myths about small firms, unfounded on fact or academic research.

Chapter 1 defines SMEs and outlines some of the considerations involved in comparing official SME statistics. Chapter 2 gives a profile of small business, mainly but not entirely in a UK context, and draws attention to the rich variety of small firm experience. Chapter 3 attempts to sketch how small firms fit into the wider economic picture and gives a little of the history of the subject. Chapter 4 discusses the constraints facing small firms from the points of view of business owners and outside observers, with special reference to finance. Chapter 5 discusses the impact of regulation and taxation on SMEs, and Chapter 6, entrepreneurship, especially in growth companies. Chapters 7 and 8 deal with government policies towards small firms. Chapter 9 continues with the subject of policy, this time in developing and transition countries, with a view of the business environment, the contribution of SMEs to development and the roles of governments and international donors in these countries. Chapter 10 concludes with a summary of some of the findings of the book, some policy prescriptions and a brief perspective on the future outlook for small firms around the world.

My debts to other authors are acknowledged in the text and in the bibliography, but in the interests of readability I have not attempted to document every point. I wish to acknowledge the valuable experience of working with my former colleagues at the Economists' Advisory Group, Bannock Consulting and their clients and in particular, help from Matthew Gamser, an authority on small business in the developing world. I have discussed some of the ideas in this book with several British academics, including Martin Binks, Jim Curran, Alan Gibb, Colin Gray and John Stanworth, over many years, as I have with Thomas A. Gray, former Chief Economist of the Small Business Administration (SBA); Dr Gunter Kayser of the *Institut für Mittelstandsforschung*; Yassi Hamada of Sapporo University; and Hiroshi Teraoka of Chukyo University. The UK Department for International Development (DFID), the Organisation for Economic Co-operation and Development (OECD), the European Commission and the World Bank have provided me with invaluable opportunities to carry out consulting assignments, and I have learned much from their officials. Various people in small business representative bodies, including Denny Dennis of the National Federation of International Business (NFIB), Dr Bernard Juby of the Federation of Small Businesses (FSB), and John Bulloch and Stan Mendham, the last two being founders, respectively, of the Canadian Federation of Independent Business and the Forum of Private

Business, have given me insights into the small firms scene. Inspiration and advice on broader economic issues from two distinguished friends, Alan Peacock and Angus Maddison, also deserve acknowledgement, as do three anonymous referees who made useful comments on the original plan of the book. Alan and Angus, as well as John Stanworth, Denny Dennis and Matthew Gamser, were kind enough to read and comment on parts of the book. Finally, thanks to Alex Allan for sensitive help with messy manuscripts. The author alone is, of course, responsible for the views expressed.

Graham Bannock
March 2004

Abbreviations and acronyms

3i	Investors in Industry (formerly ICFC, q.v.)
AIM	Alternative investment market
ANVAR	Agence Nationale pour la Valorisation de la Récherche
BCC	British Chambers of Commerce
BDS	Business development services
BES	Business expansion scheme
BIA	Business impact assessment (EU)
BIC	Business Information Center (US)
BIC	Business Information Centre (EU)
BLO	Business link operators (UK)
BRTF	Better regulation task force
BSC	Business support centres
BTI	British Trade International
BVMA	Business Volunteer Mentoring Association (UK)
CBI	Confederation of British Industries
CEB	Central and Eastern Europe and the Baltic
CEE	Central and Eastern European
CEO	Chief executive officer
CGPME	Confédération Générale des Petites et Moyennes Entreprises
Chaebol	Large conglomerate (Korea)
COSA	Commission for Administrative Simplification (France)
CSBRC	Cambridge Small Business Research Centre
CVC	Corporate venture capital
D&B	Dun & Bradstreet
DAB	Deutsche Ausgleichsbank
DEC	Digital Equipment Corporation
DFID	Department for International Development (UK)
DTI	Department for Trade and Industry (UK)
EAS	Enterprise allowance scheme (UK)
EASDAQ	European Association of Securities Dealers Automated Quotation System
EBRD	European Bank for Reconstruction and Development
EC	European Commission

ECB	European Central Bank
EDU	Enterprise and Deregulation Unit (UK) *see* RIU
EEA	European Economic Area
EIF	European Investment Fund
EIMI	Euler International Mathematical Institute
EIMS	European Innovation Monitoring System
EIS	Enterprise investment scheme (UK)
EMU	European Monetary Union
EOMMEX	Hellenic Organization of Small Medium Sized Enterprises (Greece)
ENSR	European Network for SME Research
EPZ	Export processing zone
ERISA	Employee Retirement Income Security Act (US)
ESAP	Economic structural adjustment program (World Bank)
ESBA	European Small Business Alliance
EU	European Union
EU-14	European Union members excluding Luxembourg
EU-15	European Union members prior to enlargement
Europe-19	European Union members plus Iceland, Liechtenstein, Norway and Switzerland
EUROSTAT	Statistical Office of the European Communities
EVCA	European Venture Capital Association
EZ	Enterprise zone
FCPI	Fonds Commun Placement pour l'Innovation
FDI	Foreign direct investment
FRFA	Final regulatory flexibility analysis (US)
FSA	Financial Services Authority (UK)
FSB	Federation of Small Businesses
FY	Fiscal year
G8	Group of Eight (Canada, France, Germany, Italy, Japan, Russia, United Kingdom, United States)
GDP	Gross domestic product
GEM	Global Enterprise Monitor
GSP	Growth and Stability Pact (EU)
HRD	Human resource development
IAPMEI	The Institute for the Support of Small and Medium-sized Enterprises (Portugal)
IBRD	International Bank for Reconstruction and Development (World Bank)
ICFC	Industrial and Commercial Finance Corporation *see* 3i
IfM	*Institut für Mittelstandsforschung*
ILO	International Labour Organisation
IMF	International Monetary Fund
IMPI	Institute of Small & Medium-sized Industrial Enterprises (Spain)

IPO	Initial public offering
IPR	Intellectual property rights
IRC	Innovation relay centres (EU)
IRFA	Initial regulatory flexibility analysis (US)
IRR	Internal rate of return
IT	Information technology
JASMEC	Japan Small and Medium Enterprise Corporation
JB	*Berliner Industriebank*
JV	Joint venture
KfW	*Kreditanstalt für Wiederaufbau*
Land (pl. Länder)	Unit of local government (Germany)
LDC	Less developed country/Least developed country
LEAs	Local enterprise agencies (UK)
LFS	Labour Force Survey (UK)
LGS	Loan guarantee scheme
LLP	Limited liability partnership
MES	Minimum efficient scale
MITI	Ministry of International Trade and Industry (Japan)
MNC	Multinational corporation
MSC	Manpower Services Commission (UK)
MSE	Micro- and small enterprise
NAO	National Audit Office (UK)
NASDAQ	National Association of Securities Dealers Automated Quotation System (US)
NFIB	National Federation of Independent Business (US)
NGO	Non-governmental organisation
NIC	Newly industrialised country
NICs	National Insurance Contributions
NSSBF	National Survey of Small Business Finances (US)
NTBF	New technology-based firm
NVCA	National Venture Capital Association (US)
NYSE	New York Stock Exchange
ODA	Oversees Development Administration
OECD	Organisation for Economic Co-operation and Development
OFT	Office of Fair Trading (UK)
OMB	Office of Management and Budget (US)
ONS	Office of National Statistics (UK)
PAED	Polish Agency for Enterprise Development (Poland)
PBA	Personal business adviser
P/E	Profit/Earnings, Price/earnings
PLC	Public limited company
PPPs	Purchasing power parities
R&D	Research and development
RDB	Regional Development Bank

RIA	Regulatory impact assessment
RIU	Regulatory impact unit
SBA	Small Business Association (Hungary)
SBA	Small Business Agency (US)
SBC	Small Business Council
SBDB	Small business database (US)
SBDC	Small Business Development Center (US)
SBIC	Small Business Investment Companies (US)
SBIR	Small Business Innovation Research (program) (US)
SBRC	The Small Business Resource Center
SBRT	Small Business Research Trust (UK)
SBS	Small Business Service (UK)
SCF	Survey of Consumer Finances (US)
SCORE	Service Corps of Retired Executives (US)
SDS	Scientific Data Systems
SEE	South-eastern Europe
SF	Small firm (UK)
SFLGS	Small Firms Loan Guarantee Scheme (UK)
SFS	Small Firms Service (UK)
SIC	Standard Industrial Classification
SMART	Small Firms Merit Award for Research and Technology
SMEA	Small and Medium Enterprise Agency (Japan)
SME	Small and medium-sized enterprise
SSBIC	Specialized Small Business Investment Company (US)
SSE	Small-scale enterprise
STTR	Small Business Technology Transfer (program) (US)
TBF	Technology-based firm
TBA	Total Entrepreneurial Activity Index
TEC	Training and Enterprise Council (UK)
TFP	Total factor productivity
TNC	Transnational corporation
USM	Unlisted securities market
VAT	Value added tax
VCT	Venture capital trust (UK)

1 Defining and counting small firms

Definition

How you define 'small business' is not an issue of great importance in the economics of the subject, although it raises interesting questions, and at least one book has been entirely devoted to the subject (HERTZ 1982). The essential point is that 'small' is a relative, not an absolute concept and where the line is drawn in the continuum of businesses from 'momma and poppa' shops to General Motors is inevitably arbitrary.

The reasons why people are interested in small business have to do with the juxtaposition of its perceived desirability and vulnerability. Small and medium-sized enterprises (SMEs) are desirable because they promote competition and employment and because a few innovate and grow into large firms that potentially generate even more of these things. There is more: starting a small business can be a means for an individual to achieve independence and self-expression and even wealth; and small firms serve wider, and perhaps less well understood social purposes – for example, by recycling local expenditure and savings into communities in ways that large firms may not, or by keeping streets alive at night and thus helping to reduce crime (see JACOBS 1961). The presence of SMEs also helps to avoid an overconcentration of political and economic power, a role traditionally greatly valued in the United States (BRUCHEY 1980; BUNZEL 1962).

The vulnerability of small firms arises virtually by definition from the small scale of their human and financial resources. Hundreds of thousands of firms open and close each year in the major countries, the vast majority of them very small. Businesses close for a variety of reasons and, as we explain in Chapter 2, starting a small firm can be a fairly risky thing to do. Certainly, the smaller and younger the firm, the more likely it is to close: about two-thirds of closures take place within three years of start-up. Evidence of failure is evident enough on city streets, where hopeful entrepreneurs spend money on fitting out new small shops and restaurants only to close again, perhaps their capital exhausted, when the firm cannot make money. These, however, are only the more visible signs of the vast 'churning' that goes on all the time in the business population. This churning comprises a large variety of experience, from people dropping out from employment, perhaps to do bed and breakfast from a new and cheaper home in the country, to new well-planned and funded manufacturing businesses and the kind of person that closes or sells out a firm to retire after thirty years of ups and downs, but nonetheless triumphant survival.

One approach to defining the small firm is to focus specifically on the features which distinguish the small firm from the (obviously) big firm. The Committee of Inquiry on Small Firms, chaired by the late John Bolton (BOLTON 1971) identified three characteristics in its economic definition of a small firm:[1]

- A *small market share*, that is not large enough to influence national prices or quantities. (Even though a village shop may be the only one, its prices cannot get too far out of line from those of major national retailers in the nearest town, even though people will pay something for local convenience.)
- *Managed in a personalised way*: the owners actively participate in all aspects of the business, unlike in a large firm where the shareholders and management are usually almost entirely separate.[2]
- *Independence or the exercise of ultimate management responsibility*. A small subsidiary of a large firm which has a head office to report to does not share this characteristic.

These three characteristics are to be found in the vast majority of all businesses (and, therefore, most businesses are small) but the economic definition is of no use for statistical purposes since business statistics are not classified in terms of market share, owner-management and independence. For this and other reasons, small firms are usually defined in terms of numbers employed. There is a difficulty here, in that in the employment dimension, a threshold that seems appropriate to define a 'small firm' in one activity may not be appropriate for another. For example, a manufacturing enterprise employing fewer than 250 people could be considered 'small', while a retail organisation with 250 employees and perhaps 10 or 15 branches is clearly quite a large firm, relatively speaking. However, employment numbers are generally superior to other measures of firm size as the data are easily collected (every SME owner knows how many people are employed); they are not 'sensitive' like turnover, nor are they affected by inflation.

Governments, for simplicity, tend to use one definition for statistical purposes and other, sectoral or asset- or turnover-based definitions for specific policy purposes. The European Commission and many member states, including the UK, define SMEs as those with fewer than 250 employees.[3] Other countries use other thresholds for statistical purposes: the United States uses 499 employees as the overall threshold for large firms. Japan uses different thresholds for manufacturing (299 employees), whole-sale distribution (99 employees) and retail distribution and other services (49 employees).

For policy implementation, as distinct from statistical purposes (for example, in determining eligibility for subsidised loans), official definitions are usually different and try to take into account the fact that the concept of what is 'small' must vary between different activities. The Bolton Committee, for the purposes of its Inquiry, came up with small firm definitions for nine different activities. The Small Business Administration (SBA) in the United States, using the wide discretion under the Small Business Act,[4] went further and individually determined thresholds in terms of employment or sales for each of the four-digit standard industrial classifications (SICs). This led to some anomalies – including, famously, in 1966, the classification of American Motors, then one of the 200 largest US corporations, as a 'small' firm for SBA procurement assistance programmes (PARRIS 1968). (American Motors was small relative to the Big 3 – General Motors, Ford and Chrysler – and had a share of less than 5 per cent of the market for passenger cars. Its vulnerability was proven by its later absorption into Chrysler which, later still, merged with Daimler–Benz.)

Statistics

There are as yet no universally agreed and observed standards for international small firm statistics. In their official figures, most countries exclude agriculture (the UK is an exception) and many do not include the self-employed without employees ('O' employee firms) in their overall totals of business enterprises. Another difficulty, among many, in making international comparisons is that some figures do not exclude establishments that are owned by large firms and which are not therefore properly interpreted as 'small independent enterprises'. Problems of statistical coverage are greatest in developing countries, where most small firms are in the informal sector and may not be registered or appear in official statistics at all. However, even among the advanced countries there are sometimes major differences in statistical coverage which offer pitfalls for the unwary. For example, it is not generally appreciated in Europe that the official enterprise statistics for the United States and Japan do not include enterprises without employees – which can mean a difference of 50 per cent or more in the enterprise total!

The inevitable conclusion is that SME statistics must everywhere be interpreted with caution. While statistics are generally improving – people are much more interested in SMEs than they were 50 years ago – it takes very many years for significant improvements to be made, and often requires changes in the laws governing statistical inquiries and the exchange of information between arms of government. The European Union (EU) has issued a directive which requires the adoption of *unique enterprise identifiers* and the compilation of enterprise registers in all member states, but results are not expected before 2006. The Appendix at the end of this book (p. 206) provides a fuller discussion of the coverage and sources of SME statistics and makes some detailed international comparisons.

Meanwhile, some general conclusions can be drawn. The first conclusion is that, however defined, the vast majority of all business enterprises are very small. In the United Kingdom, for example, 99.1 per cent of the 3.7 million business enterprises employ fewer than 50 people – there are only 3,500 with 500 or more employees. In employment terms, SMEs with fewer than 250 employees, the EU definition, are less dominant: they account for 55.4 per cent of all private sector employees. In the rest of Europe, SMEs are in fact even more predominant than in the United Kingdom.

The second conclusion is that there do appear to be differences in the total number of enterprises (and therefore of SMEs) in relation to the population between countries. Table 1.1, for example, suggests that southern European countries have relatively more small firms than those further North. This table also indicates that Zambia, a country typical in this respect of sub-Saharan Africa, and perhaps surprisingly, has a comparable number of SMEs to some European countries.

Finally, and contrary to common opinion, Japan has fewer SMEs than the United States, which in turn has roughly the same number as the United Kingdom. Although the figures used in Table 1.1 have been adjusted for comparability for Europe by the Statistical Office of the European Communities, and those for the United States and Japan by the author, we still cannot be certain that like is being compared with like. All the adjustments made have tended to reduce the differences in the importance of SMEs between countries, and the suspicion lingers that, with the possible exception of the EU Mediterranean states, differences in SME density, particularly for countries at similar stages of economic development, owe more to differences in coverage rather than real differences, though some undoubtedly remain. We shall find some support for these suspicions elsewhere in the book, for example in comparisons of business mortality (Chapter 2).

Table 1.1 Non-primary enterprises per 10,000 of the population, selected countries, number *c.* 2000

Europe	No.	Elsewhere	No.
Greece	759	USA	577
Italy	721	Japan	512
Spain	684	Zambia	368
UK	584		
Germany	432		
France	423		
Denmark	337		
Austria	278		

Source: Appendix.

The final conclusion to be drawn from the review of SME statistics in the Appendix is that the numerical importance of small firms *changes in character* as countries move through different stages in economic development. There is evidence that across large numbers of countries the share of SMEs in output and employment tends to decline with economic development, and the average size of SMEs tends to increase. There is also evidence that small firms are important drivers of economic development (a full discussion of this is deferred until Chapter 9). Next, in Chapter 2 we look at some of the characteristics of small firms, and the people who own them, in advanced countries.

Notes

1 The Bolton definition echoes that of the US Small Business Act (1953), which says that 'a small business concern shall be deemed to be one which is independently owned and operated and which is not dominant in its field of operations'.
2 This separation of ownership and control, first analysed by BERLE & MEANS (1932), lies at the root of the endless debates about the governance of large corporations. It is interesting to note that the owners of these large businesses are generally separated from management at one remove, since between management and beneficial shareholders are the large pension funds and insurance companies that control the majority of equity shares. Even where private individuals own shares directly, since the late 1960s these shares have generally been held electronically through nominee companies registered with (in the UK) CREST and, unless special arrangements are made, shareholders are invisible to their companies and do not receive communications from them.
3 The European Commission further defines an SME as having fewer than 250 employees, not more than 25 per cent owned by enterprises not satisfying that criteria, and with either a turnover or balance sheet total of less than €40 million and €27 million, respectively.
4 The US 1953 Small Business Act says: 'Where the number of employees is used as one of the criteria [*sic*] in making such definition for any of the purposes of this Act, the maximum number of employees which a small-business concern may have under the definition shall vary from industry to industry to the extent necessary to reflect differing characteristics of such industries and to take proper account of other relevant factors.'

2 Some characteristics of small firms and their owners

Heterogeneity and rationality

It is best to begin this chapter with recognition of the variety which exists in the small business population. Obviously SMEs differ greatly in size, in their activity sector, their growth rates and in other dimensions. In fact, it is well established that there is far greater variability in some SME characteristics than among large firms: profitability is a good example. In a non-economic sense, the 'personality' of a small firm, reflecting as it does the ideas and idiosyncrasies of its owner(s) is also bound to vary, as individuals obviously differ from one another. It is no exaggeration to say that *each small firm is unique*. This contrasts with large firms, where the separation of ownership from control and the group pressures for conformity among its numerous managers erode (but do not entirely eliminate) idiosyncrasy. Common observation suggests, for example, that large firm management frequently falls into the grip of the latest management fads and fashions from which most SME owners, less interested in the art of management as an abstraction, are largely free.

Some researchers have been so overwhelmed by the variety exhibited in small business as to deny that meaningful generalisations about the subject can be made at all. This is not the view taken in this book, though it is acknowledged that caution is necessary in making generalisations. What gives the small business population some coherence are the characteristics discussed in the Definition section of Chapter 1: personal ownership, independence and lack of market power. These characteristics produce the constraints on management and financial resources that are an inevitable consequence of small scale. While SMEs may be all different from one another, they do share many characteristics that differentiate them from large firms as a group. Failure to appreciate the nature of these differences is at the root of many of the contrasts drawn later between received opinion about the nature of small firms and small business policy and what is advocated in this book.

All businesses, large and small, have to be – or must try to be – *rational in their pursuit of profit and survival*. In small business the need for rationality, the objective weighing up of the pros and cons of alternative courses of action, is heightened by their vulnerability: they cannot afford too many mistakes. Mistakes can exhaust their limited resources and lead, in the face of competition, to the demise of the firm and possibly the ruin of its owner(s). Most of the puzzles about SMEs compared with large firms and which bemuse policymakers – for example, their reluctance to make business plans, take external equity or use more external training – simply reflect a rational response to their situation rather than, as is often supposed, ignorance and lack of sophistication.

A topical illustration of SME rationality, for example, is their generally more hostile view, compared with large firms, to the adoption of the euro by the United Kingdom. This is, of course, a politically highly charged subject that raises legitimate concerns about the consequences of a 'one size fits all' monetary policy and a feared further loss of independence within the European Union. Naturally, small business owners have often conflicting views on these issues, but their attitudes are heavily influenced by the simple facts that relatively few SMEs engage in foreign trade and would therefore not gain as much as large exporters and importers from the potential reduction in currency conversion and exchange rate uncertainty that is to be expected from adoption of the euro. All businesses would, however, have to bear the costs of conversion. A detailed study shows that although from a national standpoint the conversion cost of euro entry would be recouped in only two and a half years, in contrast to 8 per cent of the benefits, SMEs would bear 72 per cent of the private sector's total costs of conversion (BANNOCK CONSULTING 2001a).[1]

Ownership and family business

The vast majority of SMEs are owned by individuals or families, perhaps half being under sole ownership. These proportions vary with size of firm: the larger the firm, the less likely it is to be solely owned and the more likely other family members and non-family persons share ownership. For example, in a 2002 survey in the United Kingdom the proportion of sole owners fell from 62 per cent for firms with a turnover of less than £50,000 to 18 per cent in the £500,000 to >£1 million size band. Part-owners, with non-family part-owners, rose from 7 per cent to 31 per cent over the same size ranges. Part-owners in family-owned businesses rose from 27 per cent to 44 per cent over these ranges.[2]

Thus, although 40 per cent of all small businesses are family-owned, that percentage rises with size. LEACH (1992) estimated that 76 per cent of larger UK companies have substantial family ownership. Although family control may have been diluted with growth and the need to raise capital, some quoted companies (such as Sainsbury and Cadbury Schweppes) and very large unquoted companies (such as Clarks the shoe manufacturers and Rothschild the merchant bank) remain under family control or influence.

This may well be true to an even greater extent in continental Europe, where stock markets are somewhat less important than in the United Kingdom: for example, Heineken (brewing), Henkel (chemicals), troubled Fiat, booming BMW and Porsche (cars) as well as many of the great French and Italian fashion houses.

If we define 'family firms' only as those controlled and managed businesses inherited from an earlier generation, as many of the examples just quoted are, then the numbers fall away rapidly. All smaller businesses, family-owned or not, are subject to high mortality rates. According to LEACH (1992), of larger family companies, 'only 24 per cent survive as such through to the second generation, and only 14 per cent make it beyond the third'. This is not to say that family businesses, which naturally adopt a long-term perspective, perform worse than others. HAY & MORRIS (1984) found that larger unquoted businesses, most of which are family-owned, performed better in terms of profit and growth than quoted companies, even after size differences were allowed for. However, second- and third-generation businesses do often collapse or decline because of, as Leach puts it, 'a failure to manage the complex and emotion-laden issue of succession from one generation to the next'.

Multiple business ownership

Many SME owners are involved in more than one small business (*portfolio entrepreneurs*). SBRT 9/02 found that 28 per cent of respondents were a director/owner of another business, ranging from 17 per cent of those in the smallest firms to 37 per cent of those with 20 or more employees. Over 40 per cent of all firms were involved in another firm: 28 per cent as owners, 9 per cent as advisers, 4 per cent as informal sources of advice and 3 per cent as trade investors or minority business owners.

It is not really surprising that successful SME owners should make use of their expertise and funds to help or invest in other businesses. Peter J. Rosa and Michael G. Scott, in DONCKELS & MIETTINEN (1997) had similar findings. They also found a gender dimension, men being more likely than women to own another business. However, the SBRT 9/02 survey found that women were more likely to be an informal source of advice. Rosa and Scott note that multiple business ownership has been neglected by researchers, but that it could be argued that this phenomenon is sufficiently common to suggest that the unit of analysis in SME research should be the individual rather than the firm. See CARTER & RAM (2003) for a more recent study of portfolio entrepreneurship.

A related and overlapping phenomenon with multiple ownership is the *serial entrepreneur*, who starts a business, grows it, sells out and starts again. We return to the question of business ownership in Chapter 6.[3]

Motivation

The prime motivation of most SME owners seems to be *independence*: that is, freedom to express their own personality. SBRT 12/99 and also an earlier survey in 1996 found that respondents selected the following as 'closest to your main motivation for running your own business' (Table 2.1).

Several of these responses cluster around the notion of independence: certainly 'To be my own boss' and 'To work by myself' (a total of 46.3 per cent for the 1999 survey), but also 'To create a secure future' and 'To earn respect' (making up to 61.8 per cent) reflect similar motivations. The decision to work for oneself or others is surely mainly motivated by the need to earn a living, but purely economic motives – 'To make money' and 'To avoid unemployment' (totalling 24.8 per cent) come well after the desire for autonomy. Under 5 per cent of respondents were simply following family tradition. There was not much difference in the results of the surveys in 1996 and 1999, and such differences as there were can partly be explained by a change in sample composition.[4]

Respondents were also asked about their objectives, which again clustered around a theme of independence and self-expression: 'To support your preferred lifestyle', 'To protect your future or build up an asset for your children', 'To develop products and ideas/innovate' (totalling 59.4 per cent). Economic motives: 'Growth in employment, sales and profits', 'To improve your standard of living' totalled only 32.2 per cent. This includes, significantly, only 0.5 per cent whose objective was to increase employment. The vast majority of SME owners do not want to increase employment for its own sake (which means more hassle for them) but only as necessary to meet other economic objectives.

Table 2.1 'Which of the following is closest to your main motivation for running your own business?', 1996 and 1999

Motivation	1996	1999
To be my own boss/responsible for my own organisation	44.1	38.9
To make money	15.8	16.7
To create a more secure future	9.8	14.2
No alternative/avoid unemployment	10.5	8.1
To work by myself/not be told what to do	7.4	7.4
Family tradition	4.5	4.8
To earn respect/status	0.8	1.3
Other	6.5	7.7
No response	0.5	0.9
Sample	753	1,121

Source: SBRT 12/96; 12/99.

These results echo the findings of a study by C.W. Golby and G. Johns, *Attitude and Motivation* (Research Report No. 7), commissioned for, and quoted in, the BOLTON (1971) Report (emphasis in the original):

> This need for 'independence' sums up a wide range of highly personal gratifications provided by working for oneself and not for anybody else. It embraces . . . the personal supervision and control of staff, direct contact with customers, the opportunity to develop one's *own* ideas, a strong feeling of personal challenge and an almost egotistical sense of personal achievement and pride – psychological satisfactions which appeared to be much more powerful motivators than money or the possibility of large financial gains.

International comparisons of survey data on SME attitudes are complicated by the statistical issues discussed in Chapter 1 and by differences in the framing of questions and sample composition. However, the high importance of independence and self-expression and the relatively small importance of making money emerge in all surveys of SME owners around the world. The EUROPEAN COMMISSION (2002a, 2002b) ENSR Survey of SMEs throughout Europe found that although the main focus of business policy was growth (29 per cent of respondents), for 20 per cent it was survival or consolidation (21 per cent). Only 9 per cent were focused on higher profits; for more (11 per cent), it was a focus on higher quality, while for 7 per cent it was innovation.

In a survey in the United States, the most important motivations for owners of new small business were: 'Use my skills and abilities' (57 per cent); 'Greater control over my life' (54 per cent); 'Build something for my family (54 per cent); and 'Like the challenge' (49 per cent). 'Earn lots of money' was mentioned by only 18 per cent, the same percentage as those who selected 'Gain more respect/recognition' (multiple mentions were possible) (COOPER *et al.* 1990).

There is a vast literature on the motives, personality traits and psychology of entrepreneurs which is broadly consistent with these survey findings (though entrepreneurs and SME owners are not necessarily the same thing – see Chapter 6). There is controversy, but it does not seem possible to identify the traits that will predict highly successful entrepreneurs in advance, though entrepreneurs do often have similar traits. Entrepreneurs are made by their social situations and experience and often have a deviant personality, which makes it difficult for them to fit into large organisations or accept authority (CHELL 1985). STANWORTH & CURRAN (1973) argue persuasively that SME ownership is often a solution to 'social marginality' (it helps to explain why immigrants are overrepresented). The BOLTON (1971) Report stated that:

> small business continues to offer one of the few remaining career opportunities for the able and ambitious youngster who has not passed

through the higher educational 'mill'. For one of the advantages conferred by higher education, the ability to persuade and impress others by sophisticated argument, is certainly less important for the independent businessman than it is for a member of a large organisation … In a large organisation it is not only necessary for an individual to be capable of doing things and of seeing better ways of doing things, it is also necessary to be able to persuade others to give him the freedom to act or to obey or support him. In a small firm the owner-manager can act very much on his own initiative.

Legal form

Table 2.2 shows that only about one-quarter of business enterprises in the United Kingdom are incorporated: most are sole proprietorships (62 per cent) or partnerships (15 per cent). Whether or not firms are incorporated is very much a function of size: almost all firms with 100 or more employees, but only 11 per cent of those with fewer than five employees, are incorporated.

Incorporation brings with it the protection of limited liability, and possibly tax advantages, at the expense of more transparency, legal formalities and paperwork.[5] For very small firms limited liability may be largely illusory, since directors' guarantees may well be necessary for property leases, bank borrowings and other major indebtedness. This means that if the firm goes into receivership, in many cases it will be quite small trade creditors that suffer with (until recently) the tax authorities taking precedence over them.

Table 2.2 Private sector enterprises, by legal form and employment size band, United Kingdom, number and percentage, 2001

No. of employees	Sole proprietor-ships		Partnerships		Companies and corporations		Total	
	No.	*(%)*	*No.*	*(%)*	*No.*	*(%)*	*No.*	*(%)*
0	1,958	84.2	327	58.6	311	36.1	2,596	69.3
1–4	301	13.0	155	27.7	292	33.8	748	20.0
5–9	47	2.0	41	7.4	113	13.1	200	5.3
10–19	15	0.6	23	4.1	74	8.6	113	3.0
20–49	4	0.2	10	1.8	41	4.7	55	1.5
50–99	1	–	2	0.3	16	1.8	18	0.5
100–199	–	–	–	0.1	7	0.9	8	0.2
200–249	–	–	–	–	2	0.2	2	–
250–499	–	–	–	–	3	0.4	3	0.1
500+	–	–	–	–	3	0.4	4	0.1
Total	2,327	100.0	558	100.0	862	100.0	3,746	100.0
%	62.1		14.9		23.0		100.0	

Source: Small Business Service (SBS); includes public corporations and the primary sector.

From an economic point of view legal form has little significance and the decision to incorporate or not, for very small firms in particular, will be largely driven by tax considerations; for larger companies the ability to raise capital and other considerations may be important.[6] Smaller limited companies are permitted to file abbreviated accounts and only public limited companies (PLCs) are allowed to issue shares to the general public so that decisions on legal status are quite complicated and a business may wish to change its status as it grows. There were 1,822,000 companies of all types registered in the United Kingdom (2003). This number is much larger than the 862,000–company total given in Table 2.2 because many are subsidiaries and very many are also inactive.

Although company law and structures differ, the broad picture presented here for the United Kingdom seems similar in most other developed countries. In Japan, the role of incorporated business is unclear on a comparable basis, but it may be more important than in the United Kingdom or United States. Table 2.3 presents some data for the United States. It can be seen that, as in the United Kingdom, over three-quarters of business tax returns are from unincorporated firms.

Self-employment

Owner-managers of unincorporated businesses are by definition self-employed persons. So, too, in logic, are owner-managers of incorporated businesses, though for tax purposes they are treated as employees of the company which has a legal personality distinct from that of its owner(s). This distinction can be a source of confusion in small business statistics.

Table 2.3 Non-farm business income tax returns by legal form, United States, 1970, 1980, 1990, 1997, and percentage of total and percentage change, 1970–97

Form	1970 (000)	1980 (000)	1990 (000)	1997 (000)	1997 (% of total)	1970–97 (% change)
Proprietorships	5,770	9,730	14,783	17,177	72.6	297.7
Partnerships	936	1,380	1,554	1,759	7.4	187.9
S-Corporations[a]	257	545	1,175	2,647	11.1	1030.0
C-Corporations	1,408	2,166	2,542	2,063	8.8	146.5
Total[b]	8,371	13,821	20,054	23,646	100.0	282.5

Source: NFIB Policy Guide.

Notes
a Sub-chapter S corporations with 35 or fewer non-corporate shareholders may elect to be subject to income tax rather than corporation tax. This may be advantageous – for example, where, as in a partnership, shareholders may wish to offset losses in the corporation against other personal income. Changes in the numbers of partnerships, S and C corporations are partly the result of the 1986 Tax Reform Act and subsequent legislation.
b These totals are much greater than the number of enterprises, because of multiple returns (see Chapter 1).

In 2001 (1st quarter) in the United Kingdom there were 3.2 million persons in the labour force classified as self-employed, an increase of over 80 per cent over the estimates for the late 1970s.[7] Some of these persons will be in partnerships, some in companies and most will be sole proprietors; some are working full-time, some part-time and some will be employing others. The upsurge in self-employment in the 1980s (which has levelled off since the early 2000s) has brought the proportion of the labour force that are self-employed back to near the levels at the beginning of the twentieth century (Table 2.4).

Women are less likely to be self-employed than men. In 2001, some 26 per cent of the self-employed were women whereas 47 per cent of all persons in employment were women (though the gap is closing slowly: numbers of men in self-employment fell by 9 per cent in 1995–2001, while that of women increased slightly). Women are also less likely to be employers than men but this, too, is changing. In the decade ending 1996, the growth rate of the number of women-owned businesses in the United States was 78 per cent, compared with 47 per cent for all firms. By 1996, one in every four American workers was employed by a business owned by a woman (BLACKFORD 2003).

By contrast, the self-employed are a higher proportion of all in employment among ethnic minority groups, bearing out the 'social marginality' theories reviewed above. It is not true, as has been commonly supposed, that the large increase in employment in small firms in the 1980s was mainly the result of the upsurge in self-employment. Over the period 1979–86, the growth in the number of self-employed contributed only 49 per cent of the increase in employment in firms with fewer than 20 employees (BANNOCK & DALY 1994).

Table 2.5 shows self-employment ratios for a number of OECD countries. There appear to be quite large differences, but on closer examination it can

Table 2.4 Self-employed as percentage of the labour force, United Kingdom, selected years

Year	(%)
1911	12.8
1921	10.1
1951	7.2
1960	7.0
1970	7.4
1980	7.5
1990	11.7
2002[a]	10.7

Source: *Annual Abstract of Statistics and Monthly Digest of Statistics*, HMSO.

Note

a 1st quarter.

Table 2.5 Non-agricultural self-employment as percentage of non-agricultural civilian employment, selected countries, 1973, 1989, 1998

Country	1973 (%)	1989 (%)	1998 (%)
France[a]	11.4	10.5	8.2
Germany[a]	9.1	7.7[d]	9.4
Italy[b]	23.1	n.a.	22.7
Japan[c]	14.0	n.a.	9.7
United Kingdom[a]	7.3	n.a.	11.4
United States[c]	6.7	7.5[d]	7.0

Source: *OECD Employment Outlook*, June 2000.

Notes
a Including most owner-managers of incorporated businesses.
b Classification of owner-managers of incorporated businesses is unclear.
c Excluding owner-managers of incorporated businesses.
d 1990.

be seen from the notes to the table that the treatment of owner-managers of incorporated businesses also varies. Whether 'employees' or incorporated businesses are counted as self-employed or not can affect these ratios by several percentage points. Allowing for this and other factors, it seems unlikely that there is much difference between the ratios for France, Germany, Japan, the United States and the United Kingdom though, as we found in Chapter 1 for SME density, Italy does appear to have a significantly higher ratio of self-employment than the other countries shown. The trend over time in these ratios is flat or downwards, with the exception of the United Kingdom, but in quite a few of the other countries included in the OECD review on which the table is based (but not shown here) there had been a resurgence of self-employment in the latter half of the period.

Productivity and profitability

There was at one time a debate about the relative efficiency of SMEs and large firms. Output per person employed is generally positively correlated with firm size: in general, the bigger the firm the higher the value added per employee. This relationship can be observed even within the SME sector, at least in the upper echelons. The 1997 UK Census of Manufacturing, for example, gives net output per head for firms with 100–199 employees as over 21 per cent higher than for firms below that size-band. However, the data also show that net capital expenditure as a percentage of net output is 19 per cent higher for the larger of these two size groups (there are no figures for the size of the capital stock). This is the explanation for the difference: labour productivity is higher in large firms because they are more capital-intensive than small firms. The BOLTON (1971) report documented this point in some detail and also found that profitability, defined as rates of return on net assets, was higher in small unquoted and quoted companies than in all quoted companies, though not greatly so. It was also noted that the dispersion of rates of return was greater for small than large firms. This was attributed both to the fact that large firms were more likely to be diversified and therefore able to offset profits on some activities against losses on others, and less likely to be dependent upon the efforts of single, fallible individuals. The Committee concluded that there was 'no evidence for assuming that small firms are, in general, any less efficient than large, or vice versa'.

There are enormous difficulties in the way of measuring the relative efficiency of small and large firms in addition to the apparently insoluble problem of separating out the contributions of labour and capital. Profitability is particularly difficult to measure for small firms since unincorporated businesses do not in general keep comprehensive accounts including balance sheets. This is why studies of profitability are usually confined to incorporated businesses. There are no comprehensive databases with financial information on unincorporated businesses, so that research has to be based on samples that are almost never fully representative.[8] Moreover, as STOREY (1994) points out, profitability in small firms is, to an extent, 'discretionary' in the sense that owners may 'underpay' or 'overpay' themselves and invest or not in the business, and may choose, or not, by these means to make small or large profits. Storey also recognises that there are a wide variety of approaches to record-keeping and accountancy, particularly in the smallest firms. For unincorporated businesses, analysis has been made much more difficult by the progressive exemptions for reporting requirements which were introduced since the 1980s and the Office of National Statistics (ONS) at that time ceased publication of its Business Monitor MA3, *Company Finance.*

'By the 1980s smaller companies had become less rather than more profitable than larger ones' according to Andy Cosh and Alan Hughes ('Size, financial structure and profitability: UK companies in the 1980s', in HUGHES & STOREY 1994). This apparent sea change in the relative profitability of at least small and large manufacturing firms, as found by the Bolton Committee and later confirmed by the Wilson Committee (1979), is mirrored in the well-known and more recent break in the persistent tendency for small quoted companies to outperform their larger brethren, as well as other data, but no satisfactory explanation has been advanced for it. There seems to be little doubt about the sea change, but we have to conclude that once again data problems may be obscuring the full picture. The fragility of any conclusions to be drawn is illustrated by Cosh and Hughes' finding, based on their own panel data set, that adding back directors' emoluments reverses the position and leaves the profitability of small firms as higher than that of large firms. Moreover the comparison is much less clear-cut for non-manufacturing small firms, which on some measures were more profitable than large firms. The greater dispersion (variance) of small firm profitability still seems to exist, though even this has not been con-firmed in some sample studies (STOREY *et al.* 1987).

A more recent and important study of returns on the equity of private and quoted companies in the United States also shows a deterioration in the relative profitability of private compared with public companies over the period 1990–8 (MOSKOWITZ & VISSING 2002). It can be seen from Table 2.6, based on the results of this study, that returns for both types of business rose in the period but were somewhat higher in private companies in 1990–5 and fell below public companies in 1996–8. However, when a salary was imputed for owner-managers not taking one, returns for private businesses were below those for public ones throughout, with a flat trend in the ratio between the two compared with a downward trend in that ratio on an unadjusted basis. It should be noted that these US figures include unincor-porated firms.

However measured, it seems that there is not much difference between the profitability of small and large businesses and that the earlier superiority of the former has been eroded. Given the greater capital intensity of large firms we should expect their returns on assets to be higher, but it may be that small firms are becoming more capital-intensive (there is some evidence of this for the service sector). Nevertheless this still leaves the question of the relative risk faced by the two. This risk is higher for small firms, as we demonstrate later. Theory suggests that higher risk should be compensated for by higher returns. MOSKOWITZ & VISSING (2002) make this point and comment that 'the majority of household investment in private companies is concentrated in a single, risky, privately-held firm in which the household has an active management interest'. The reason why people are willing to invest in risky small firms when they can reasonably expect, despite recent events, to get similar long-term returns from investing in the stock market, is perhaps to be explained by the non-financial rewards discussed earlier in this chapter.

Table 2.6 Post-tax returns on market value[a], private and quoted businesses, pairs of years United States, 1990–8

Year	Private[b] (%)	Private with salary imputation (%)	Public (%)
1990–2	12.3	8.2	11.0
1993–5	17.0	12.7	14.6
1996–8	22.2	18.4	24.7

Source: MOSKOWITZ & VISSING (2002).

Notes
a Profits were adjusted for retained earnings. Estimated market values for private businesses imply a profit/earnings (P/E) ratio of 5.6 compared with 11.6 for public companies. Unincorporated businesses accounted for 19.3 per cent of total market value, incorporated private businesses for 24.9 per cent and public companies for 55.9 per cent.
b For private businesses, equity holdings by households were based on the NSSBF and the Survey of Consumer Finances (SCF).

Earnings of owners and employees

BOLTON (1971) established that employee earnings in small firms were lower – about 20 per cent lower than in large firms – although some of this large difference was reduced if account were taken of age and gender structures. Similar findings have been made subsequently and in many countries. For example, in 1989, labour costs in manufacturing (firms with more than 1,000 employees = 100.0) were 72.8 in firms with 20–99 employees in Italy and 61.4 per cent in Japan. For firms with 100–499 employees the ratios were 87.0 and 69.7, respectively (BOLTHO *et al.* 2001). The authors point out that the low Japanese earnings reflect the presence of large numbers of low-productivity subcontractors in the economy. The *Japan Statistical Yearbook 2003* shows that earnings of all employees in firms with over 1,000 employees were 37 per cent higher for men and 27 per cent higher for women than in firms with 10–99 employees in 2001). Earnings data do not normally include a valuation of fringe benefits and if these were included in the comparisons made above, the differences between small and large firms would be greater.[9]

The reason why earnings are lower in small firms generally is that labour productivity is lower than in large firms, a point already made above in relation to profitability comparisons. Employees in large firms have been able to capture part of the higher value added per head that results from capital intensity and perhaps, in some instances, monopoly power. Small firm owners pay lower wages to their employees than big firms, therefore, because they cannot afford to pay more. The well-attested fact that wages are lower in small firms is often referred to with disapproval, with the assertion that the jobs offered by small firms are of poor quality and the implication that owners are exploiting their staff. A study by DENNIS (2000) shows that in the United States, and we should expect elsewhere, owner income is correlated with the level of wages the business pays and the fringe benefits it provides: small businesses that do well and yield higher than average owner earnings pay their employees well, and vice versa. As Dennis puts it, 'the business's owner and the business's employees are in the venture together. They jointly prosper or they jointly fail'.

This partnership in the fortunes of owners and employees in small firms does not mean that the interests of the 'partners' are always perceived to be symmetrical. If the firm fails, then generally the owner loses financially more than the employee, who only has her job at stake. The owner can lose both her job and her savings – and, in extreme cases, her home where it has been mortgaged to provide capital for the firm. If the firm succeeds spectacularly, then the owner stands to make a substantial capital gain and not simply enhanced income.

It may well be that many employees in small firms accept lower earnings than their counterparts in large firms because there are more opportunities for learning (see Chapter 8) or that human relations are more familial and participative. Equally, however, many employees may not have the choice between working in a small firm and a large one with higher wages and fringe benefits. The Bolton Committee, which took the former interpretation, was later criticised for having adopted a rosy view of employment relations in small firms which, being largely ununionised, provided little evidence of conflict to the public view. In Chapter 9 of STANWORTH & GRAY (1991), it was pointed out that, compared with the immense literature on entrepreneurship, little attention had been given to employment relations in small firms, and this remains true today. Such research as had been done, and that has been done subsequently, does suggest that things are not quite as rosy or as straightforward as the Bolton Committee asserted, though there is controversy – see John Atkinson and David Storey, 'Small firms and employment', in ATKINSON & STOREY (1994). This, in retrospect, is hardly surprising given the fact that conditions in small firms vary enormously from sweatshops to professional partnerships and that owners cover the gamut of human nature from the mean and autocratic to the benevolent and fraternal.

STOREY (1994) presents UK data on earnings by the full-time self-employed compared with all employed. Self-employed earnings are more variable, with a higher proportion of employees in both the bottom and the top of the distribution, and their arithmetic mean is 30 per cent higher. We should also expect self-employed earnings to be more variable over time than those of the employed, since profitability is variable. Earnings will also be less per hour worked, since it is well established that average hours of the self-employed are higher than for the employed.[10] Since incorporated businesses tend to be larger than unincorporated, it is quite possible that earnings for owners of incorporated firms are higher than for the self-employed. However, as Storey acknowledges, some of the income of the self-employed, and of owners of incorporated businesses, will be a return on capital invested in the business. Also fringe benefits, probably much higher for the employed (at least those in larger firms), need to be taken into account. Another reason why the earnings of the self-employed can be higher than employees in general is that the self-employed tend to be older and to have better educational qualifications than the employed. This is true both for the United Kingdom (BANNOCK & DALY 1994) and the United States (NFIB 2000). Once again we find that data problems prevent firm conclusions, but there is no convincing evidence that on average small firm owners generally make more money than employed people for equivalent hours, occupations and qualifications, even though, given the risks they face, they might be expected to. At least among the minority of small business owners driven by material considerations, there is always the oxygen of hope. In fact a large proportion on the lists of the most wealthy people owe their wealth to business creation and growth. However, there is also evidence that the self-employed are disproportionately represented among the poor.

'Births' and 'deaths'

There is intense interest in statistics on new 'births' and 'deaths' of businesses, since the former are taken to be an indicator of entrepreneurial vitality and the latter of weakness in business conditions and wasted resources. As we shall argue, both these interpretations, to some extent at least, may be misapprehensions. UK Government spokesmen have commented that new business 'birth rates' are lower than in the United States and in Germany that they are lower than in Britain. However, data are not available to draw reliable comparisons of these kinds. Data on business 'births' may include new subsidiaries of larger enterprises, mergers, changes of name and legal form and even relocations. As with business stock data, the self-employed are often excluded.

The Fourth Annual Report (EUROPEAN COMMISSION 1996) of the European Observatory for SMEs contained a study of the demography of enterprises. Using national data, this report gave 'birth' rates as a percentage of the business stock for 1988–94 ranging from 2 (Portugal) to 17 per cent (Germany), with the United Kingdom at 13 per cent. The report recognised that widely different definitions were used, and after attempted adjustments the range fell to about 5–11.5 per cent, but still with unresolved definitional problems. Unadjusted 'death' dates ranged from 1 (Portugal and Spain) to 13 (Germany), with the United Kingdom at 12 per cent.

The Global Enterprise Monitor (GEM), also referred to in the Appendix, produces a Total Entrepreneurial Activity Index (TEA) based on large surveys of the adult population and which reflects the percentage of population involved in creating nascent ventures and new firms up to 42 months old. For 2001 and 2002, the TEAs for the G8 countries (all down on the previous year) were as in Table 2.7.

The GEM data are difficult to interpret as an indicator of 'births', given the definition of entrepreneurial activity. In fact, the GEM report for the United Kingdom for 2002 states that 'The data here should not . . . be

Table 2.7 TEA Index, G8 countries, 2001–2

Country	2001 (%)	2002 (%)
United States	11.6	10.5
Canada	10.0	8.8
United Kingdom	7.7	5.4
Germany	8.0	5.2
Japan	5.2	1.8
France	7.4	3.2
Italy	10.2	5.9
Russia	6.9	2.5

Source: GEM website. The source notes that the United Kingdom comes 23rd out of 37 countries, with countries in Asia and South America heading the rankings.

interpreted as an accurate measure of actual numbers of business start-ups in particular communities, regions or sectors. Instead it should be taken as a measure of the number of businesses that are likely to exist if appropriate framework conditions prevail.'

One of the issues in interpreting 'birth' and 'death' data is that these two are related: high 'births' are associated with high 'death' rates, and low 'births' with low 'death' rates. This association can be observed in all SME demographic data and means that the difference between the two (the net rate which measures the extent to which the business stock has grown or declined) tends to vary less than the 'birth' or 'death' rates. For example, in the European Network for SME Research (ENSR) study, the unadjusted range for 'death' rates was 1–13 percentage points, but the range of net rates was only 1–4 per cent (one country, Iceland, had a net rate of –1, indicating a declining business stock). The association of gross 'birth' and 'death' rates could be saying something about the coverage of the data but it could also mean, for example, that high 'births' entail greater risks being taken, resulting in high 'death' rates, and vice versa.

While international comparisons of 'births' and 'deaths' are clearly hazardous, it does seem that differences between countries have some significance and do not simply reflect definitional problems. Certainly within countries, where like is presumably being compared with like, there are considerable variations between regions. 'Birth' and 'death' rates also seem to vary cyclically over time and between activity sectors.

Various studies have attempted to explain variations in *new firm formations* and *terminations* (probably more suitable terms than 'births' and 'deaths'). There has been some debate about the relative importance of 'push factors' – founders starting businesses through lack of alternative employment opportunities – and 'pull factors' – for example, market opportunities for profit. We agree with STOREY (1994) that both 'pull' and 'push' factors are at work, with their impact varying according to activity sector, location and time.

The same conclusion was reached in a very interesting study by FOREMAN-PECK (1985) of the regional pattern of firm foundation 1919–29, a period when comprehensive data for Britain existed.[11] Areas with high incomes and rising populations were likely to have higher 'birth' rates. Foreman-Peck, and later GUDGIN *et al.* (1979) and others noted that small firms breed more small firms. This is because workers in small firms get experience in a wider range of jobs and, in their proximity to the owner-manager, get to see how the business is run.

UK data on value added tax (VAT) registrations and deregistrations have been extensively analysed and allow us to illustrate some of the points made in this section, as well as the greater volatility and risk of small firms, which we have asserted but not yet quantified.

Caution is needed in interpreting VAT numbers because registrations and deregistrations do not necessarily correspond to business openings and closures. There are many reasons why a firm may deregister without ceasing business: for example, its turnover may have fallen below the registration threshold (£54,000–56,000 in 2003/4), or it may have been taken over and absorbed into another enterprise The same is true for new registrations, which may mean simply that a long-standing business previously below the turnover threshold has grown above it or decided to register voluntarily, which any firm below the threshold is free to do. These factors and others are very important, and possibly 40 per cent of deregistrations or registrations do not represent true business closures or openings. However, only about 45 per cent of all businesses in the United Kingdom are registered for VAT. We should expect opening and closure rates to be higher for those smallest firms than for those above the threshold; it may therefore be that these statistics are not as misleading as one might suppose.

Table 2.8 presents the basic UK VAT data for 2001. It can be seen that overall registrations were 10.5 per cent of the stock of VAT-registered traders and deregistrations 9.8 per cent, giving an increase in the stock of 0.7 per cent.[12] The net change varied from –6.3 per cent in the extractive industries to +3.3 per cent in hotels and catering. It will be noted that even though the number of manufacturers is declining, 'exit' rates are lower than in some of the expanding sectors such a hotels and restaurants and business services, which have relatively high 'entry' rates. Part of the explanation for this is that barriers to entry (e.g. capital requirements) are generally lower in these expanding sectors.

Registration and deregistration rates by region (not shown) also vary, being highest in London and lowest in the north east of England, Wales, Scotland and Northern Ireland.

There have been changes over time. The VAT stock rose by one-third between 1980 and 1990, with a net increase in every year of the decade. In the 1990s growth ceased and the stock was still below 1990 levels in 2001.

Table 2.8 VAT registrations and deregistrations and net change as percentage of the stock at start of 2001, by activity sector, United Kingdom, 2001

Item	Registrations	Deregistrations	Net	Stock at year end
Agriculture, fishing	2.1	3.3	–1.2	149.7
Mining, energy, water	12.5	19.8	–6.3	1.6
Manufacturing	7.2	9.6	–2.4	149.3
Construction	10.8	9.6	1.2	171.7
Wholesale, retail, repairs	8.3	9.8	–1.5	380.0
Hotels, restaurants	17.9	14.6	3.3	107.3
Transport, communications	12.6	10.9	1.7	75.3
Finance	10.3	10.3	–	15.5
Business services	14.2	11.5	2.7	440.5
Education, health	10.0	7.6	2.4	21.0
Other services	10.4	7.7	2.7	152.4
All industries	10.5	9.8	0.7	1664.4

Source: Calculated from SBS data.

Risk and survival

The SBS publishes three-year survival rates of VAT businesses, which show that in 1998, the percentage of firms first registered three years previously and still trading was 64 per cent (up from 60 per cent in 1993). The fact that of all businesses 'closing', 36 per cent do so within three years of 'start-up' (remember the qualifications attaching to the VAT data) has always attracted a great deal of comment. However, although personal losses may have been caused to owners, from a social point of view these closed businesses have for the most part been replaced with new businesses, often using the same assets such as premises and equipment, and the closures are the price of the management learning that takes place and of a continuously changing and adapting economy. The proportion of VAT closures that result in bankruptcy and voluntary arrangements with creditors is also undoubtedly quite low. In England and Wales the number of insolvencies in 2000, not an exceptional year, was, according to the *Annual Abstract of Statistics*, under 10,000 self-employed persons (not all through business failure) plus 14,317 insolvencies of companies. That makes a total of, say 25,000 at most, or only 1.5 per cent of the total number of registered firms and 14 per cent of the number of deregistrations in the year 2000.

Table 2.9 demonstrates that the percentage of registrations and deregistrations in the VAT business population falls fairly steadily by size of sales turnover. The higher rate of deregistration for very small firms is consistent with the survival data given earlier, showing that, of firms which deregister, about 36 per cent do so within three years of first registration.

Small firms are thus particularly vulnerable in the first three years after start-up. While, as recognised earlier, there do seem to be differences in 'birth' and 'death' rates over time and between regions, and probably between countries, the pattern of early closure is remarkably similar in all countries for which reasonably reliable figures are available.

Table 2.9 Registrations and deregistrations as a percentage of the stock of VAT-registered firms, by turnover sizeband, United Kingdom, 1980

Turnover (£000)	Registrations (%)	Deregistrations (%)
0	14.5	13.5
1–14	15.4	24.1
15–49	14.4	12.0
50–99	11.0	7.2
100–499	8.5	4.4
500–1999	6.1	3.6
2000+	4.9	3.8
Total	12.1	10.9

Source: GANGULY (1985); no later figures are available.

Earlier we showed that only 64 per cent of new businesses in the United Kingdom survive for three years or more; in other words, 36 per cent of new firms cease to trade within three years. Figures for the United States (SBA 2001), the Netherlands and other developed countries are remarkably similar[13] and do not seem to vary very much between activity sectors. Equally remarkable is that in at least those developing countries for which data are available, over 50 per cent of all closures were also three years old or less (LIEDHOLM & MEAD 1999; PARKER 1996), a figure which is roughly consistent with that for advanced countries. Indeed, Liedholm and Mead say that 'this pattern of early closure is similar to that observed in India and the United States'. It seems that in terms of survival rates at least, different environments do not produce different results. We discuss the relationship of this important finding to issues in small business growth in Chapter 6.

Exports and internationalisation

The vast majority of SMEs are local in their operations and rooted in local communities. Nevertheless many export to customers in other markets, particularly in manufacturing but increasingly also in service activities. Small firms also contribute to exports indirectly through supplying goods (including components) and services to larger direct exporters. Some small firms do not export directly but through domestic wholesalers. In the early 1990s, it was estimated that there were about 100,000 direct UK small firm exporters and that in some European countries, SMEs accounted for 25 per cent or more of total exports (BANNOCK & DALY 1994). All the evidence is that export activity by small firms has been increasing.

SME exporters have played an even greater role in the dynamic economies of East Asia. For example, in Korea in 1985, SMEs accounted for 40 per cent of commodity exports (38 per cent in 1965) (NUGENT & YHEE 2002). In Taiwan in 1998, SMEs accounted for 56 per cent of exports (KUO & LI 2003).

Various studies have shown that the proportion of firms that export increases with size – as one would expect – as does the export ratio (percentage of sales turnover exported), but that among firms which do export there is a much weaker relationship, if any, between firm size and the export ratio. Overall, including exporters and non-exporters, in Europe-19 (for definition see page 213), according to EUROPEAN COMMISSION (2002b), the export ratio for enterprises in 2000 was 7 per cent for micro-, 14 per cent for small, 17 per cent for medium and 21 per cent for large enterprises.

SMEs are surprisingly important in invisible exports. For the United Kingdom, PRINGLE (1994) estimates that invisible earnings by SMEs exceed those from the financial services of the City of London and are particularly important in the rapidly growing sector of business, education and leisure services.

SMEs also go beyond exporting (and importing) to shift part or all of their economic activities abroad: for example, by foreign direct investment (FDI), in sales or production affiliates and in licensing technology. They are thus participating fully in the continuing process of globalisation. Sometimes SME globalisation will follow that of its large domestic customers, but many specialised small manufacturers are shifting activity to China and other low-cost countries. Venture capitalists in Silicon Valley report that most of the new projects they invest in have an element of development work or programming carried out in India or elsewhere. (Dan Roberts, 'Hunt begins for millions of missing jobs as US recovers', *Financial Times*, 17 February 2004).

BANNOCK & PARTNERS (1994) estimated that there were about 10,000–15,000 UK exporting SMEs that also had overseas establishments, joint ventures (JVs) or licensing arrangements. These were not necessarily multinationals in the usual sense of the term (say, more than 25 per cent of world assets outside the country of origin). The study reported that the UN programme on transnational corporations (TNCs) estimated that there were some 35,000 TNCs worldwide, of which 20,000 employed fewer than 500 people. Currency convertibility, freedom of capital movements, reductions in tariff barriers, the emergence of new industrialised countries (NICs) providing opportunities for low-cost sourcing and technological developments, have all favoured globalisation. For example, many thousands of Japanese SMEs have shifted operations abroad since the appreciation of the yen began in the mid-1980s (MITI 1991). Many manufacturing SMEs in the advanced countries have actually reduced their domestic employment and become design and marketing organisations with no domestic production facility.[14]

It used to be observed that SMEs would go through a series of stages from domestic to export as they gained experience and globalised activity, but more recently, and particularly in new niche technologies, SMEs are exporting from start-up (KUNDU & KATZ 2003). The 'born-international' phenomenon is partly explained by the fact that for some innovating new technology-based firms (NTBFs) the domestic market will be too small, while with short product cycles it is necessary to block off imitative competition and exploit the international market quickly.

Conclusion

A lot of ground has been covered in this chapter, which has demonstrated both that there is enormous variety in SMEs and their circumstances and that despite this some fruitful generalisations can be made, particularly about commonalities between countries. The theme introduced in Chapter 1, that published statistics on small firms can easily mislead and are in any case full of gaps, has been further illustrated and developed and, hopefully, some widespread misconceptions corrected.

Perhaps the most striking feature to emerge is the extraordinary turbulence below the surface that characterises this large sector of the economy. In the United Kingdom in 2001, 176,000 firms registered for VAT and another 163,000 deregistered, and changes on this scale continue year after year. In the United States, even for firms with employees only, well over half a million enter and leave the field every year. Over one-third of new businesses do not survive beyond three years. Yet in both countries, and as far as we can tell, everywhere else, owner-investors in small firms on average – and their employees – make no more, nor less, money than they could if they invested – or worked – in large firms. The explanation of this paradox, for owner-managers at least, seems to be that for many it is the opportunity for *self-expression* rather than money alone which is the prime motivator, though the hope of business success in the face of all the risks borne is undoubtedly a factor.

It is as well that, everywhere, so many people are willing to face the challenges of running a small business, or of working in one, because they matter so much in all market economies. This, and the history of research on the economics of small firms, is the subject of Chapter 3.

Notes

1 The surprisingly high proportion of conversion costs borne by SMEs follows from their large number, limited size and the fact that conversion costs are only a weak function of firm size. Any administrative burdens imposed on all businesses end up falling most heavily on SMEs, a fact of some importance discussed at length in Chapter 5. Conversion costs are largely irrelevant to the decision on euro entry but, if that decision were taken, there is a case for compensating SMEs.

2 We draw heavily in this chapter and elsewhere in the book on the regular *NatWest SBRT Quarterly Survey of Small Business in Britain*, in this case the report for September 2002. Henceforth references to this survey are designated thus: SBRT 9/02. The Small Business Research Trust (SBRT) survey has a sample of about 1000 enterprises employing up to about 100 persons in all sectors of the UK economy, including the primary sector. Like all surveys, it underrepresents micro-businesses.

3 Since we define SMEs as independent enterprises, we are not concerned here with small establishments or subsidiaries owned by large firms. In the general absence of comprehensive enterprise censuses, we do not know how many establishments are owned by enterprises in the business population as a whole. In UK manufacturing in 1987, the number of 'businesses' exceeded the number of 'enterprises' by 9.4 per cent but, as noted in Chapter 1, these figures are no longer published. For 1963 the number of establishments exceeded the number of enterprises by 40.6 per cent (BOLTON 1971) but these figures are not comparable with the 1987 data. In Japan, the excess of all establishments over enterprises in 1999 was 27.5 per cent. In the United States, for employer firms only, the excess was 21.4 per cent.

4 See GRAY (1998) for an in-depth interpretation of these results.

5 Partnerships can also incorporate as limited liability partnerships (LLPs) in the United Kingdom and some other countries.

6 Few simple, accurate statements can be made about taxation. Owners can pay themselves in dividends which, unlike a salary, do not bear National Insurance contributions (NICs), the highest marginal rate of income tax is 40 per cent plus employee and employer contributions totalling 23.8 per cent, and the full rate of corporation tax is 30 per cent with less for small profits and start-ups. The tax authorities might disallow corporate tax treatment if it is regarded as a disguised form of employment (2003/4).

7 Some of the apparent increase in self-employment in the United Kingdom results from changes in the basis for estimation of the business population.

8 The Board of Governors of the US Federal Reserve system do carry out a sample interview survey, the National Survey of Small Business Finances (NSSBF), which includes comprehensive data on 5,000 private businesses with fewer than 500 employees.

9 SBRT 12/02 showed that only 42 per cent of small firms with employees had active pension schemes (by law in the United Kingdom, employers must offer stakeholder pensions which become active only if employees wish to contribute or the employer voluntarily does so). The proportion with active schemes rose steadily from 12 per cent for firms with only one employee (other than the owner) to 78 per cent for firms with 20 or more employees. Well over 80 per cent of small business owner-managers aged between 40 and 70 have a pension scheme of their own. For a large proportion of business owners these pension schemes will be at best barely adequate and in SBRT 3/01, 38 per cent of all respondents aimed to sell their business when they retired – though many of these, particularly the smallest firms, will probably be unable to do so.

10 Trevor Jones, David McEvoy and Giles Barrett, 'Labour-intensive practices in the ethnic minority firm', in ATKINSON & STOREY (1994) cite various studies, including CURRAN & BURROWS (1988) that show that small business owners work significantly longer hours than employees. Their own survey found that only one-quarter of owners worked fewer than 40 hours a week (the national average for employees), with an average of 53.2 hours. Asian owners worked even longer hours but, interestingly, perceptions of profits and incomes were not related to hours worked.

11 The registry of business names and owners was established by an Act of 1916 intended to prevent enemy aliens from avoiding confiscation of property.

12 From SBA (2001) we can calculate new starts of employer firms for 1999 at 10.2 per cent of the stock, and terminations at 9.1 per cent. These figures are of the same order of magnitude as those for the United Kingdom but do not include firms without employees. It is not surprising that bankruptcies were only 0.65 per cent of the stock in the United States, given the coverage of the figures.

13 'Failure – an iron law', *Small Business Perspective*, 6, 1992.

14 KUO & LI (2003) review the literature on the SME role in FDI. They note that this role is important, with SMEs accounting for 50 per cent of the value of all US FDI in 1982 and for 66 per cent of the number of FDI investments by the UK in 1981.

3   Do small firms matter?[1]

The large firm/small firm paradigm

In a superficial sense, the answer to the question posed by the title of this chapter is obvious. As shown in the Appendix, SMEs account for about 60 per cent or more of employment and 20–30 per cent of GDP in the advanced countries, and perhaps for more in the developing world. Of course, small firms must matter. Yet SMEs are generally regarded as poor cousins to large firms: less productive – look at the disparity between their shares in employment and value added – less sophisticated, less powerful and, well, smaller. That is the static view; in a dynamic perspective, it has not been possible to ignore the fact that almost all large firms started out as small, many of them quite recently. Think for example of Pfizer (1942), Honda (1948), Intel (1968), Wal-Mart (1969), Microsoft (1981) and Cisco (1984). The seedbed role of the small business sector has been accommodated into conventional thought through the perfectly correct perception that only a tiny minority of small firms ever do grow to really significant scale. The mass of SMEs are still seen as vestiges of the agricultural, craft-dominated past – indeed, almost as a backward peasantry. The universal persistence of official measures for the support and modernisation of small firms bears witness to the prevailing view that while SMEs are in need of help and are something of a drag on the economy, the real motor of economic growth is large enterprise which can benefit from economies of scale, investment, research and development (R&D) and scientific management.

It is easy to see why this should be so. As we shall show, the long rise of western economies to historically unprecedented levels of income per capita has been accompanied by a reduction in the share of SMEs in output and employment, despite some reversals, especially in the 1960s. Economic advance seems always to have been led by large firms. The Industrial Revolution – in Britain in the eighteenth and nineteenth centuries – saw a concentration in the control of household manufacturing into the hands of smaller numbers of merchant entrepreneurs under the 'putting-out' system, then its progressive enclosure into factories and, finally, as capital-intensive technology developed, the factories became larger. A similar pattern occurred in Belgium, France, the United States and Germany and, apparently, also in the later stages of the more recent examples of industrialisation, including those in south-east Asia (see Chapter 9).

The belief in the driving role of large firms has been reinforced more recently by their high visibility in the continuing globalisation of economic activity – for example in oil, motor vehicles, aerospace, pharmaceuticals, consumer electronics, computers and other advanced industries.

The theme of this chapter is that arguments about the relative value of small and large firms to the economy are beside the point; like the red and white corpuscles in blood, in the market economy both small and large firms are necessary and complementary. We begin by extending the analysis of Chapter 1 to cover the long history of the aggregate shares of small and large firms in the advanced economies. We then go on to review how economists have interpreted these past trends and the radical reassessment of economic thinking that is now beginning to take place. Finally we try to explain what the complementary roles of small and large firms actually are.

The fall and rise of small firms in Britain

Given the difficulties already described of using small firm data even for recent times, it will be no surprise to the reader that the study of long-term trends is more difficult still. For Britain, although more detailed and reliable data on population began to be available from 1801, it was not until the early 1830s that inspectors started systematically counting factories. It is clear from several sources that micro-enterprises and large firms co-existed in the last quarter of the eighteenth century in Britain, and no doubt much earlier. The British East India Company was chartered by Elizabeth I in 1600. The Royal Exchange Assurance and London Assurance, both substantial corporations, had been founded in 1720.[2] CLAPHAM (1950) refers to Defoe's description of silk mills at Stockport in the 1720s, where 'six engines, the buildings of which are of prodigious bulk' employed some 2,000 people. These would be quite significant medium-sized firms even by today's standards (DEFOE 1724).

There seem to be no comprehensive statistics on the size distribution of enterprises in Britain, however, even for the last quarter of the nineteenth century. CLAPHAM (1952) discusses at length the Return of Factories and Workshops Act 1871. This showed that there were 127,000 separate manu-facturing working places (oddly, the *Census of Production* revealed exactly the same number for *enterprises* in 1985: there were 143,000 establishments) employing some 2.4 million people (5.0 million in 1985) – an average of 19 persons each (35 in 1985). Clearly there was a considerable increase in the average size of manufacturing establishments over this period, but in fact this comparison understates the increase because the 1871 figures do not include such activities as milling and wheelwrights – and, more importantly, because they exclude outworkers.

It is not until 1924 that we have reasonably reliable numbers on the size distribution of firms in manufacturing from successive *Censuses of Production*. Chart 3.1 shows that the share of small enterprises (fewer than 200 employees) in total UK manufacturing employment fell continuously from 1935 and, by analogy with the establishment data, also from 1924 (though with a significant upward blip in the 1930s) and continued to fall again until the late 1960s. Since then the share of small firms increased to the mid-1990s and now appears to have levelled out.

Data on the early size distribution of firms are sparse outside manufacturing, particularly so for the service sector. It seems, however, that the Agrarian Revolution was accompanied by the rapid disappearance of the very small landowner in England even before the Private Enclosure Acts peaked between 1760 and 1780, and the General Enclosure Acts speeded up the process from 1801 (JOHNSON 1909). This process of concentration in

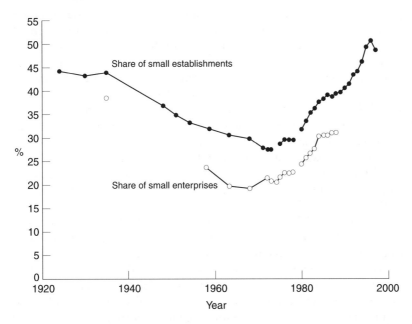

Chart 3.1 Share of small establishments and enterprises in total manufacturing employment, United Kingdom, selected years, 1924–97

Sources: BOLTON (1971); Business Monitor PA 1002; *Census of Prodution Summary Tables*, HMSO. For a discussion of changes in the coverage of data, see HUGHES (1990). For the absolute numbers and data on numbers of firms from 1924 to 1998, see STANWORTH & GRAY (1991, Chapter 1).

Note
'Small enterprises and establishments' are defined as those with fewer than 200 employees. Comparable enterprise data are not available after 1988.

farming seems to have continued very slowly to the present day, though it remains essentially a small-scale activity in Britain.

The BOLTON (1971) Inquiry (which did not cover agriculture) found that concentration had increased in retail distribution between 1950 and the mid-1960s, though not markedly so, and that:

> the contribution of small firms to economic activity was declining in most industries with the possible exceptions of road transport and some of the miscellaneous service trades. Although there have been exceptions, we think it likely that in most industries this decline has been going on at least since before the war.

From 1979, estimates of the whole enterprise population in the United Kingdom, including agriculture, construction and services, show that the reversal in the trend in concentration, which was probably general from the late 1960s, continued rapidly between 1979 and 1991, though it seems to have ceased after the 1989–92 recession. The total number of SMEs, including the full-time self-employed without employees, rose from 1.8 million in 1979 to 2.7 million in 1991, and the overall share in employment of enterprises with fewer than 200 employees rose from 49 per cent to 58 per cent over the period. Much of this increase was accounted for by very small firms, and the number of large firms employing 500 or more people, and their total employment, fell absolutely (BANNOCK & DALY 1994). By 2001 the SBS estimated the total enterprise population at 3.7 million and the employment share of enterprises with fewer than 200 employees at 53.8 per cent. However, there have been at least two upward changes in the coverage of the total enterprise population estimates since 1979. The self-employed and VAT numbers in Table 3.1 suggest that the enterprise population, and therefore the number of SMEs, has not increased further since the early 1990s.

Despite the formidable data problems, the long-term picture is fairly clear: the quantitative importance of small firms in Britain probably declined, no doubt with fluctuations, at least from the beginning of the statistical era in the nineteenth century right down to the mid-1960s, when a reversal of trend took place that may now have run its course. Small firms have always accounted for the vast majority of all firms by number, of course, and in terms of employment for a smaller majority.

Statistics on large firms have always been easier to compile, and for the period since 1909 we have a series on the share of the 100 largest firms in net manufacturing output (Chart 3.2). This series shows a rise in aggregate concentration over the whole period 1909–68, interrupted only by the Second World War; then a plateau of stability until the early 1980s, followed by a sustained decline. This picture, dealing as it does only with the top of the distribution, is not the mirror image of that for small firms, but it adds continuity and credence to that picture.

Table 3.1 Self-employed and businesses registered for VAT, United Kingdom, total number, 1979, 1990, 1994–2001

Year	Number of self-employed (000)	VAT stock year end
1979	1,906	1,289
1990	3,298	1,709
1994	3,301	1,609
1995	3,361	1,600
1996	3,300	1,603
1997	3,351	1,621
1998	3,280	1,652
1999	3,202	1,658
2000	3,139	1,664
2001	3,147	1,677

Sources: Self-employed: *Annual Abstract of Statistics* 1992, 2002; VAT stock: SBS for 1979 and 1990; BANNOCK & DALY (1994).

Note
In 2001, 45 per cent of the SBS estimate of the total number of enterprises were registered for VAT. The number of self-employed (with and without employees) is about twice that of VAT traders, which of course includes incorporated businesses, since the majority of the self-employed are not registered and some are in partnerships.

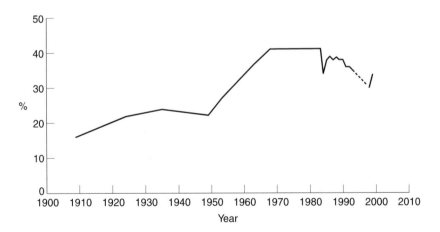

Chart 3.2 Share of the 100 largest private sector enterprises defined by size of net output in UK manufacturing, selected years, 1909–99

Sources: PRAIS (1976), updated by the author from successive issues of the *Census of Production*. For 1998 and 1999, special tabulations from the ONS.

Note
There were changes in coverage in 1993 onwards and 1999 onwards.

Trends in concentration in other countries

Figures on numbers of small firms and their share of employment before the Second World War are also hard to find for other countries, though some data, reaching back into the nineteenth century, are available for a few countries.

Markovitch, cited in BRAUDEL (1990), calculated that in the years 1835–44, craft production (defined as firms not using machinery) accounted for 75 per cent of industrial product in France, and that by 1855–64 this average had fallen only to 63 per cent. On a different basis, defining craft (*artisanat*) production as that carried out in firms where the owner was a production worker as well as a manager, the craft share in output rose to over 80 per cent for 1855–64. Moreover, these figures seem not to include family or homeworkers which, according to Markovitch, accounted for at least 8 per cent of textile employment in France as late as 1860–5 (MORSEL 1987).

Other data for France reproduced in Table 3.2, and which also probably exclude outworkers, show that average employment per firm in industry, transport and commerce doubled from 1851 to 1921, though there was a decline between the 1896 and 1906 censuses. Table 3.3 shows that the share of establishments with fewer than 10 employees in total industrial employment in France fell from 58 per cent in 1906 to just 16 per cent in 1974, with a temporary recovery in the 1930s. In Germany, on a whole-economy basis, a similar shift is apparent for the smallest firms (under six employees), though again there was a pronounced recovery between 1925 and 1933 (SEGENBERGER *et al.* 1990, citing R. Stockman and W. Kleber).

Some data are available for long-term trends in the numbers of small manufacturing establishments in the United States. Harold G. Vatter, in 'The position of small business in the structure of American manufacturing 1870–1970', in BRUCHEY (1980), notes that 'the hundred year record shows that ... small firm numbers proliferate when the economy and the [manufacturing] sector are strongly expanding during an intermediate time period; the numbers decelerate when ... general expansion slows'. He

Table 3.2 Employees per firm, average number, selected years, France, 1851–1921

Year	Industry, transport and distribution (men)	Industry (men and women)
1851	2.26	2.57
1866	2.44	
1881	2.63	
1896	3.51	3.16
1906	3.20	2.71
1921	4.50	3.77

Source: MORSEL (1987), citing P. Simiand, *Le Salaire, l'Evolution Sociale et la Monnaie*, Paris, 1932.

Table 3.3 Employment by industrial establishment employment size band, France, selected years, 1906–81

Year	0 employees (%)	1–9 employees (%)	>10 employees (%)	Total (%)
1906	27	31	42	100
1926	14	27	59	100
1931	12	22	66	100
1936	17	22	61	100
1954	6	19	75	100
1962	5	16	79	100
1966	4	16	80	100
1974	3	13	84	100
1981	4	14	82	100

Source: SEGENBERGER *et al.* (1990), citing Didier, *Economie et Statistique*, 144, 1982, and 2, 1969, INSEE.

observes, for example, an increase in the numbers of US manufacturing establishments between 1869 and 1919, with reversals in the 1870s and early 1900s and again in the 1930s, a slight increase during the Second World War, growth in 1947–53, and two decades of decline from 1950. BLACKFORD (2003) observes similar fluctuations, with a resurgence of SMEs in the United States from the 1970s to the close of the 1990s.

The finding that the role of SMEs in the United States has been pro-cyclical does not necessarily contradict our earlier discussion in Chapter 2 of periods of 'recession-push' factors in new business formation, because the US data mostly exclude the self-employed without employees. The enormous growth from 123,000 to 355,000 in the number of manufacturing establishments shown in DODD (1993) for the period 1850–90 was during a period of rapid industrialisation and population growth (in this period, the self-employed were included). Growth in the number of SMEs has also been experienced more recently in the 'Asian Miracle' (see Chapter 9). Another source shows that despite the rise of large establishments as US industrialisation proceeded over the period 1820–70, concentration in terms of output hardly changed because of the rapid expansion of SMEs (ATTACK 1986).

As Segenberger *et al.* (1990) show, more recently there has been a general international trend for the number of small firms and their share in employment to increase since the middle 1960s. We have given some detail on this for Britain. For the United States, the position is less clear-cut: the SBA annual report for 1987 (SBA 1987), commenting upon the long-term concentration of the US economy, stated: 'In more recent years, this long-term secular decline appears to have reversed.' The report gave the percentage of total employment in firms with fewer than 100 employees from the US *Enterprise Census* as 39.9 in 1967 and 40.1 in 1977 and 1982. However, the percentage share of firms with fewer than 500 employees rose from 53.2 to 54.1 over the period. We cannot conclude from this that the

United States is an exception to the recent international trend because, as noted in Chapter 1, the US data exclude the smallest firms.[3]

For Japan, there also seems to have been a long-term increase in concentration, at least in manufacturing, up to 1926. There was some reversal in the early 1930s and a resumption of concentration during the Second World War; however, again these long-term figures exclude the smallest firms (Table 3.4). Better data are available for Japan from 1969 and these also indicate a resurgence of small firms, with the employment share of firms with fewer than 100 employees increasing again up to the onset of Japan's economic crisis in the early 1980s with some resumption of concentration since then (Table 3.5).

Table 3.4 Employment by employment size band (five or more employees only), manufacturing, Japan, selected years 1909–42

Year	5–99 (%)	100–499 (%)	500+ (%)	Total (%)
1909	58.0	21.3	20.7	100.0
1914	52.5	22.3	25.2	100.0
1919	45.2	23.3	31.5	100.0
1926	47.7	22.3	30.0	100.0
1926	41.0	21.6	37.4	100.0
1931	49.0	25.4	25.6	100.0
1937	45.0	20.9	34.1	100.0
1942	41.0	17.8	41.3	100.0

Source: Adapted from MITI, quoted in TERAOKA (1996).

Note
Break in comparability from 1926.

Table 3.5 Establishments, private sector employment and percentage shares in establishments and employment by employment size band, Japan, selected years, 1969–96

Year	No. of establish- ments (000)	Employ- ment (000)	1–4		5–9		10–29		30–49		50–99		100+	
			Est (%)	Emp (%)	Est (%)	Emp (%)	Est (%)	Emp (%)	Est (%)	Emp (%)	Est (%)	Emp (%)	Est (%)	Emp (%)
1969	4,666	35,239	72.2	19.6	14.8	12.6	9.3	19.6	1.8	9.0	1.2	10.4	0.7	28.8
1978	5,870	45,521	70.1	19.1	16.4	13.5	10.0	20.4	1.8	8.5	1.1	9.0	0.6	29.5
1981	6,291	45,961	69.3	20.5	6.9	14.8	10.3	22.2	1.8	9.3	1.1	10.4	0.6	22.8
1991	6,559	55,014	64.4	16.7	18.6	14.4	12.7	24.0	2.2	9.9	1.3	10.8	0.8	24.2
1996	6,522	57,583	62.6	15.4	19.0	14.0	13.7	24.7	2.4	10.3	1.5	11.2	0.8	24.4

Source: Adapted from Establishments and Enterprise Census, *Japan Statistical Yearbook*, 2003.

Note
All industries, includes primary sector.

In summary, we may conclude that over the long period, the share of small firms in employment and output has certainly fallen, but there were important reversals of this trend, even in the nineteenth century. There was a widespread reversal in the inter-war recession (1919–39), and a fairly vigorous one from the 1960s until the early 1990s.

Explaining the resurgence of small firms

There is no agreement on the causes of the recent resurgence of small firms. It cannot be explained by the continuing shift to services in the industrialised countries, because the trend has been common to both service and manufacturing sectors. For the same reason we can probably rule out explanations based solely on a technological shift in favour of small-run production, though on balance technological change has favoured smaller firms.

The previous reversals of trend in the 1930s can be explained by an 'escape to self-sufficiency' in times of high unemployment. This effect also seemed to be operating in the recessions of the early 1980s, but the growth in the number of small firms, in the United Kingdom at least, actually accelerated in the second half of the 1980s after unemployment stopped rising and started to fall.

The shift to small firms began well before the 1979 UK Thatcher government declared itself committed to expansion. Perhaps it has gone further in the United Kingdom than elsewhere because the small firm share in economic activity had earlier fallen further and faster than elsewhere. Government policy may have reinforced the shift to smaller firms, especially in the United Kingdom, but it did not initiate the process and the impact of policy specific to SMEs was probably negligible.

The international nature of the recent shift towards small firms, and its vigour and duration, are probably a reaction and readjustment to the excessive concentration of the 1950s and 1960s. The unwinding of the inflationary momentum of that period, and the thrust of competition from the developing world and the NICs, were major causal factors. Very large companies, in reaction to these competitive pressures, have flattened management structures, disposed of subsidiaries and concentrated on core activities. Large firms emulated the greater use of subcontracting to small firms that has been such a striking feature of the economies of south-east Asia, where much of the competition has come from (see Chapter 9). PIORE & SABEL (1984), to whom we return in Chapters 7 and 10, argue that SMEs and flexible production methods can cope much better than large firms with high fixed costs in periods of fluctuation and uncertainty such as the 1970s and 1980s.

The views of economists

The long rise of big business has inspired a deep tradition, particularly in British and American literature on economic organisation, business history and economic development, in favour of the virtues of continued concentration, or at least in the virtues of large-scale enterprises. An early and still powerful figure in this tradition was Joseph Schumpeter, who argued that it was large firms that drove innovation. He wrote (1943):

> innovation itself is being reduced to routine. Technological progress is increasingly becoming the business of teams of trained specialists who turn out what is required and make it work in predictable ways.

What Schumpeter was really saying was 'forget small firms, big business is the future'. In this, he was a convert to the reality of the continuing concentration of business in America.[4] BERLE & MEANS (1932), published at the time Schumpeter moved from Germany to the United States, were the first to document fully the concentration of economic power into big firms. This process had been going on for a long time, and with it a decline of proprietary capitalism which they labelled the 'separation of ownership and control'. Berle & Means showed that American industry was increasingly owned by pension funds and other financial institutions, it was being run not by owners but by salaried managers who owned a negligible proportion of the equity.

Alfred Chandler, whose meticulous work on organisational development of large US corporations (CHANDLER 1962) was influenced by Schumpeter, has had enormous influence on the literature on big companies. Chandler did not argue that small firms were unimportant; he simply ignored them.[5]

J. K. Galbraith, also in the Schumpeterian tradition, wrote: 'By all but the pathologically romantic, it is now recognised that this is not the age of the small man' (GALBRAITH 1967). More recently, William Lazonick made the surprising assertion that 'proprietary capitalism has long since vanished' (LAZONICK 1991).[6]

In a way, the authors cited were attacking the basic premises of the equilibrium-based neo-classical theory of the firm that had its origins in a period in which most economic activity was conducted by small proprietary firms.[7] In this theory, there is no place for new firms or entrepreneurship; firms are just there in large numbers, facing infinite competition that forces operation at optimum scale and price-taking at marginal cost – a fair description of the situation of many small firms today. The theory was later adapted to take account of the presence of large firms (oligopoly),[8] but that added little to an understanding of the dynamics of the market system in which, we shall argue, small firms play a vital part in addition to their static role.

The Schumpeter–Chandler tradition is largely silent on the origins of large firms, and the role of small firms in market economies. Either the neo-classical model does, more or less, prevail – in which case the small firms would not be there unless they were making efficient use of resources and were playing some role – or the Schumpeter–Chandler school's assertions about the superiority of the large corporation over the small firm would have resulted in the virtual disappearance of small business. There is a missing element here.

A few economists have pondered on the reason for the persistence of small firms in the economy. Alfred Marshall struggled with this question in his *Principles of Economics* (MARSHALL 1890). In his later *Industry and Trade* (MARSHALL 1919) he commented that in less capital-intensive industries 'the number of small businesses is constantly growing; since their products are ever finding new vents in these markets, as well as in the supply of special materials and machines to large businesses'. Marshall was well aware of the contributions of small firms and the role of the small entrepreneur:

> at any given time and in any given condition of industrial technique, there is likely to be a point beyond which any further increase in size gives little further increase in economy and efficiency. And that is well; for small businesses are on the whole the best educators of the initiative and versatility, which are the chief sources of industrial progress.

Much later, Edith Penrose (PENROSE 1959) recognised the dynamic role of small business in the economy. She showed that the existence of *economies of growth*, as important for firms of all sizes as economies of scale, had been neglected, and feared that by 'artificially' protecting themselves against competition the success of large firms could restrain the growth of the economy:

> To the extent that small firms are prevented from taking advantage of economies of growth by artificial restrictions on their ability to expand into those areas not occupied by the larger firms (which we have called the 'interstices'), resources in the economy would be inefficiently used.
> (PENROSE 1959)[9]

The obsolescence of the economics of industrial organisation

A whole branch of applied microeconomics, the economics of industrial organisation, emerged in the 1950s[10] to explain the predominance of large firms and to reconcile the benefits of the large corporation and the dangers of monopoly power (neo-classical theory showed that under monopoly, equilibrium output could be expected to be lower and prices and profits higher than under perfect competition).

It would take us too far from the thrust of this book to review all the theoretical and empirical underpinnings and disagreements of the economics of industrial organisation.[11] We must content ourselves with a caricature, not too far from the truth, of the findings of this and related branches of economics that predominated in the post-Second World War period and which still prevail to a large extent today.

The main pillar of support for the large firm is the undeniable existence of *economies of scale*. As everyone knows, capital-intensive techniques can manufacture hundreds of thousands of cars more cheaply than a few. This is why, not only in many technologically advanced sectors such as motor vehicles, electronics and aviation, but in many others such as brewing, cigarettes and soap, large firms account for the majority of output. In some industries the declines in unit cost, as Marshall noted, seem to level off beyond a certain point. Economists have calculated a minimum efficient scale (MES).[12] In a few industries, the MES is very high: passenger jet aircraft seem to be a case in point. However, research shows that about 50 per cent of firms in most, though not all, industries operate below the MES (AUDRETSCH 2001). How is it that SMEs survive in these cases?

There are several answers to this question. One answer is that production economies of scale do not by any means apply to, or cover, all business costs. For example, a small brewer serving a local market can compete with a giant brewing at a fraction of the cost per barrel because the giant is burdened with heavier marketing, transport and other costs.[13] The same reasons explain why a local carpenter can often tailor-make a fitted kitchen for a similar or lower cost than mass-produced units. Another reason is that technological development can rapidly change MES, for example as in mini-steel plants or electrical generating. Many SMEs do not compete directly with large firms at all but operate in *niche markets*, too small to be of interest to mass-producers. The small firm may be able to charge premium prices for some products and services, even where they are competing with larger firms; this is why small corner shops survive in competition with super-markets. This last point brings out the fact that the MES concept is frequently of doubtful applicability to service activities, which now account for the bulk of gross domestic product (GDP). Most research has been focused on manufacturing but in the growing service sector, now some three-quarters of the economy, SMEs have substantial advantages. In law and medicine, large firms have always been in a minority position, for example, as in many other sectors of personal and business services (Philip Scranton, 'Moving outside manufacturing: research perspectives on small business in twentieth-century America', in ODAKA & SAWAI 1999). The MES concept is clearly an oversimplification, above all because it reflects a static view. In reality all new firms are likely to be below the MES; they start that way because they hope to grow (AUDRETSCH 2001).[14] There are also diseconomies as well as economies of scale. It is a common observation, for example, that co-ordination costs, and with them overheads, increase rapidly with employment size.

Finally, we have been writing about what Marshall called *internal economies of scale* but, as he was the first to emphasise, there are also *external economies of scale* which are accessible by firms of all sizes. The ability to buy cheap materials and components that are produced on a large scale, together with access to new technology, knowledge and skilled labour can, in many circumstances, offset to a large extent the scale disadvantages of the small firm. Marshall thought that the availability of these external economies was growing all the time and this process is probably still accelerating. A small firm, for example, can buy in through wholesalers a range of electronic components from all over the world and assemble them in innovative ways without being disadvantaged in its field of, specialised computers, say, by its lack of scale. Marshall emphasised the importance of industrial districts to the delivery of external economies, and there is a large literature on clusters of small firms in, for example, Silicon Valley in the United States, and the clusters of small export-oriented manufacturers of ceramics, leather and other goods in Northern Italy. However, with improved communications, some of the benefits of external economies are increasingly available to small firms everywhere.

Economies of scale are, or were, also thought to apply uniformly to R&D. There is some truth in this, particularly where research is capital-intensive, and it is a fact that most *recorded* R&D is conducted by large firms or government/higher educational establishments. However, it is again an oversimplification to conclude that large firms always have an overwhelming advantage in R&D. It is not easy to facilitate the necessary freedom of thought and action and to accommodate the radical innovative spirit in large organisations, or to insulate research units from the pressures of bureaucracy and sometimes short-time horizons of senior management.[15] It has often been noted that many large firm innovations have been instigated and developed without the sanction of, and even in defiance of, senior management: the first DEC minicomputer was a case in point.[16] In OAKEY (1994) this process is termed 'bootlegging'. The author can vouch from personal experience that the launch of the Range Rover from the then British Leyland in 1973 had its origins in unofficial back-of-experimental-workshop activity in the mid-1960s.[17]

It is true in a sense that, as Schumpeter foresaw, most innovation activity in large firms has been routinised, but this activity in reality is mostly about improving or extending existing technology and products. BAUMOL (2002), whose recent work attributes a large proportion of steady economic incremental growth to these types of activity, admits that radical innovations often come from outside the big corporations. This is a well-established fact: small firms continue to contribute disproportionately to inventions and innovations (ACS & AUDRETSCH 1990; JEWKES *et al.* 1969). Probably most R&D in small firms goes unrecorded (ROPER 1999) and SMEs are generally reluctant to patent original ideas because of the cost both of registration and defence and because in modern global technologies (large) competitors will work round patents and steal a march. It is worth emphasising that R&D expenditure is an input not an output (innovative outputs are hard to measure), and the statistics can again mislead. The probability is that the productivity of R&D in small firms (outputs over inputs) is vastly higher than in large firms. Moreover, there are external economies in R&D: as AUDRETSCH (2001) points out, technological knowledge gets diffused, for example by shifts in technical personnel between firms.

The general superiority of labour productivity in large firms over small was shown in Chapter 2 to be the result of higher capital intensity and not an unambiguous sign of greater efficiency, which it is often supposed to be. Another element in the case for the invincibility of the large corporation is its alleged use of better-qualified and better-trained personnel. On the first point, it was shown in Chapter 2 that the self-employed are not inferior overall in terms of qualifications to those employed in large firms – though their employees may be in some countries. We shall show in Chapter 8 that it is a myth that large firms do more and better training than small firms. In fact, the small firm sector is a net supplier of trained and experienced personnel to the rest of the economy.

The latest view on why the role of small firms must shrink (continue to shrink long-term) is that small firms cannot hold their own with globalisation. The theory is that SMEs will lose out in two respects: first, because their domestic markets will contract as large foreign firms extend their penetration by exports and local production, and second because SMEs are at a natural disadvantage in exporting and operating abroad because of their limited financial and managerial resources. These views belie the facts. We have already shown in Chapter 2 that although most SMEs do not export directly or operate abroad, many do. The foreign activities of SMEs and their share of global exports and FDI, we showed, are substantial and even increasing. Moreover, globalisation brings greater complexity and specialisation, which creates new roles for SMEs. We established earlier in this chapter that recently, in a period of rapid globalisation, the share of SMEs in total employment has actually been increasing. Technology, notably the spread of new media for communication such as the Internet but also new techniques for batch production tailored to ever-changing consumer requirements, has increased the capacity of SMEs to compete globally.

The fear of world dominance by multinationals is not new. After the Second World War it was believed that American multinationals would annihilate European companies thanks to their superior economies of scale and supposedly more advanced management techniques. A flood of books and articles urged European companies to merge together to respond to the *American Challenge* (the title of a book by the French author, see SERVAN-SCHREIBER 1968). In fact, European and Japanese companies did meet the challenge, in some industries such as car and consumer electronics to the point where there was concern in the United States about the survival of its major industries. This challenge, too, was met and consumers have benefited greatly by the enhanced competition (ABERNATHY *et al.* 1983). The pressures of global competition have not diminished the role of SMEs: GUILLEN (2001), on the evidence of his case studies of Argentina, South Korea and Spain, says: 'SMEs can and do thrive in the context of globalisation if only state policies do not overwhelm them by artificially diverting too many resources to business groups, large firms, and/ or state-owned enterprises.'

The complementarity of small and large firms

The key to an understanding of the persistence of small firms is their *complementarity* to large ones; the one is not superior or inferior to the other. SMEs tend to be local, or specialised, or both; individual, client-oriented, inventive and labour-intensive. Large firms tend to be international, mass-oriented, diffusion-oriented and capital-intensive. In a static sense, SMEs carry out functions that it would not be economic for a large firm to perform because of the limited scale of the market, or where personal service can give a competitive edge. For example, repair and maintenance of buildings and equipment is very much the province of the small firm.

In a dynamic sense, the role of SMEs, or at least some of them, is to pilot small-scale innovations. If successful, the firm may grow or be taken over, or simply emulated, by a large firm more suited to mass-marketing. While only large firms may innovate in certain capital-intensive activities, they almost always rely upon SMEs at some stage in the process, either as specialist suppliers or in the marketing of the result. Boeing and Airbus passenger jets could not be produced without many thousands of small suppliers, and their seats would not be filled without hundreds of thousands of travel agents around the world. There is no fixed borderline between small and large firm activities. New ways are found of organising old activities: coffee bars used to be the exclusive province of the small firm, now there are large chains alongside them; some markets where demand has shrunk – for example, the manufacture of smokers' pipes – get recaptured by small firms.

Historically, and still today, SMEs play key roles in economic development. In the early stages of development, small firms helped to develop markets. Itinerant pedlars, for example, created markets for small manufacturers of pots and pans in Britain and America before the industrial revolution and still do today in developing countries (BLACKFORD 2003, BROWN 2000).[18] The service sector develops first, as in the role of merchants in creating the putting-out system. As economies develop to the advanced stage, agriculture (small firms again) shrinks as a proportion of total output, then manufacturing rises and finally the service sector (small firms predominantly) accounts for the greater part of economic activity. The service sector not only develops markets but, as with the early merchant activity, helps to accumulate capital for larger firm investment.

In Chapter 9 we show that the role of SMEs changes somewhat as development continues; they become less important as a share of output (though not necessarily of employment) and more medium-sized firms emerge – SMEs grow larger, on average. SMEs help to diffuse a widespread commercial culture and a trained labour force with the necessary skills, disciplines and organisation upon which further developments can be built.[19]

In later stages of development, as more larger organisations emerge and continue to grow, SMEs increasingly perform specialised activities which cannot be carried out optimally on a large scale. Large firms become increasingly capital-intensive as development proceeds, creating more value added and wealth. This wealth, and the expenditure that results from it, allows new, more labour-intensive firms to emerge and create new markets. These new markets, in turn, may be occupied by large firms as the new activities mature to the point where large-scale operations are viable.

Since the late 1970s, there has been a revival of interest in the economic role of SMEs, but until very recently that interest has been mainly focused narrowly on job creation by the small firm sector. In 1979, more or less simultaneously, David Birch and Graham Gudgin found that small firms, nationally in the United States and regionally in Britain, accounted for a disproportionate share of new jobs (BIRCH 1979; GUDGIN *et al.* 1979). These findings were later replicated elsewhere (SEGENBERGER *et al.* 1990) and despite fierce academic debate and scrutiny they have been confirmed as basically sound, though it is the very small firms (the ones harder to measure) that seem to account for most of the superior job creation performance of small firms.[20] The interest aroused by these obviously important findings at a time of high unemployment is understandable, but they did not result immediately in any advance in thinking on the role of SMEs in the economy. If anything, the job generation debate has distracted attention from the way that small firms are actually an integral and essential part of the whole capitalist economic system. To conclude that small firms are important because they create jobs is to miss the real point. As argued in this chapter, SMEs perform many functions in the economy and as a result create jobs to perform those functions. Employment is a by-product, even though it is a very welcome one.

Conclusion

Since the earliest times, small and large firms have coexisted wherever markets have been allowed to work with some degree of freedom.[21] There is nothing new, even in the process of globalisation. The Bardi and Peruzzi companies of Florence in the thirteenth century were the largest companies in the world at that time: they owned ships, wagon and mule trains, banks and even metal mines, all over Europe. The great chartered companies, such as the East India companies of the seventeenth century, had an even wider sphere of operations, owning plantations and having depots, offices and factories. Alongside these big firms in both periods were many thousands of smaller and itinerant traders, artisans, farmers (even though there were serfs in various degrees of bondage in various countries) and merchants and others, such as mercenaries – all recognisably antecedents of the small firms of today.

As mentioned earlier, satisfactory data on numbers of enterprises and their shares in overall economic activity did not exist until the nineteenth century and then, as now, are imperfect. It is fairly clear, however, that in the advanced countries the number of small enterprises and their share in employment has fallen since the nineteenth century, with some important reversals of the downward trend – a widespread one in the inter-war recession and a vigorous one from the 1960s until the late 1990s. None of the reasons earlier evinced for a permanent superiority of large firms over small and a continuously shrinking role of the latter in the long run are sustainable. But this is subject to the proviso that markets are allowed to work with reasonable freedom. The persistence of small firms is all the more remarkable given the constraints they face in terms of managerial resources and finance, and the administrative burdens they bear in the highly regulated modern economy, as we show in Chapter 5. The reason SMEs persist is that their role as complements to large firms is essential in the market economy.

Most (not all) economists and economic historians have until recently been fixated on large firms.[22] The reason for this must be that the statistical information on SMEs is fragmentary and unsatisfactory, especially for earlier times. Most small firms are born and die without leaving any records: these records are not cherished and preserved as are those of the big corporations.[23]

To some extent the blind spot about SMEs – if that is not too harsh a phrase for it – is an Anglo-American characteristic. As already mentioned, Schumpeter's earlier work emphasised the role of individual entrepreneurship but shifted to a preoccupation with the large bureaucratic corporation after he moved from Germany to the United States. There is, again as mentioned, a strong constituency in favour of small firms in the United States and a suspicion of the giant firm and its connotations of monopoly. However, as BLACKFORD (2003) points out, action in favour of SMEs in the United States has been largely symbolic. In Chapter 7, we argue that this is a general phenomenon.

In continental Europe (and also in Japan) there is rather more statistical information available on SMEs than in the English-speaking countries, and there is a longer tradition of government support and encouragement. This may, in the case of continental Europe, be partly the result of the survival of some types of craft or guild traditions which remain in legal form today, for example in the *artisanat* and *handwerk* systems of France and Germany, respectively (DORAN 1984).

Notes

1 This chapter draws heavily on two unpublished papers by the author presented at seminars: 'Small firms in modern economic history: a missing element',

London School of Economics Business History Seminar Group, May 1995; and 'The neglected majority: the role of SMEs in economic development', Buckingham University, October 2001. The Seminars were chaired by Professor Leslie Hannah and Professor Martin Ricketts, respectively. The author is indebted to these chairpersons for the invitations and to all participants for comments.

2 M.W. Kirby, 'Big business before 1900', in KIRBY & ROSE (1994).

3 The census definition of 'establishments with one or more employees' was introduced in 1947, but the exclusion of the self-employed in US enterprise statistics has deeper roots. It can be seen from DODD (1993) that data on the number of manufacturing establishments on this basis go back to 1899. From 1850 to 1890, 'neighbourhood, household and hand industries' (self-employed) were included, as mentioned above.

4 This was the later Schumpeter; in his earlier writings, for example SCHUMPETER (1934) first published in 1912, that we refer to again in Chapter 6, he emphasised that the role of individual entrepreneurship was not fixated on large firms whose apparent dominance had yet to be established.

5 Chandler's first major book, *Strategy and Structure* (CHANDLER 1962), does say that before 1850 industrial enterprises were very small and were usually family affairs. His main concerns in this and his subsequent books, *The Visible Hand* (1977) and *Scale and Scope* (1990) are the development and organisation of US and, in the latter, British and German companies. Chandler concluded that Britain delayed too long in adopting managerial capitalism.

6 Lazonick's thesis was that proprietary capitalism began to give way to managerial capitalism, in which ownership and control were separated, around the beginning of the twentieth century and that this was now giving way to 'collective capitalism', thought to characterise Japan (and Germany).

7 Neo-classical economics, built on the foundations laid by Adam Smith, Ricardo and John Stuart Mill in the period 1776–1848, was dominated by Alfred Marshall (MARSHALL 1890, 1919).

8 CHAMBERLIN (1933), ROBINSON (1933).

9 Penrose was not by any means persuaded that the persistence of small firms was explained entirely by their role in a well-functioning economic system. She accepted many of the views of STEINDL (1945), who thought that small firms survived in large numbers only through market imperfections and the 'gambling instincts' of small firm entrepreneurs who accept very high risks for low remuneration, most of whom were doomed to failure only to be replaced by more unrealistic optimists. Steindl and Penrose both assert that large firms 'tolerate' small competitors either as not worth their attention or as a fig-leaf to cover monopoly power. Steindl's book, perhaps the only one to be devoted wholly to the heart of this subject, concludes: 'The survival of small firms is thus dependent on a series of factors not very creditable to our economic system: monopsonistic exploitation of labour, imperfection of markets due to irrational reasons, unemployment and the gambling preferences of small entrepreneurs with all the waste of energy attendant on the high turnover of small businesses. In other cases their continued existence is only due to toleration by big business.'

10 For example, see BAIN (1959), SCHERER (1970), though these authors are not to be identified necessarily with the views critiqued here.

11 In this very brief review of economists' thinking, it is perhaps necessary to mention the views of the Chicago School associated with the Economics Department of Chicago University, and Milton Friedman in particular. The Chicago School was, and is, sceptical of government intervention, believing that markets allocate resources efficiently and that monopolies will attract competitors and break down if they are not in the interests of consumers. The School was

also of course influential in the monetarist revolution. The Chicago School is not particularly interested in small firms, but its views are consistent with those expressed in this book.

12 MES are often measured as the average size of the largest plants accounting for half an industry's output. The term can be misleading, since small-scale entry can still be attractive if the penalty for suboptimal scale is not substantial. (See Richard Schmalensee, 'Inter-Industry Studies of Structure and Performance,' in SCHMALENSEE & WILLIG 1989. Also see PRATTEN 1971 for comprehensive studies of economies of scale in various UK industries.)

13 Many years ago the author helped to write and present a television programme for the UK Open University. The programme contrasted the oil refinery-like plant of a large brewer with that of a small local brewer (Young & Co., now a quoted company) that sold its beer at similar prices. To add force to the visual paradox, the small family brewer delivered its beer to its pubs by horse and dray!

14 In a way, the MES is simply the scale at which a firm can survive in competition on a sustained basis (STIGLER 1950).

15 The President of Bell Telephone Laboratories, inventor of the transistor among many other things, said many years ago: 'one thing a director of research must never do is to direct research, nor can he permit direction of research by any supervising board' (quoted in JEWKES *et al.* 1969). More recently, Smith Klein Glaxo heavily decentralised their R&D activity in an attempt to increase the productivity of their enormous R&D spend. The company also bought in products and ideas from small biotechnology companies.

16 We are writing here of *innovation*, which is putting new goods and services on the market. Innovation may be preceded by invention outside the innovating company.

17 The concerns of corporate management about achieving innovation are amply reflected in the management literature. Modern texts give considerable space to this subject, even those on small firms (e.g. DEAKINS & FREEL 2003). There is even a specific stream of literature on how large corporations can learn to act with the flair and flexibility of small firms through releasing the energies of their innovative staff members (for a recent example, see BUCKLAND *et al.* 2003). *Intrapreneurship*, or 'in-venturing', in a big organisation by setting up well-rewarded product groups with a large measure of independence, for example, may help but ultimately management imperatives never allow complete freedom of action. The history of corporate venturing (in which large firms set up programmes to take minority stakes in small enterprises to open windows on new technologies) demonstrates how frequently a new chief executive, or a downturn in big company fortunes, lead to the plug being pulled (see Chapter 6 for more on corporate venturing). An elephant cannot be as nimble as a mouse.

18 Brown quotes Matthew Boulton, a prominent figure in the British Industrial Revolution, as writing in 1795: 'hawkers, pedlars and those who supply petty shops . . . do more towards supporting a great manufactory than all the Lords in the nation.'

19 For some econometric evidence for the assertions in this and the preceding paragraph, see G. Bannock and M. Binks, 'SMEs in the development process', in BANNOCK & DALY (1994). See also Chapter 9.

20 Assessment of the role of SMEs in job creation is not simple because firms move between size classes, up and down; because there is job creation from new entrants and job destruction from exits, from expansions and contractions and for other reasons, including the different experience of large and small firms in recessions. The issues are conveniently summarised in EUROPEAN COMMISSION (1997).

21 POLANYI (2001) reminds us that there never have been unregulated markets, and that regulation has permitted markets to work in a way that would otherwise be precluded by social dissent (see also Chapter 5).

22 Among the exceptions, BERG (1993), who has made use of less conventional data sources to illustrate the range of firm sizes in the pre-modern period, referring to the Chandler school, writes that 'many of these histories are fundamentally teleologies, charting the emergence of the outstandingly large, wealthy or successful firms and entrepreneurs as the yardstick of industrialisation. The result is a historical chasm between the known – the factory system and the large-scale production – and the unknown – the artisan and the small- and medium-scale producer.'

23 The Schumpeter–Chandler view has not gone unchallenged. For example, Chandler's view that Britain delayed too long in adopting managerial capitalism, and that this was the main cause of its relative decline, has been effectively refuted (CHURCH 1993).

4 The constraints on small firms

Rankings of constraints

External perceptions

As we saw in Chapter 3, the economists' view of the constraints on small firms is that smallness denies access to economies of scale. This problem applies to virtually all the resources used in the production process. Economists describe these resources as the *factors of production*: land, labour, capital and usually also entrepreneurship. All are subject in some sense to scale economies: for example, premises tend to cost more per square foot for small surface areas; there are economies in the recruitment of skills (intensified by the lower wages paid in small firms); it is cheaper per pound to borrow £10 million than £10,000 and small firms do not have access to public securities markets; management in large firms benefits from the division of labour – a large firm can have specialists while the small business owner has to try to be an expert in everything. Not least, and as we shall demonstrate in Chapter 7, there are also economies of scale in dealing with the growing administrative requirements of regulation by government. To be sure, small scale confers certain advantages, notably initiative, flexibility, low co-ordination costs and the ability to offer specialised and personal service, as we have seen, but the constraints are formidable.

Economists and other researchers, and the governments they influence, have focused heavily on these scale-related problems and especially upon entrepreneurship (defined broadly to include management) and finance. There is also an emphasis on the issues of innovation and information (the former embracing the problems of growth companies, especially technology-based firms) where there are thought to be market imperfections which discriminate against small firms.

The relative interest in various aspects of small business studies is illustrated in Table 4.1, which breaks down a database of some 340 recent important research articles and reports on SMEs by subject. It can be seen that only four areas account for almost two-thirds of the total, with entrepreneurship and finance accounting for 42 per cent.[1]

Table 4.1 SME research reports and articles, by subject, 1997

Topic	(%)
Entrepreneurship and management (including female and ethnic)	26.7
Finance (including late payment)	14.9
Innovation (including growth companies)	12.9
Information, networking and support (including subcontracting, franchising)	10.3
Employment generation, flexibility and relations	6.0
Training	6.0
Demography, macroeconomic relationships and statistics	5.7
Exports and Europe	5.4
Tax and regulation	4.5
Local economic development	3.3
Competition	2.1
Policy evaluation	2.1
Total	100.0

Source: Calculated from *SME Research Database*, Department of Trade and Industry (DTI), Institute for Small Business Affairs and the Small Business Research Trust (SBRT), 1998.

The preoccupations of governments in small business policy also focus heavily on finance, information, advice and training, although recently there has been a growing interest in administrative burdens. For example, the European Commission Third Multiannual Programme for SMEs (1997–2000) (COM (96)98final) allocated half of its budget of Ecu 180 million to its European Information Centres and enterprise co-operation services. The priorities set at the 1995 Madrid Summit were, in order of importance: (1) administrative simplification; (2) information; (3) training; and (4) research and technological development. The financial environment for SMEs was in seventh position. However, government spending on SME policy heavily reflects the preoccupations with finance, information and support (see Chapter 7).

SME owners' perceptions of constraints

There have been many surveys on barriers to growth and on the problems experienced by SMEs in general. Constraints and problems are not necessarily the same things, and somewhat different results are obtained from the two types of survey.[2] A survey of major business constraints conducted across the whole of the European Economic Area (EEA) by the Observatory of SMEs (EUROPEAN COMMISSION 2002b) ranked 'lack of skilled labour' followed by 'access to finance' and 'administrative regulations' as the most often selected constraints, though many respondents selected 'other' and 15–22 per cent of respondents had no constraints. Other surveys (using different lists), for example those of the UK Cambridge Small Business Research Centre, bring out the importance of market demand, but also suggest that access and cost of finance is an issue, indeed of first rank for fast-growing firms. Marketing, management skills and the availability of skilled labour were also ranked quite highly again, especially by fast-growth firms (reviewed in STOREY 1994).

The World Bank surveys mentioned in the Appendix allow us to look at the relative perceived importance of various constraints on a global basis (Table 4.2), and SCHIFFER and WEDER's (2001) analysis of the large database of the 1999–2000 survey further allows us to see how perceived constraints vary with firm size. These authors, on the basis of regression analysis, conclude that 'smaller firms face more obstacles than medium-sized firms, and these in turn face more obstacles than large firms'. This was particularly true for financing, taxes and regulations, corruption and anti-competitive practices. There were 'no significant differences in how much infrastructure, policy instability . . . affect firms of different sizes'. These relationships can be seen from an inspection of Table 4.2 which also shows that taxes and regulations everywhere come top as obstacles (and are ranked especially high in the transition countries), followed by financing. Corruption is a particular problem in Africa. Generally, scores are highest in the transition countries, followed by Africa and East Asia, and are lowest in the developed countries of the OECD; in other words, they follow levels of development, as one might anticipate.

Table 4.2 Ranked obstacles to doing business, worldwide and selected regions, by firm size, 1999–2000[a–c]

Obstacle	World			Africa			East Asia and Pacific			Transition economies			OECD		
	S	M	L	S	M	L	S	M	L	S	M	L	S	M	L
Financing	2.88	2.86	2.59	2.96	2.83	2.78	2.61	2.52	2.61	2.99	3.10	3.00	2.34	2.17	1.94
Infrastructure	2.24	2.27	2.38	2.77	2.83	2.77	2.26	2.34	2.06	2.13	2.08	2.05	1.72	1.85	1.72
Taxes and regulations	2.90	2.96	2.63	2.19	2.23	2.23	2.41	2.60	2.31	3.28	3.25	3.12	2.79	2.79	2.45
Policy instability	2.80	2.84	2.71	2.40	2.49	2.32	2.72	2.70	2.60	2.96	3.00	2.89	2.25	2.14	2.12
Corruption	2.60	2.50	2.45	2.89	2.86	2.73	2.38	2.52	2.13	2.58	2.42	2.20	1.69	1.63	1.52
Anti-competitive practices	2.43	2.37	2.20	–	–	–	2.41	2.43	2.16	2.48	2.41	2.17	2.02	1.96	1.83
Average	2.64	2.63	2.49	2.64	2.65	2.57	2.47	2.52	2.31	2.74	2.71	2.57	2.14	2.09	1.93

Source: Adapted from SCHIFFER & WEDER (2001).

Notes

S = small firm, 5–50 employees; M = medium-sized firm, 51–500 employees; L = large firm, more than 500 employees.

a Rankings are based on scores selected by respondents on a 4-point scale: 1 = no obstacle, 4 = major obstacle.

b Base is 10,000 firms in 80 countries.

c This table omits some constraints included in the source (inflation, exchange rate, judiciary, street crime and organised crime) and does not give detail for Latin America and the Caribbean and South Asia, which are included in the World total.

Owners' problems

The longest-running survey of small business problems as such in the United Kingdom is that of the Small Business Research Trust (SBRT), already mentioned in Chapter 2. Recent results for the SBRT survey and those for a similar survey conducted by the National Federation of Independent Business (NFIB) in the United States are shown in Table 4.3. The two surveys are not strictly comparable for various reasons, the most important of which is that the NFIB survey lists 100 problems while the SBRT only lists only 14, and this required considerable and possibly arbitrary regrouping. What is striking is that government administrative and tax burdens are of critical importance (United States) and most important (United Kingdom) for 38.8 per cent and 21.9 per cent of mentions by respondents, respectively. This means that government itself is the biggest problem in the United States and second only to market demand in the United Kingdom. Lack of skilled employees or high pay come next. Finance, by contrast, is only of major concern to 2–3 per cent of respondents. It is important to be aware that there are sometimes large variations over time in these rankings: for example, in 1989 when UK interest rates (bank base rates) were as high as 15 per cent, finance was the most important problem for 39 per cent of respondents, by far the highest-ranked problem. There are also variations in rankings according to respondent firm size. For example in the SBRT survey cited in Table 4.3, concern about skilled labour shortages were greater among larger firms (which recruit more frequently) but market demand was more of a problem for smaller firms.

Table 4.3 Ranking of concerns of small business owners, United Kingdom and United States, *c.* 2000

Concern	United Kingdom (%)	United States (%)
Economic climate/sales	22.9	6.9
Government regulation/paperwork	15.6	20.2
Lack of skilled employees/high pay	10.4	13.7
Cashflow	9.4	4.2
Lack of time/capacity	9.4	2.0
Other problems	8.3	11.0
Competition	7.3	3.5
Tax burden	6.3	18.6
Marketing problems	4.2	1.1
Finance/exchange rates/interest rates	2.1	2.8
Other costs (e.g. premises, transport)	2.1	14.7
Inflation/supply costs	1.0	1.3
Total	100.0	100.0

Sources: United Kingdom: SBRT 12/02; United States: NFIB (2000), data re-allocated to fit UK categories and expressed as a percentage of total mentions citing problem as 'critical'.

The high importance given to government-related problems by SME owners is not restricted to the United Kingdom and the United States, nor is it a recent phenomenon. It so happens that an international survey carried out in 1984 used the same problem categories as the SBRT surveys and the relevant results are shown in Table 4.4. It can be seen that Japan was exceptional in giving a low ranking to government-related problems,[3] while financing and interest rates were then a major concern in several countries, including the United Kingdom, as was competition from big business.[4]

Surveys of problems experienced by small firms in developing countries produce very different results from those in developed and transition countries, as could be anticipated from Table 4.2. The proportion of respondents in micro- and small enterprises surveys in Africa mentioning lack of access to markets and capital is much higher in the United Kingdom and the United States, as are problems with inputs of materials, semi-finished goods and transport (Table 4.5).

Taxation and regulation and labour issues are of relatively minor importance compared with the results of problem surveys for OECD countries shown in Tables 4.3 and 4.4. Labour is in chronic surplus in the developing world. Taxation and regulation do not rate as problems because most of the respondents to these surveys are in the informal sector, where direct taxes are not in general applied and most regulations are not enforced. This does not mean that regulation is not an issue in the developing world; indeed, it is a major issue, as we show later in Chapter 9. As LIEDHOLM & MEAD (1999) point out, access to capital and other inputs 'is often constrained precisely because of government controls and regulation'. However, respondents do not perceive the regulatory causes behind their problems.

Table 4.4 Most important problems faced by small business, selected countries, 1984

Problem	Canada	Japan	West Germany	Nether- lands	United Kingdom	United States
Government regulation and paperwork	16.4	2.5	14.0	24.8	20.8	18.3
Taxes	9.2	9.2	8.6	10.2	15.8	12.5
Subtotal	25.6	11.7	22.6	35.0	36.6	30.8
Interest rates and financing	20.8	7.2	19.7	5.8	17.5	11.0
Realising sales	8.6	37.8	4.6	11.8	9.7	8.4
Competition from large business	8.9	11.9	13.7	11.8	10.8	9.7
Other	36.1	31.4	39.4	35.6	25.4	40.1
Subtotal	74.4	88.3	77.4	65.0	63.4	69.2
Grand total	100.0	100.0	100.0	100.0	100.0	100.0

Source: SKIM (1984).

Table 4.5 Most important problem at time of survey, average of five African
countries, *c.* 1992

Problem	Respondents reporting any problems (%)
Capital	22.4
Markets	23.8
Tools, equipment and repairs	4.4
Raw materials, intermediate inputs	25.3
Taxes and regulation	4.3
Transport	4.9
Labour force	1.0
Other problems	13.8
Total reporting any problems	100.0
Percentage reporting any problems	85.4

Source: LIEDHOLM & MEAD (1999).

Note
Based on Growth and Equity through Microenterprise (GEMINI) surveys of firms with up to
50 persons in Botswana, Kenya, Malawi, Swaziland and Zimbabwe.

Although the percentage of respondents mentioning them varies over
time, the problems themselves (government burdens, market demand,
competition from big business and, except in times of high interest rates,
finance for a minority – lack of skilled personnel is also a highly cyclical
problem) are eternal.

They were certainly all preoccupations of the BOLTON (1971) report.
Commenting on this continuity, STANWORTH & GRAY (1991) stated
that:

> these eternal problems of small firms are an inevitable consequence of
> their small scale. Small business owners are acutely subject to time
> pressures and can easily be criticised for the lack of specialised
> knowledge which is available within the more elaborate management
> structure of the larger firm. These time pressures explain the low toler-
> ance of small business owners for the bureaucratic burdens imposed by
> government. The risks faced by small firms, their exclusion from
> organised securities markets and their weak bargaining power vis-à-vis
> suppliers of capital, explain their concerns about both taxation and
> financing. The same lack of bargaining power with other suppliers, and
> their individual weakness against larger competitors, explain their
> concern about monopoly policy.

Research on problems and constraints

One cannot help noticing, when comparing the allocation of research topics
in Table 4.1 and the rankings of constraints and concerns in Tables 4.2–4.5,
that researchers and SME owners' preoccupations are not very closely

matched. For example, entrepreneurship and management accounts for 27 per cent of the research publication volume in Table 4.1 but this subject does not achieve substantial mention in owners' problem rankings.[5] This mismatch seems to occur in other countries. William J. Dennis, Jr, in 'Research mimicking policy: entrepreneurial/small business policy research in the United States' (in SEXTON & LANDSTROM 1999) cites a study by BROCKHAUS (1987) in which a comparison of topics in academic journals and those voted as of greatest concern at the White House Conference on Small Business in 1986 showed them to be unrelated.

The fact that SME owners see their problems as almost entirely external to the firm does not necessarily mean that they are unaware of any management limitations of their own (though some may not be) but is often implicit in the listings they select from. The intensity and duration of the problems they select will, of course, depend partly on how owners handle them, and in this sense all the problems have a management element.[6] This does not alter the fact that the problems as ranked do arise in the external business environment. We return to entrepreneurial and management issues in more depth in Chapter 6, but we have commented upon them here because responses of these kinds to problem surveys are sometimes taken as evidence of ignorance and a justification for subsidised training programmes for SME owners. In general, most SME owners with some experience are only too well aware that their fate lies largely in their own hands – indeed, that is why they are in business on their own account in the first place.

Despite the mismatch between SME owners' preoccupations and the research done on them there is, of course, no reason why the two should coincide. Much research is driven by fashion and policy concerns that are often directive in intent. In addition, the volume of research might be proportional not to the importance of issues to SME owners but to the complexity and intractability of the problems studied. This is certainly the case in financing issues, as we shall see. All this said, however, and with very few exceptions – competition policy being one of them – most small firm problems have been fairly thoroughly looked at.

Macroeconomic conditions in terms of market sales, interest rates, the exchange rate and inflation together consistently appear as problems in the rankings, although their incidence is cyclical (the level of interest rates is not a serious problem in OECD countries at the time of writing). STOREY (1994) found that although there is controversy, some macroeconomic variables are correlated with some measures of business failure.[7] It is also probable that in a given country, high proportions of employment in SMEs contribute to economic efficiency, stability and growth (see a very interesting exercise in comparing SME density, productivity, output, unemployment and wage inflation across 48 US states, ROBBINS *et al.* 2000). Several studies, e.g. ROBSON (1996), have confirmed that inflation is bad for small firms. This may be because small firms, with little if any market power, are less able to raise prices than large firms, and because high inflation is associated with high interest rates on the bank borrowings on which many rely.

There is not space in this book to review all the research on SME constraints and problems. We restrict ourselves to a summary treatment on the two broad issues at or near the top of the rankings. In the remainder of this chapter we discuss financing, where there has long been controversy and which is perhaps overresearched. In Chapter 5, we consider government regulation and taxation, which is a rather more recent topic for research and one whose importance has received insufficient attention. Because of the sheer volume of material on financing, we deal almost entirely with the United Kingdom and to a lesser extent the United States, but the issues are very similar in all developed countries. Taxation and regulation are discussed in Chapter 5.

Is finance a constraint?

The characteristics of small firm financing

For the United Kingdom at least, there are considerable difficulties in drawing conclusions about the financial structure of small firms as a whole because, as pointed out in Chapter 2, there are no comprehensive data on unincorporated businesses. Box 4.1 summarises what is known about the balance sheet structure of incorporated businesses in the United Kingdom, but even here interpretation is difficult because the findings are largely based on data which is well over 10 years out of date.[8] Comparisons between the 2000 largest companies and the remainder undoubtedly conceal important differences within these samples. Moreover, the averages derived from aggregated company accounts also conceal wide variations between firms. Finally, company accounts data can tell us little about the detailed sources of equity finance.

Table 4.6 is based on SBRT surveys of both incorporated and unincorporated firms from singleton self-employed to companies with up to about 100 persons. These figures show the percentage of respondents using the sources of finance listed, not the percentage of the total volume of finance obtained. However, a detailed breakdown is given of the sources of equity used as well as debt.

The figures in Table 4.7 for the United States are on a different basis again. They have the merit of being based on the value of capital employed and include unincorporated as well as incorporated businesses. The coverage of the US data is restricted to 'small' firms, with those below the high cut-off of 500 employees split into two (above and below 20 employees), but the breakdown of sources of finance is fairly detailed.

The three disparate pictures certainly agree upon the fact that the source of borrowing for SMEs from financial institutions is predominantly from banks. It is also clear that the main source of equity is the principal owner;

Box 4.1 Small firm (limited company) financing characteristics, United Kingdom

1 Small companies rely to a greater extent than large firms upon *debt* (as opposed to equity), particularly short-term debt (they are more highly geared). However, owner's capital in small firms is understated because of the importance of directors' loans, which may effectively be a form of equity. Fast-growing firms are financed to an even greater extent by means of borrowed funds.

2 Small firms are more reliant upon *bank finance* than are large firms. Small firms are much more reliant on short-term loans than large, but within total bank lending the proportion of term lending has increased. Small firms also make greater use of *non-bank finance* such as hire purchase and factoring.

3 *Trade credit* (both debtors and creditors) is a larger proportion of the balance sheet total for small than for large firms, and small firms generally give more credit than they receive.

4 A lower proportion of assets in the balance sheet are *fixed tangible assets* in small than in large firms (particularly in non-manufacturing).

5 The dispersion of *financial structure and performance* of small firms about the average is greater than that for large firms. This diversity means that generalisations can be misleading. For example, although in most periods small firms (particularly in non-manufacturing) in total have a larger proportion of cash in the balance sheet than large firms and may be net depositors with the banking system, while as many as 30 per cent have no recourse to financial institutions for borrowing at all, a large proportion – perhaps over 40 per cent – are net borrowers.

Source: adapted and updated from Chapter 3, in STANWORTH & GRAY (1991) using SBRT 6/99; *Quarterly Report on Small Business Statistics*; Bank of England; July 2002 and Andy Cosh and Alan Hughes, 'Size, financial structure and profitability: UK companies in the 1980s', in HUGHES & STOREY (1994). Balance sheet structure data relate to limited companies, 'large firms' being defined as those ranked in the top 2,000 in terms of capital employed in the non-financial sector.

family and friends and angel finance are more important than venture capital, but both are of relatively minor importance.[9] The US data do not indicate that very small firms are more highly geared than larger small firms, nor that the former are more dependent upon bank finance, as do the British company accounts data. However, the data are not necessarily inconsistent and the differences may well have to do with differences in sample composition and definition. For example, a breakdown of the SBRT sample by firm size (not reproduced here) shows that a much smaller proportion of

Table 4.6 Sources of borrowing and equity by small firms, 1991 and 1999, UK

Source	Respondents (%)	
	1991	*1999*
A Borrowing		
Bank overdrafts and term loans	89.2	71.1
Loans from owner, director or proprietor	28.0	31.2
Hire purchase or leasing	24.3	23.7
Mortgage for business premises	18.1	16.6
Credit card or similar short-term loans	13.1	15.8
Loans from family or friends	10.1	9.0
Long-term business loans from other financial institutions	4.4	3.1
Debt factoring/invoice discounting	1.6	3.1
Loans or grants from government, local authority or enterprise agency	4.1	2.9
Loans from other private individuals	1.6	1.3
Other	1.8	1.1
No response/none	17.5	24.4
B Equity		
Yours or other personal sources	67.3	64.0
Retained earnings	40.8	49.9
Family and friends	10.2	8.9
Other private individuals (inc. BES/EIS)[a]	3.0	2.1
Venture capital company or other professional investors	0.8	1.1
Trade investors	0.5	0.6
Other	0.6	1.8
No response/None	17.0	15.8
Base	835	619

Source: SBRT 6/99.

Note
a BES = Business Expansion Scheme; EIS = Enterprise Investment Scheme.

very small firms (under five employees) have bank overdrafts and term loans than in the 10–50 employee size-bands. It also seems that although small firms as a whole do make more use of asset-based finance (such as hire purchase and leasing) as indicated in the UK company accounts data, this again does not apply to the smallest firms. The US data also confirm the greater importance of director (owner) loans for the smallest firms referred to in item 1 of Box 4.1.

The disadvantages of SMEs in financing

We have seen above that very few SMEs say that finance and interest rates are their most important problem, except at times of exceptionally high interest rates. Most small firms are not expanding at a rate that requires more external finance: yet when asked to identify constraints on growth, a

Table 4.7 Capital employed, by source of funding, SMEs,[a] United States, 1993[b]

Source	Total equity plus debt		
	All (%)	Smaller (%)	Larger (%)
Principal owner	31.33	44.53	27.22
Angel finance	3.59	n.a.	n.a.
Venture capital	1.85	n.a.	n.a.
Other equity	12.86	n.a.	n.a.
Total equity	49.63	56.00	47.67
Commercial banks	18.75	14.88	19.94
Finance companies	4.91	3.08	5.47
Other financial institutions	3.00	3.53	2.83
Trade credit	15.78	11.81	17.01
Principal owner	4.10	5.59	3.63
Other debt	3.83	5.11	3.45
Total debt	50.37	44.00	52.33
Total debt plus equity	100.00	100.00	100.00

Source: BERGER & UDELL (2000).

Notes
a 'Smaller' are defined as fewer than 20 employees or $1 million in sales.
b Underlying data are from NSSBF (1993); data relate to firms with fewer than 500
  employees in non-farm, non-financial and non-real-estate businesses.
n.a. = not available.

very much larger proportion name finance as an issue. Because of the
perceived social importance of growth, the question of whether or not there
are gaps in the provision of finance has received enormous public attention
since at least the 1930s,[10] as well as a large volume of academic research.

We have already noted that there are sound reasons why small firms
should be disadvantaged compared with large firms in raising finance. Small
firms present higher risks to lenders; information about their past record and
prospects is more difficult and more costly to obtain; it costs relatively more
to administer small than large loans, and small firms do not have access to
public securities markets. There is also the paradox that although small firm
owners complain about the availability of external finance, they are often
reluctant to borrow – and particularly to seek external sources of equity
which might be more appropriate for the risks they present – for fear of
compromising the independence which we showed in Chapter 2 is their main
motive.

In addition to the survey results that finance is a constraint, academic and
other observers have adduced other evidence. Studies have shown that in
both the United Kingdom and the United States, investment by smaller
quoted companies is sensitive to *cashflow* and *liquidity* (that is, they invest
when they have the money) whereas for larger firms, investment is more
independent of these factors as they can raise the money when they need it

(DEVEREUX & SCHIANTARELLI 1989; FAZZARI *et al.* 1988). It has also been found that the number of start-ups is related to levels of aggregate wealth, that wealthier persons are more likely to become entrepreneurs and, less convincingly, that finance providers discriminate against ethnic minority groups (see DE MEZA 2002 for references). Moreover, the great majority of small firm borrowers from banks have to provide security (COMPETITION COMMISSION 2002 found that it was 59 per cent) and this security is in most cases of much greater value than the value of the loan (BINKS *et al.* 1993).

None of this evidence conclusively shows that capital markets for small firms are imperfect in the sense that viable borrowers are being denied funds on which providers can obtain economic returns.[11]

The finding that investment by smaller quoted companies varies more with their cashflow than that of large quoted companies could reflect the probability that they face relatively more profitable investment opportunities, while their greater vulnerability in the face of illiquid markets in small company stocks inspires both caution and a desire not to dilute their equity. While large company executives often complain about a lack of investment opportunities, small company managers are more often heard to complain that they do not have enough resources, capital and management to pursue theirs. In short, there are economies of scale in finance.

The finding that there is a positive relationship between wealth and small business start-ups is also ambiguous. Wealthier people may be more willing to invest because, relative to their wealth the risk is lower; this is part of the basis for angel finance (see Chapter 6). This propensity of the wealthy to invest does not mean, however, that these investors would be prepared to try to borrow the money if their wealth disappeared, and it therefore tells us nothing about the availability of finance.

There is in fact no objective way of establishing funding shortfalls, since there is no information available on firms which do not start up through lack of funding, or fail to expand for that reason as distinct from other reasons. It is possible that some firms with good prospects do not approach external funders because they assume they will be rejected through lack of collateral security or for some other reason, but this again is almost impossible to establish, even though attempts have been made (KON & STOREY 2003).

Recourse has therefore been had to pure theory to help resolve the question. STIGLITZ & WEISS (1981) found that if borrowers' projects differed in probability of success (which they must) and banks could not, through lack of information, select the best prospects, they would not set interest rates at the highest level that would balance demand and supply. This is because to do so would lead only the highest-risk borrowers, who expect higher returns, to pay the high rates (adverse selection). The result would be losses for their banks, who therefore ration credit. In fact it is well known that the range of interest rates charged by banks is quite narrow (BINKS *et al.* 1993). DE MEZA & WEBB (2002) on the other hand, who, unlike STIGLITZ & WEISS (1981), assumed that the returns on firms' projects differed not only in their probability of success (risk) but also in the rate of return achieved, reached precisely the opposite conclusion: i.e. that there would be an *oversupply* of credit. This arises because banks know less about their customers' prospects than the firms themselves do (information asymmetry) and therefore offer loans on terms that do not depend upon in-depth credit assessment but on collateral and other factors. The optimism of their customers (Steindl's 'gambling instinct' (STEINDL 1945)) and their potentially irresponsible use of other people's money (moral hazard) result in excessive borrowing, not a deficiency of credit.

We conclude that while capital markets are certainly not perfect in the neo-classical sense, the financing problems of SMEs are largely inherent in their situation. Banks can be criticised for not doing more to reduce information asymmetries by relationship lending that involves developing contact with customers over time, but concentration in banking has been working against this. Large impersonal organisations not rooted in local communities find relationship banking difficult to manage[12] and there is some evidence that the German and US banking systems, which are more fragmented, have performed better as far as SME lending is concerned – but the differences are probably less important than the similarities.[13]

It is true that the COMPETITION COMMISSION (2002) report was critical of the UK banks' finding that they had been overcharging SMEs. The evidence for this indictment can, however, be criticised in turn on the grounds that the profitability calculations did not adequately take account of the losses sustained on small business banking at some points in the economic cycle. It is easy to criticise banks but it has to be remembered that, in lending, the best a bank can hope for is to get its interest paid and the loan repaid; if the borrower fails, the bank may lose both, especially where there is no collateral or the collateral cannot be realised. In a loan contract, as STOREY (1994) recognises, the bank bears the full downside risk but the upward gain is limited to the interest paid. In fact, bank lending to SMEs has increased at a time when the growth of the SME population has been arrested while, as the Commission's report shows, the Forum of Private Business surveys have been suggesting improved relationships between banks and SMEs over a six-year period.

Conclusion

Despite controversy, academic opinion is now moving against the belief that there are significant market failures in the provision of finance for small firms, and certainly against the need for government intervention in this field (CRESSY 2002).

To conclude that financing is not a significant problem is not to deny that some apparently good business projects of talented entrepreneurs may fail to obtain backing. How many of these there are, and whether or not other managers with similar projects have raised the money and substituted for them, is unknowable. Very commonly, successful entrepreneurs look back to their early days and recount how their first attempts to raise money were unsuccessful and that they were forced to start in a small way, accumulate some capital and demonstrate a track record before external finance became possible. This is the classic route for the small firm which starts in a garage and ends up in a large factory (60 per cent of all small firms are home-based). As we argue in Chapter 6, this may not be a bad thing, since the hard way is a learning process that sorts out the talented from the less talented. It is not enough to have a good project: you need also the knowledge and experience to bring it to fruition. (High-tech businesses may be a special case, and this is also discussed in Chapter 6.) The foregoing has been mainly about OECD countries; in the developing world, financial markets function less well and indeed a precondition for advanced development is the elaboration of capital markets (see Chapter 9).

It is also a fact of life that there are economies of scale in finance just as there are in other spheres of business operation. Large companies can raise finance more cheaply than small ones. This is true even in the public securities markets to which small firms do not have access. The average costs of a new equity issue in Europe, for example, fall from about 10–15 per cent of the gross proceeds for issues in the range of €5–€10 million to 4–8 per cent for issues in the range of €25–€30 million (BANNOCK CONSULTING 2001b).[14]

The widespread belief in the phenomenon of capital market imperfections in the supply of finance for SMEs may be scarcely more scientifically based than the belief in flying saucers (UFOs). In both cases there have been many sightings; there are passionate believers and non-believers, and you can even look the subject up in learned books. Hard evidence, however, remains elusive.

Notes

1 Less than 10 per cent of the material on entrepreneurship dealt with management as such; most dealt with the entrepreneurial personality and regional, gender and ethnic differences in enterprise activity. The sample will have been influenced by the interests of the sponsors and the compilers (for example, it is UK-oriented) and somewhat different results might have been obtained by a more comprehensive analysis of the literature. Nonetheless the specialised journals do seem to be dominated by coverage of the same subjects.
2 In both cases, usually, respondents are asked to select issues from a list and often to rank issues in order of importance. Results can obviously be influenced by what is included in the list and by the sample characteristics. The relative importance of issues also varies over time and between activity sectors.
3 The Japanese exception probably owes something to a reluctance to be critical of government at a time of emphasis on 'administrative guidance'. The author's conversations with Japanese small business people, then and more recently, make it clear that they actually feel much the same about government as

businessmen in other countries (see also FRIEDMAN 1988). Certainly by the mid-1990s, 72 per cent of SMEs in Japan were in favour of 'active deregulation', according to a survey by MITI (1995).

4 The figures in Table 4.4 and for the United Kingdom in Table 4.3 relate to the 'most important problem'. A fall in the percentage of respondents selecting a particular issue does not necessarily mean that the issue has become less of a problem: it may have simply been displaced by more pressing concerns. Another important consideration in interpreting these surveys is that the problems ranked are *immediate* problems. Financing, for example, may be an issue only when the firm is at an early stage in its life, or wishes to expand: most surveyed firms are not in either of these positions. This is why financing gets a much higher ranking in surveys of constraints. Finally, it needs to be borne in mind that these surveys cover only *existing* enterprises: entrepreneurs in the process of starting new enterprises, or who have attempted but failed to do so, are not included.

5 In Table 4.3 management issues are lumped in with 'time capacity', which includes production capacity. In fact, in the SBRT surveys, 'internal management difficulties' was first distinguished as a separate category from the beginning of 1990 but mentions have accounted for only 0.6–3.3 per cent in the ensuing period.

6 Thus cashflow/payments/debtors' problems can be partly mitigated by more rigorous credit control procedures, competition by seeking out market niches, financing by more thorough and persuasive applications for loans and so on.

7 Many small business research results are controversial, often because samples are not fully representative or because of the choice of different countries, time periods and data sets. Contrary to the (qualified) conclusions of Chapter 2 on 'push' versus 'pull' theories of new firm formation, ROBSON (1996), cited above, did not find a positive association between unemployment and new firm formation, perhaps because the VAT data used exclude the smallest firms and also because the time period (1980–90) was exceptional.

8 Nevertheless, the broad findings are quite similar to those of the BOLTON (1971) Committee report.

9 This is not necessarily true for high-growth small firms; see Chapter 6.

10 The Macmillan Committee in 1931 in Britain identified a gap in the supply of small sums of long-term capital. Subsequent inquiries included the Radcliffe Committee in 1969, the Bolton Committee (BOLTON 1971) and the Interim Report of the Wilson Committee in 1979. In the course of each investigation, financial institutions argued that capital markets were functioning adequately but it is interesting that each Inquiry ultimately led to new initiatives which cumulatively seem to have improved the situation. Macmillan ultimately led to the creation of the Industrial and Commercial Finance Corporation in 1945 (ICFC, later absorbed into 3i–Investors in Industry); Radcliffe led to the greater availability of term loans from the commercial banks and Wilson to the Business Start-up Scheme, later the Business Expansion Scheme (BES) and the Loan Guarantee Scheme (LGS). The latest inquiries were those of the Cruikshank Committee in 2000 and the subsequent COMPETITION COMMISSION (2002) report.

11 In the neo-classical state of perfect competition that assumes large numbers of suppliers and perfect information, all borrowers with viable projects would obtain finance. These assumptions are not, of course, satisfied in the real world. There are not large numbers of commercial banks, at least in the United Kingdom, where four groups account for 90 per cent of the number of accounts and 84 per cent of value (COMPETITION COMMISSION 2002) and banks

have only limited information on their small borrowers – certainly less than the borrowers themselves (asymmetric information).

12 See BERGER & UDELL (2002).

13 At one time, it was fashionable to compare the British banking system very unfavourably with the German system in relation to both small and large firms, but on closer examination most of the advantages (and, indeed, differences) with the German banks have proved illusory. See EDWARDS & FISCHER (1994).

14 It is an interesting paradox that, unlike economies of scale in production, economies of scale in finance do not necessarily provide any social benefits. As SCITOVSKY (1952) points out, being able to borrow funds more cheaply than the average means that providers get a lower return – it is simply a transfer of resources. Economies of scale in production, by contrast, result in actual savings in real resources.

5 Business owners and government

Small business in society

SME owners' attitudes to government are ambivalent. They have a strong vested interest in law and order and strongly support competition policy, which they see as a potentially restraining influence on big business, but are generally hostile to taxation and all forms of regulation and interference. Politically, these attitudes incline small business owners to the right of the spectrum, though they feel that governments of all political complexions undervalue their role in the economy and society and, despite the rhetoric, often discriminate against them. For example, the UK Federation of Small Businesses (FSB) notes that: 'There is insistence always on employees' rights but what about the [small] employer's rights: we have no rights.'

Although SME owners are numerous in the business scene and perhaps only somewhat less represented as members of trades unions or persons of pensionable age, their strong sense of independence combined with time pressures mean that they are 'non-joiners' and not organised to defend their interests.[1] To most SME owners rooted in their local communities, central government seems remote and, above all, uncomprehending of their day-to-day business realities. This is not surprising, since few members of the legislature have experience in small business and it would be most unusual for a civil servant to have worked in a small firm.[2] It is not clear, however, how important knowledge is in determining government policies towards business, though it can be very important in the design of specific regulatory measures – or, as we show in Chapter 8, support systems.[3]

Much of the difficulty governments experience in understanding small business stems from *cultural differences*, which in turn result from the quite different circumstances in which civil servants and SME owners find themselves. The civil servant is salaried and secure, the SME owner is remunerated ultimately by the uncertain profitability of the firm; the civil servant sees her job and herself as quite separate whereas for the owner her firm is an expression of herself. The civil servant has strictly regulated discretion, the owner has total discretion, prescribed only by the business environment. One has to be careful in generalising about the heterogeneous population of small firms, but although both the government administration and the SME owner need a common core of skills in decisionmaking, problem-solving and information processing, in other respects their managerial requirements differ.[4] The entrepreneur at the executive level focuses on negotiation, troubleshooting and interpersonal communications, the government administration on organisation, co-ordination, formal communications and monitoring. At the policy level, although the SME owner usually has a general strategy and objectives in mind, she is more concerned with tactical planning, innovation and risk-taking; does not, typically, write out objectives and policies or plan strategically; and is working to shorter timescales. In short, the owner is more concerned with doing things than with abstractions.

These contrasts between the government administrators and the SME owner obtain to a large extent also between large firm and small firm executives. GIBB (2000) lists 14 contrasting characteristics of the business approach in government/corporate and small business, ranging from 'accountability/trusting' to 'functional expertise/holistic' and 'planning/ intuitive'. These differences are functions of *organisational size*: a small business owner does not need to spend much time on co-ordination (there are few people in the firm) and can function without written plans or frequent meetings for the same reason (though a plan may be necessary to raise external finance).

There are differences, of course, between management in large firms and government, but they are very much closer to each other than to the small firm. Governments prefer dealing with large firms: they are more predictable, there are fewer of them and they speak much the same language as government departments. John Kenneth Galbraith called this 'bureaucratic symbiosis'. Governments 'do deals' with large firms and persuade them to pursue policies or take actions in the light of the broader social interest, such as in treatment of minorities, training, the environment or tax revenue. There is a long history of this going back to medieval times. Large firms can be encouraged to pursue corporate social responsibility.[5] None of this is possible with small firms, nor does it appeal to them. In short, governments can understand much more about big firms than small ones.

We now go on to discuss the two aspects of government activities which can create most problems for small firms: taxation and regulation. These two things are in fact aspects of the same thing – taxation actually results in regulation of part of financial record-keeping and management and is a levy on the financial resources of the firm, while regulation as such, in terms of compliance costs, is a levy on the firm's personnel resources and professional support.

Taxation

The rise of taxation and complexity

During the past 200 years or so, the role of the state in the economy has increased greatly. Because of growing expenditure on health and education and transfer payments, the share of tax revenues of central and local government (including social security contributions) has had to rise.

It can be seen from Table 5.1 that tax ratios vary considerably between countries. These ratios are very much higher in Scandinavia and the European Union than in the United States or Japan, but have tended to increase everywhere.

Although there are important differences in detail between countries, the broad shape of tax structures is remarkably similar. Personal and unincorporated business incomes are subject to progressive income tax; company income is subject to corporation tax; while both employers and employees pay social security contributions. There are taxes on expenditure increasingly in the form of VAT (though not in the United States, where sales taxes are used). Most countries tax capital gains both at personal and corporate levels, and wealth at death, although only a few tax the wealth of the living except in the form of real estate taxes. There are a host of other taxes such as import duties, excise taxes, licences and stamp duty. All countries, and particularly those with a federal political structure, levy taxes at local as well as national levels of government.[6]

With the rise in the tax ratio there has been a growth in the complexity of tax systems everywhere. The increasing tax ratio has led to greater rewards for tax avoidance and evasion and a parallel rise in concern for fairness. Tax avoidance and evasion have led to complex regulations designed to close loopholes and provide the necessary information and controls for tighter enforcement. In the same way the alleviation of the burden of taxation on the least advantaged has taken the form of complex exemptions, thresholds, rebates and welfare payments.[7] Complexity has been further increased by modifications designed to further particular policy objectives such as the encouragement of R&D expenditure, investment or saving.

Table 5.1 Total tax revenues as percentage of GDP, selected countries and years, 1965–2001

Country	1965	1975	1985	1995	2000
United States	24.7	26.9	26.1	27.6	29.6
Japan	18.3	21.2	27.2	27.6	27.1
France	34.5	35.9	43.8	44.0	45.3
Sweden	35.0	42.3	48.5	47.6	54.2
United Kingdom	30.4	35.3	37.7	34.8	37.4

Source: *Revenue Statistics 1965–2000*, OECD.

These developments in taxation have several kinds of differential effect on small as compared to large firms, and therefore can be expected to distort the size distribution of the business population away from the optimum resulting from the interplay of scale economies and other factors discussed in Chapter 3.

The depletion of after-tax resources for investment

The first and most important of these differential effects is that taxation *depletes the resources* of working proprietors and their families and friends. This is important because SMEs, as shown in Chapter 4, rely heavily on owner equity and short-term borrowing. It is true that interest on debt (but not generally dividends for equity) is tax deductible, but short-term borrowing is expensive and the availability of debt may be restricted by lack of collateral (which has to be saved out of taxed income) or by the policies of banks which do not wish to see debt equity ratios (gearing) exceed unity.

Large firms are in a different position in respect to taxation – they have access to cheaper sources of both equity and debt finance. Also, being more capital-intensive and R&D-intensive, large firms benefit from the general bias in tax systems towards favouring capital investment and penalising employment through investment reliefs, R&D expenditure reliefs and social security contributions, as well as discriminating against smaller firms which tend to be more labour-intensive and which carry out less measurable R&D. Another way in which income tax systems can discriminate against SMEs results from their greater variability of profits mentioned, in Chapter 2. Under progressive taxation, taxes bear heavily in good years so that the average tax rate will be higher than if profits did not vary from year to year or were averaged over, say, three-year periods. It is difficult to assess how important net discrimination in the tax burden against small firms actually might be, but there is some evidence. Studies by the SBA in the United States many years ago indicated that, as a proportion of turnover, taxes were higher for SMEs than for large firms. Turnover is not an idea measure for this purpose, but in practice there is little alternative. Another issue is that large firms benefit to a greater extent from negative taxes – for example, grants and subsidies under regional policy or to encourage inward investment. BANNOCK (1990a) cites a dissertation by Gerhard Kern of the University of Mainz (1984): this study showed that as a percentage of turnover, all business taxes net of grants and subsidies were estimated at over twice as high in small firms as in large ones in Germany in 1970; ten years later this difference had narrowed to 25 per cent, still a considerable difference.

The impact of tax incentives for savings

The second main way in which tax systems divert resources from small to large firms is through incentives for *contractual savings*. Working proprietors, friends and families obtain no tax relief on earnings invested in their own business, but they and everyone else are eligible for various forms of relief on savings. All the major developed countries provide some form of tax relief for savings in life assurance, and almost all in the acquisition of pension rights. Since the capacity of financial institutions to invest in unquoted companies is limited by law, prudence and the high unit costs of small investments, the effect of these fiscal inducements to savings is to channel funds away from small to large firms.

It should be noted that the tax-induced diversion of funds away from SMEs affects not only investment by the working proprietor but also by third parties. While working proprietors have to invest in the equity of their own business out of taxed income they, and third parties, may obtain tax relief on investment in large firms. It is true that there are schemes in some countries to provide tax relief on investment in unquoted and unincorporated firms for third parties (not owner-managers) but these schemes are hedged with restrictions and limited in extent.

Tax compliance costs and incentives effects

The third way in which taxation discriminates in favour of large firms and against SMEs is associated with the *compliance burden*, which has risen inexorably with the growth of complexity of tax systems. By 'compliance burden', we mean the incidence of the cost of tax administration and the use of professional advice borne by a business both in assessing and paying its own tax and in collecting taxes from shareholders, employees and consumers. These costs, thanks to economies of scale in compliance, fall more heavily on small firms, but in this respect they are similar to the other costs of regulation and are discussed in more detail below.

The foregoing does not exhaust the ways in which the operation of tax systems may discriminate against small firms and reduce their role below the optimum. There is the whole question of the effects of taxation on incentives for hard work and risk-taking. It may be that, by taxing business success and failing to compensate for failure, taxation by its very nature reduces the incentive to start up and expand a small firm. Death duties and inheritance taxes, where they apply to business assets as they do in all countries (although reliefs are available), may also threaten the continuation of some small firms on the death of a predominant owner.[8] However, these effects of taxation are impossible to measure.[9]

The evidence on tax discrimination against SMEs

We believe that the capital market and compliance cost distortions resulting from modern tax systems have played a part in reducing the share of SMEs in economic activity below the theoretical (but unmeasurable) level that would obtain in the absence of taxes. It would be reasonable for the reader to ask what evidence there is for this belief. Certainly the long-term increase in taxation has been associated with a long-term decline in the role of SMEs. There have been reversals, but the most recent one seems to have been associated with some reduction in (or at least a slowdown of the growth of) aggregate tax ratios, though only from the mid-1980s. We also find, as shown in Chapter 9, that in cross-section studies of many countries, tax ratios tend to rise with levels of GDP and that the share of SMEs tends to decline with development. Of course many factors other than taxation affect the role of small firms. It should be noted that the extent of tax avoidance and evasion can affect the outcome. It may be no coincidence that tax compliance in southern European countries is notoriously low and of course these countries have much higher SME densities than the European average (see Chapter 1).

Evidence on the consequences of specific tax changes upon the role of small firms is sparse and inherently difficult to interpret because factors other than tax are always at work. It is true that the tax reforms of the Thatcher government in the United Kingdom after 1979, for example, were accompanied by a large increase in numbers of SMEs, but this trend had started earlier and the really important tax changes were not made until the mid-1980s. There were also other measures in favour of small firms such as the opening up of local authority contracting – for example, for building maintenance and refuse collection.

The 1986 Tax Reform Act in the United States was probably the most radical tax reform exercise in a major economy before or since, and was much applauded by economists. The reforms included increased personal income tax thresholds, reduced rates of tax made possible by the elimination of various deductions and some simplification of the system. The reforms were followed by some increase in numbers of SMEs, but it is difficult to attribute any general impact of the tax changes on the SME population. Various studies (reviewed in BANNOCK CONSULTING 2001c) have, however, examined the impact of subsequent changes in the Federal capital gains tax since 1978, under which the maximum rate for individuals was reduced from 49 per cent to 20 per cent for assets held for a year or more. These changes were found to have had positive effects on entrepreneurial activity, the demand for venture capital financing and economic growth, capital formation and productivity – without adverse effects on income tax yields, though inevitably not without controversy.

What can be done about tax discrimination against SMEs?

Most countries have done something to attempt to alleviate the burdens of taxation for SMEs. In some countries, unincorporated business income may be averaged over two or three years where that would reduce the total tax liability over the period. There are easements for wealth, capital gains tax and taxes on death for business assets in many countries. There are also measures to reduce compliance costs for particular taxes (see below) and measures to promote investment in small quoted and unquoted companies.

In general, tax systems for incorporated businesses are more favourable to small companies than to unincorporated businesses.[10] This is because, as mentioned in Chapter 2, dividends may be taxed at lower rates than owners' salaries and will not bear social security contributions, but also because in many countries (for example the United Kingdom, Japan and the United States) corporation tax rates have a progressive element, so that small companies pay lower rates of taxes than big ones.[11]

These palliatives may have been helpful in some cases, but they do little to alter the basic issues of discrimination against SMEs, and even what has been achieved has been at the price of complicating the tax system still further. Almost all economists believe that major tax reform is necessary for many reasons, not simply in the interests of SMEs, although their solutions vary. Various proposals have been made: economic distortions and compliance costs could both be reduced drastically if business and income taxes were restored to a true income base – that is, to eliminate all tax reliefs for savings (PEACOCK 1978) or to tax expenditure only (MEADE 1978). Less radically, major adaptations could be made to existing taxes or some – corporation tax is a candidate – could be abolished altogether.[12] An expenditure tax of the kind proposed by MEADE (1978) would allow the abolition of VAT, which is a major source of difficulty for SMEs.[13]

It is beyond the scope of this book to analyse the relative merits of the radical alternatives to the present taxation systems. None of them is under active consideration at present, although in the United States there are lively public discussions on major tax reforms from time to time. Governments are understandably reluctant to disturb tax arrangements which are the source of large amounts of revenue. All reforms would create winners and losers and therefore political fall-out. One has to be pessimistic about the prospects for effective tax reform. Moreover, the pressures from vested interests are so strong that even the limited reforms and simplifications that have taken place have generally been eroded in later years, as happened after the US 1986 Tax Reform Act.

Regulation

The nature and history of regulation

All governments seek to supervise and control the activities of private enterprise, not only in the interests of economic efficiency (such as the control of pricing in monopolistic industries), but also in the social interest (fairness, health and the environment and safety). Regulatory activities have not been restricted to government as such; the manorial system and artisans' guilds in medieval times were indistinguishable in principle from modern government market regulation (POLANYI 2001) and some activities today – for example, the legal profession – are partly subject to 'self-regulation'.

Government workplace regulation of the modern kind really dates from the nineteenth century during the Industrial Revolution.[14] In England, beginning with the Health and Morals of Apprentices Act 1802, a series of laws was introduced from then to the end of the nineteenth century to set minimum ages for employment in factories, limit the hours of work for children and, in 1844, of women; whitewash and ventilate factories, report accidents and so on (PEACOCK *et al.* 1984). Until 1853 the Factory Acts were confined to textile factories (mills), and only in 1878 was the system extended to cover all factory and workshop trades so that small firms were exempted (MATHIAS 1983). These laws were consolidated in the Factory and Workshop Act 1901, and since then the scope of regulation has widened and deepened continuously, particularly since the 1970s. By modern standards, social laws were hardly draconian – for example, the Factory Act 1809 excluded children under the age of nine from working in cotton mills and restricted those over that age to 12 hours a day (reduced to 6½ hours a day in the Act of 1833). Laws of these kinds were introduced in other countries as industrialisation developed. In the United States, legislation on child labour was not introduced until 1836 in Massachusetts, but not until the 1930s did all states have child labour legislation (FAULKNER 1960). Minimum wages, but only for certain trades, were introduced after 1900 in England, but general minima did not begin to be introduced until 1938 in the United States and were not universal until the 1990s in the United Kingdom. Today, government regulation extends to virtually all spheres of business management (Box 5.1) and almost all of the regulatory burdens which result apply to small as well as large firms, though there are exceptions.

Box 5.1 The scope of government regulations potentially giving rise to compliance costs

---

1   Employment protection

1   Legislation on dismissals, redundancy, maternity leave, employment contracts, working hours, employment of disabled persons, discrimination against race or sex.
2   Legislation on minimum wages, indexation, forms of remuneration.
3   Laws affecting collective agreements, participation and information.
4   Laws on training and apprenticeships.

2   Collection and payment of taxes and grants

1   Collection and payment of social security contributions and income taxes for employees, payments of benefit.
2   Collection and payment of value added tax, sales taxes and other special taxes such as excise duties.

---

3 Payment of national and local income taxes, payroll and property taxes.
4 Application for grants and rebates.

3 Health and safety

1 Working conditions: space, heat, light.
2 Accident prevention.
3 Fire prevention.
4 Pollution.
5 Compulsory insurance.
6 Planning restrictions on the construction of new buildings and the usage of existing buildings.

4 Provision of information

1 *Direct*: data on employees and their remuneration, statistics on a variety of matters, assistance with official inspections and investigations.
2 *Indirect*: Comments on proposed and present legislation and policy, principally via trade and employers' associations.

5 Other laws

1 Planning and construction, consumer law, privacy laws, customs and exchange control.
2 Company reporting and business registration laws, monopoly and restrictive practices laws.

6 Industry-specific

Transport, catering, alcohol, agricultural, placement agencies, home rentals, state monopolies, etc.

Source: BANNOCK & PEACOCK (1989).

The theory of regulation

The justification for some form of social legislation was obvious on humanitarian grounds. Other kinds of regulation, however, have been justified by economic theory. The theory is that left to themselves, markets are imperfect: for example, as mentioned in Chapter 3, under conditions of monopolistic competition, prices will be higher and output lower than under perfect competition. Intervention is therefore justified to promote public welfare. Externalities are another issue – private producers may not bear the full social costs of pollution, for example, and would pollute less if they were to bear these costs. Again, regulation, or the taxation of pollutants is the answer. Information which is assumed to be 'perfect' in the competitive ideal is another case where in the real world, markets do not produce a socially optimal result. This is because producers may not be able viably to satisfy market requirements for information, because much of it has the characteristics of a 'public good': it is freely transferable once known, and it is difficult to make money out of creating and supplying it. This argument justifies the provision of certain kinds of information by government or regulation to ensure that firms do so, such as in the United Kingdom the requirement under the Consumer Credit Act 1974 for providers of credit to demonstrate the effective annual interest rate charged. We return to the economics of information in Chapter 8, because it has relevance to the government provision of support to small firms.

More recently, new theories of public choice have emerged that have challenged the assumption that government regulation does help to restore markets nearer to the competitive ideal (see PEACOCK *et al.* 1984 for a succinct summary and references). One of the possible reasons for the failure of regulation is that industry 'captures' the regulators so that regulation serves the interests of specialist producer groups rather than the general welfare. We may also add that regulators themselves may end up serving their own interests, so that regulatory agencies may have budgets inflated out of all proportion to the benefits of their activities.

The effects of regulation

It can be appreciated that small firms, not as well organised or as influential as large ones, are not likely to benefit much from 'regulatory capture' and will suffer unduly from the costs imposed upon them by regulatory agencies. This last is because there are economies of scale in regulatory compliance which, as we demonstrate below, mean that compliance costs rise steeply with firm size.

Regulatory capture aside, there can be benefits to businesses (and consumers) from regulation. Consumers, for example, might have greater confidence in regulated firms so that the latter might not need to spend as much on reputational advertising as they would if unregulated.[15] If health and safety regulation reduces industrial accidents or sickness, then this will have benefits for producers. Some advantages are more obvious: for example, re-regulation following the privatisation of British Telecom in the United Kingdom has created opportunities for the formation and growth of many small alternative telecommunications firms. Regulation and competition resulted in considerable reductions in prices in telecommunications and in other privatised utilities.

As another example of private benefits from regulation, PEACOCK *et al.* (1984) point to the benefits accruing to the motor trade through the imposition of regular vehicle testing in the United Kingdom and Japan: this is achieved both through the business generated for repair stations and the enhancement of demand from manufacturers through accelerated depreciation. SYKES (2002) argues that although vehicle testing imposes cost on car owners, it benefits all road users in terms of safety and lower pollution.

One cannot reach sweeping conclusions about the effects of regulation; it can be either beneficial or damaging. It is not safe to assume that where market imperfections can be demonstrated, regulation will automatically bring markets closer to the competitive ideal – it may move them further away from that ideal.[16] Action by the UK Monopolies and Mergers Commission (MMC) to modify the tied-house system, under which brewers owned some of their sales outlets (pubs) and which was judged to be prejudicial to competition, is a case in point.[17] This action stimulated an increase in concentration in brewing and, partly through the disruption of distribution patterns, some increase in the rate of beer price increases in pubs.

Perhaps the best example of counter-productive regulation is that of the excessive regulation of labour markets in Europe. In contrast to the United States, EU countries have greater restrictions on hiring and firing and also high levels of payroll taxes, more rigid wage bargaining structures and supports for trades union activities. There is widespread agreement amongst economists that the resulting lack of flexibility in labour markets is the prime reason for Europe's poor employment and growth performance since the 1960s (see GALLI & PELKMANS 2000; SMETS & DOMBRECHT 2001).[18]

It is a characteristic of regulation that the administration costs, though difficult to assess, are more easily measured than the benefits. Since there is now growing evidence on the magnitude of the compliance costs of regulation and more particularly on their differential effect upon SMEs, most of the rest of this chapter is devoted to these.

Definition and measurement of compliance costs

The compliance costs of meeting regulatory requirements are of three kinds. First there are *direct costs*, such as those of installing equipment to control emissions. Second, there are the *administrative compliance costs*, or paperwork burdens involved. Third, there may be, as mentioned earlier, *excess burdens*, or efficiency costs, which are the costs to the economy as a whole that result from (further) distortions from the competitive ideal.[19] The first and third types of cost may be important but for our purposes, which are to look at the direct effects of regulation on SMEs, we intend to confine our attention to administrative compliance costs, for which useable survey data are available.

Administrative compliance costs consist of the time needed to understand the law, deal with the necessary paperwork and inspections by officials, visit government offices and train and pay staff, where necessary, to carry out the work. Also included under this heading are any paid-out costs to legal advisers, accountants and consultants. There may also be costs of postage, storing information or modifying computer programmes or administrative procedures to meet government requirements. It is important that only the incremental costs of meeting these requirements should be included. In other words, properly defined compliance costs are those which are incurred solely and exclusively to meet regulations. In practice, in assessing these costs quite tricky decisions may have to be made: for example, the modification of computer software or even the replacement of data processing systems might have been necessary for other reasons, and the incremental cost of meeting regulatory requirements might be negligible in these circumstances.

There are other difficulties in measuring compliance costs. Not only should these costs be *incremental* – that is, only costs which would not be borne in the absence of regulation should be counted – but they should be assessed *net of any benefits received* by the firm. The clearest case of private benefit of regulation is in the collection of VAT where registered traders add the tax to their charges to customers and then, after an average delay of perhaps six weeks where quarterly returns are required, forward the tax receipts to the authorities. In the meantime the firm may earn interest on the money.[20] Another difficulty is that costs may be unusually high where a firm starts to comply with the regulation but may settle down at lower levels as time goes by. The distinction between *transitional* and *recurrent* compliance costs can be important when attempts are made to measure the incidence of costs over time (see EVANS 2001). Finally, businesses do not normally keep records distinguishing regulatory costs from other costs, so that most research has to rely on subjective estimates by managers.[21] This is a greater problem for large firms, where many different people and departments are affected, than in the small firm where most management functions are concentrated in one or two persons.[22]

We have not so far referred to the administrative costs of government itself in operating regulatory systems. These government costs are not directly germane to the impact on SMEs since they are borne out of general taxation; however, there is scope for shifting administrative costs between government and affected firms. The long-term trend is for these costs to be shifted downwards so that companies are expected, for example, to assess their own taxes – with penalties for incorrect or non-compliance – as well as collect taxes from employees and consumers. This is no doubt an efficient procedure from a social point of view (there are more pressures on companies than on governments to minimise costs), but it is another factor in the general increase in compliance costs on business. Studies in taxation reviewed below indicate that at least 80 per cent of the total public and private costs of VAT administration are borne by business, and a dispropor-tionate share of this is borne by SMEs. SANDFORD *et al.* (1981) calculated that of the combined public and gross private operating costs of VAT, 83 per cent were accounted for by registered traders with a taxable turnover of under £100,000. In fact, the costs of collecting the tax borne by traders and the authorities exceeded the revenue obtained for these smaller firms.

Research results on overall compliance costs

Systematic and large-scale analysis and research on regulatory compliance costs dates only from the 1970s. It was pioneered in the field of taxation by Professor Cedric Sandford of the University of Bath (see SANDFORD *et al.* 1981, 1989), but more recently research has broadened to cover a wider field and many countries. Because of differences in coverage and methodology these studies are difficult to compare, but four broad findings are well estab-lished: first, total regulatory compliance costs are very large in all developed countries; second, these costs are tending to increase everywhere; third, tax compliance is the largest single element; and fourth, as a percentage of sales turnover, compliance costs fall steeply with increasing firm size.

In the early 1980s the costs of regulatory paperwork burdens for the United Kingdom and Germany were estimated at between 2 and 4 per cent of GDP (BANNOCK & PEACOCK 1989). EUROPEAN COMMISSION (1995) put the average cost of administrative burdens for SMEs at 3–4 per cent of GDP. This study indicated that obligations resulting from having employees accounted for 30–40 per cent of the total. There has certainly been a further substantial increase since these earlier estimates: the BCC estimate that the cost of new regulations introduced between 1998 and 2003 amounted to over £20 billion (about 2 per cent of GDP).[23] For the United States, somewhat more broadly defined Federal regulatory costs have been estimated by Professor Thomas Hopkins at 7.7 per cent of GDP for the year 2000 (cited in GRAY 2001). These figures are very large: for example, in the United Kingdom gross value added in agriculture, forestry and fishing, and the whole of the construction sector is about the same as the estimate of compliance costs. Thomas Gray shows that if estimated deadweight losses (costs not offset by benefits) are also allowed for (which they are not, in the US figure cited above), then the total cost of regulation could be greater than the Federal government tax take. Thomas Gray cites data showing that the cost of regulation increased by about 10 per cent between 1972 and 2000. This is probably a slower increase than has taken place in Europe.

Research results on SME compliance costs

Compliance costs are *regressive* – that is, they bear most heavily on small firms. This results from the fact that some administrative costs are fixed (for example, the fee for registering a business), while others do not rise proportionally with firm size: with computerisation, and depending on the complexity of the business, one or two book-keepers can probably handle £3 million of sales as easily as £1 million.

Chart 5.1 shows VAT compliance costs as a percentage of turnover by firm size for Britain and Germany. Both curves slope steeply downwards to the right and are typical of compliance cost curves, showing the regressive nature of the incidence of regulatory costs. It can be seen that costs were somewhat lower in Germany, but the gradients of the curves are similar.[24] Very similar results have been obtained in similar studies in a whole range of countries (see NAO 1994 and SANDFORD 1995). A 1995 study by R. Clemens and I. Kokaly at the *Institut für Mittelstandsforschung* in Germany estimated that total administrative compliance costs as a percentage of turnover fell from 3.1 per cent for firms with 1–9 employees to 0.1 per cent for firms with 500 or more employees.[25]

Research in the United Kingdom found that among small firms, for all regulation, including taxation, the average hours per person working in the business per month fell from 7.9 for one-person firms to 0.4 for firms with 50 or more employees (SBRT 9/99). After adjustment for differences in average firm size in this survey it appears that there were variations between activity sectors, with firms in construction and transport spending more time on government paperwork than retailers, for example. In 1998, 59.2 per cent of respondents reported that time taken on government paperwork had increased, and 39.1 per cent said there had been no significant change. Respondents were asked to state which three of 12 groups of regulation took

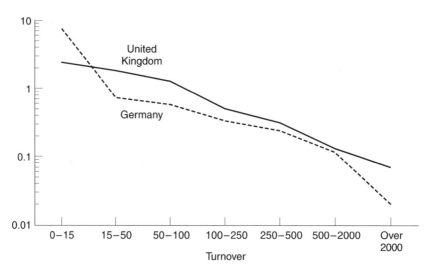

Chart 5.1 Gross VAT compliance costs as percentage of turnover, by turnover size band, United Kingdom and West Germany, 1985

Source: Graham Bannock & Partners and Professor Horst Albach. 'The compliance costs of VAT for smaller firms in Britain and West Germany', in BANNOCK & PEACOCK (1989).

the most time to deal with. Overall, VAT was the most burdensome and was included in the top three elements by 71.6 per cent of respondents. VAT was followed by 'PAYE and National Insurance contributions' (57.2 per cent) and 'Self-assessment taxation' (48.3 per cent). 'Other taxation' was included by 16.0 per cent, 'Health and safety' came in fourth position (24.9 per cent), followed by 'Other employment' with 13.0 per cent (Table 5.2). There were some interesting firm size differences in these results. Larger firms are much more concerned about health and safety, employment regulation and also statistical enquiries than smaller ones, but all are concerned about tax compliance costs.

In a small firm, much of government paperwork has to be dealt with by the owner-manager. An SBRT survey throws some light on this and also on the use of professional advisers (Table 5.3).

Table 5.2 Respondents including selected areas of regulation in the three that take the most time to deal with, United Kingdom

Area	(%)
VAT	71.6
Self-assessment	48.3
PAYE and NIC	57.2
Other taxation	16.0
Minimum wage	3.0
Working time directive	5.1
Other health and safety	24.9
Other employment	13.0
Environmental	5.7
Building and planning	3.6
Statistical enquiries	11.0
Other	8.7
Base	507

Source: SBRT 9/99.

Table 5.3 Cost of compliance time spent by owner/managers, staff and advisers, by turnover size band, United Kingdom

Turnover size band (£)	Yourself/partner/ director (%)	Staff (%)	Professional advisers (%)
Less than 20,000	79.56	7.41	13.04
20,000–49,999	72.11	5.98	21.90
50,000–149,999	64.88	14.18	20.94
150,000–349,999	53.59	20.12	26.29
350,000–749,999	43.41	34.75	21.84
750,000–1,499,999	41.13	35.53	23.34
1,500,000 and over	35.05	48.67	16.28
All	56.13	22.49	21.38
Base		396 respondents	

Source: SBRT 3/96.

International comparisons of compliance costs

International comparative research on compliance costs is still in its infancy. Indeed, apart from the Anglo-German comparison of VAT compliance costs I am aware of only one cross-country study using common methodology, and that was carried out by the OECD.[26] The OECD study, which covered 11 countries, found that administrative compliance costs averaged 4 per cent of turnover, with large differences between countries – for example, 8 per cent in Norway and 1 per cent in Australia. The perceived level of compliance (the extent to which firms thought regulations were actually complied with) also varied between countries, being lower in Australia than in Norway, for example. This helps to explain country differences in the compliance cost–turnover ratios. The survey also confirmed the regressive nature of compliance costs and brought out the fact that, even so, perceived levels of compliance were lower for small firms than for large. The majority of respondents (61 per cent) believed that administrative compliance costs had increased over the two previous years, thus also confirming the results of other surveys. Finally, the majority of the costs were incurred in complying with tax (43 per cent) and employment (34 per cent), with only 23 per cent accounted for by environmental regulations.[27]

Regulatory frameworks are increasingly alike in developed countries. Given cultural and methodological differences in available survey data we doubt that, in Europe and the United States at least, there are very great differences in the burden of administrative compliance costs between countries. As mentioned earlier, EUROPEAN COMMISSION (1995), reviewing the available material, put total administrative compliance costs for SMEs alone in EU countries at between 3 and 4 per cent of GDP (this would imply figures of 4–6 per cent for all firms, large and small). The OECD study discussed above put the comparable figure for SMEs at 3 per cent. The figures cited in GRAY (2001) for the United States, which relate to the whole economy, imply a ratio of SME compliance costs of about 4.5 per cent of GDP. Allowing for the different dates, definitions and methodologies for these studies, the differences between developed countries do not seem very significant.[28] We discuss the situation in developing countries in Chapter 9.

How important are compliance burdens?

The estimates discussed above suggest that administrative compliance costs for all businesses are now of the order of 5 per cent of GDP in the developed countries. In the United Kingdom that would put them at about £50 billion (2001). This is a staggering figure when compared with central government receipts from income tax (£113 billion in 2001/2). It is considerably more than the yield of corporation tax (£32 billion) and over three-quarters of receipts from VAT or compulsory social security contributions (£66 billion and £63 billion, respectively). There are, of course, considerable margins of uncertainty about the estimates of compliance costs, but any plausible downward adjustment would still leave a very large number.[29] Moreover, we have not allowed for the costs of government in administering the regulatory system or for efficiency costs.

What all this means is that the real resource costs absorbed by regulation per firm are very large indeed (about £1,700 on average for all firms in the United Kingdom with fewer than 250 employees), and these resources have alternative uses. Some regulation is essential to the functioning of the market system and social welfare, but if compliance costs could be reduced the rewards would be large. In theory, if compliance costs could be reduced by, say, 10 per cent, then those resources could be absorbed in higher taxes and used to improve public services without business being any worse off. Alternatively, if taxation remained unchanged and compliance costs were reduced the private sector would have additional resources to spend on investment and business development, which in turn could be expected eventually to yield higher tax revenues.

The benefits of lower compliance costs would be still greater, however, if the effects on efficiency costs were taken into account. Lower deadweight losses, or excess burdens, should benefit the whole economy. We see no way of estimating these overall, but a component of them should result from a relief from the downward pressure on the role of SMEs in the economy. This could be expected because, as shown above, SMEs bear a disproportionate share of total compliance costs and the injection of resources into the SME sector would also be disproportionately large.[30] If the SME share in economic activity is being held below the optimum (whatever that may be) by the weight of regulatory compliance costs, a reduction in that weight should yield economic benefits. The only major proviso to this argument would be if all or most of the regulatory costs were passed on to consumers. This seems unlikely for SMEs at least, and if most of the rising costs were being absorbed by them this would be consistent with the low returns being earned by SMEs and the lower wages they pay, as discussed in Chapter 2.

Why are administrative compliance costs so high?

Compliance costs have become so large mainly because of demands (from consumers, workers and others, including business itself) for more and more protection and fairness in increasingly complex and wealthy societies. Rising standards of living and security of welfare do not abate these pressures, they promote them, as do the efforts of the multiplicity of pressure groups.[31] Poorer societies in the developing world, as we shall see in Chapter 9, are for various reasons obliged to tolerate much lower standards, though their governments are increasingly importing regulatory practices from the advanced countries.[32]

The important point is that the countervailing forces against the imposition of higher regulatory standards are weak compared with those pressing for more regulation. Democratic pressures do exert some downward pressure on rates of taxation, since proposals to raise taxes are hotly debated in legislative bodies and by the public at large.[33] There is no such debate about regulation, the costs of which are unknown to the electorate – and, indeed, until recently, to the legislature. The public is largely unaware that there are any costs to regulation. Where they are aware of costs, it seems to be assumed that these costs will simply be borne by business instead of, by large firms at least, passed on to the public. From the point of view of governments, electoral demands for regulation can therefore be met at little political cost.[34]

There are, of course, other reasons for high administrative compliance costs. As noted in the discussion of taxation above, regulatory systems have become more complex in an effort to achieve fairness. As an example, if VAT were levied at a single rate with no exemptions and on the whole of consumer expenditure, the compliance cost of the tax would be greatly reduced. Pressure for exemptions (food, for example) prevents achievement of this simplicity in most countries.[35] Another reason why regulation is administratively more costly than it need be is that systems are designed and implemented in the bureaucratic culture of government by people who, understandably enough, have limited familiarity with business practices. Often regulations have to be changed after introduction to make them more compliant-friendly, but each change introduces new costs until things have settled down again. Finally, it seems to be easier to introduce new regulations than it is to remove existing ones. Vested interests build up commitments to existing regulations, and there are also always pressures on the time available in legislative assemblies. The political rewards for removing old laws are generally slight. As a result there is a 'ratchet effect', with new burdens being added and little taken away.

What can be done about excessive regulatory compliance costs?

It is not so much individual regulations that cause problems – most are well-meaning and directed at real issues of concern – but the overall burden they constitute which eats into the scarce time and resources of SMEs.[36] The relentless accumulation of compliance costs has received more and more attention since the Thatcher–Reagan governments of the early 1980s, although explicit attempts to curtail burdens have a longer history, certainly dating at least from the 1950s in the United States.

From the early 1980s in Europe, machinery began to be put in place. In late 1983, for example, the German Federal government set up an independent committee to review legislative burdens, as did the French government at about the same time. The United Kingdom established an Enterprise and Deregulation Unit (EDU) in 1986 following an in-depth review of the problem.[37] The Commission of the European Communities also set up a central SME Task Force in 1986, one of the most important functions of which was to control regulatory burdens. Since around 1990 international organisations such as the OECD, which at that time established the Working Party on Regulatory Management and Reform, have been concerned with regulatory issues. This interest has been extended to the Third World by the World Bank, UN agencies and others because it has been realised that regulatory reform is important for private sector development in these countries (see Chapter 9).[38]

Many different but overlapping approaches have been made to the control of regulation. They can be classified into two groups: the administrative control approach and the legal control approach.

Under the *administrative control approach*, machinery is set up to review regulations, particularly forthcoming regulations, and initiate change. This approach is most highly developed in the United Kingdom, where a regulatory impact assessment (RIA) has, since 1996, been required for all new regulation imposing significant costs on business.[39] The RIAs assess the costs and benefits of regulation and must specifically take into account their impact on SMEs. The regulatory impact unit (RIU), which has satellites in all major government departments, assists in the preparation of RIAs. An independent better regulation task force (BRTF) was set up in 1997 to advise on the quality of regulation.[40]

The *legal control approach* is to enact laws to lay down procedures for the review of new or existing regulations and to limit the freedom of regulatory agencies to impose compliance burdens. The United States is unique in the extent of its use of this approach. For example, the Regulatory Flexibility Act 1980 requires agencies to submit an initial impact assessment (initial regulatory flexibility analysis, IRFA) for proposed new regulations to the SBA for review (see Chapter 7). Rules may not be issued until SBA comments have been considered and a final regulatory flexibility analysis (FRFA) completed. Another example is the Paperwork Reduction Act, also first passed in 1980 and renewed and extended in 1995. This Act gave the Office of Management and Budget (OMB), part of the Executive Office of the President, authority for approval of requests for information such as statistical surveys (GRAY 2001). The Chief Counsel for Advocacy of the SBA, on behalf of small firms, can mount legal challenges to agencies that do not abide by these Acts.

Also under the legal control approach, we can mention specified exemptions for small firms from the application of regulations. FLETCHER (2001) lists a number of examples of these exemptions in the United States relating to minimum wages, unpaid leave and equal pay for men and women and other legislation. Finally, Sunset Legislation, which expires after a set period if not explicitly renewed, is another form of the legal control approach.

The administrative and legal approaches are not mutually exclusive and both are used in several countries, including the United States. A number of *technical approaches* have also been used to limit or ease particular types of compliance burden. For example, France has, in some areas such as social security, taken on central responsibility for the redistribution of information between government departments to save businesses having to submit the same information separately to several departments.[41] The United Kingdom has a Survey Control Unit in government that has to vet intentions to send out information requests to businesses.

As shown above when reviewing the survey evidence, the various approaches to controlling regulatory compliance costs do not seem to have arrested their growth, although undoubtedly burdens would have increased faster in their absence. This seems to be particularly true for the United States, where regulatory costs were estimated to have declined between 1977 and 1987, a period when the legal control approach was apparently used most aggressively. One of the difficulties in controlling regulation is that so many bodies in addition to government departments regulate business. BRTF (2003), for example, points out that large numbers of independent regulators have taken over functions previously carried out by government and says there are over 1,000 non-departmental public bodies, such as the dependent utilities' regulators, which act at arms length from government.

Controlling regulation, with all its differential impact on SMEs, is clearly a major challenge; we defer discussion of what more might be done to achieve this to Chapter 10, where we conclude that regulation is *the* major problem in assessing the future prospects for small business.

Notes

1 Assuming 7 million SME owners/spouses, this compares with 8 million trades union members and 11 million persons of pensionable age, out of a population over 18 years of 46 million. Many SME owners, perhaps 20 per cent in the United Kingdom, are members of trade associations which are concerned with special sectoral interests and therefore present a fragmented view to government, but fewer (perhaps less than 10 per cent) are members of horizontal employer organisations which represent small business or business as a whole. There are some umbrella bodies, such as the Confederation of British Industries (CBI) and British Chambers of Commerce (BCC), which have significant voices but which have problems sometimes where the interests of their small and big firm members do not coincide. Similar bodies exist in Continental Europe, where in some countries – for example, Germany – chambers of commerce are public law bodies (all firms must be members). There is a pan-European organisation which lobbies the European Commission and Parliament, the European Small Business Alliance (ESBA). In North America the National Federation of Independent Business (NFIB) in the United States and the Canadian Federation of Independent Business together have about 1 million members and strong research capabilities. In France, the Confédération Générale des Petites et Moyennes Entreprises (CGPME) unites small firm bodies in manufacturing, distribution and other services. Japan has very powerful SME representation which in the past has had a major influence on

government policy (see FRIEDMAN 1988 on the Japanese Small and Medium Business Federation). The fragmentation of small business representation is sometimes cited as a reason for inaction by government; in fact, all representative bodies agree that government is the main problem they face (see Stan Mendham, *Small Business Perspective*, 6, 1992).

2 The author once made this observation to a senior official in an African government and was told: 'Wrong, many of us are running businesses on the side – how else can we live on our salaries'! This is no doubt correct, but merely serves to illustrate how vested interests and larger political interests determine policy rather than knowledge as such.

3 In 2002 there was an outcry from the UK DTI when David Arculus, Chairman of the Better Regulation Task Force, suggested that 'officials were overwhelming business with red tape because few had enough experience of working in the private sector' (*Financial Times*, 16 May 2000). The DTI actually has a programme for short-term secondments of its officials to small firms to help the familiarisation process.

4 We draw heavily here, and also in Chapters 6 and 8, on DEEKS' excellent and wide-ranging book, *The Small Firm Owner-Manager* (1976).

5 Corporate social responsibility is very much about placating special interest groups in an era when large firms are so powerful that they have to make concessions to the primacy of profit to maintain their legitimacy – whatever their shareholders might think. Small firms can rarely permit themselves this luxury. Philip M. Van Anken and R. Duane Ireland, in 'Divergent perspectives on social responsibility: big versus small' in JUDD *et al.* (1988), argue that small firms should concentrate on not being socially irresponsible but eschew social activism. In fact, small business owners play a leading role in local communities, while NFIB research shows that charitable contributions per employee are higher for small than for medium-sized or large firms in the United States.

6 The discussion below focuses mainly on central government direct taxes (on income and wealth). Readers interested in local taxation and expenditure taxes will find a detailed treatment in BANNOCK (1990a). Value Added Taxes are not levied on firms but on consumers; firms collect the tax and in theory pass it all on to consumers, but in practice some business costs are not deductible and are taxed under VAT (see BANNOCK & PEACOCK 1989). VAT has, moreover, exceptionally heavy compliance costs which are discussed below.

7 The growing complexity of the tax system can be measured only indirectly, for example by counting the numbers of pages in the relevant legislation. The fairly drastic simplifications in the US 1986 Tax Reform Act, discussed briefly below, still left a document of 1,600 pages. Adam SMITH (1776) wrote of taxes that 'the time of payment, the manner of payment, the quantity to be paid, ought all to be clear and plain to the contributor, and to every other person'. He went on 'the certainty of what each individual ought to pay is, in taxation, a matter of so great importance, that a very considerable degree of inequality, it appears, I believe, from the experience of all nations, is not near so great an evil as a very small degree of uncertainty'. In all countries now, over two-and-a-quarter centuries later, we are so far from this ideal that uncertainty deriving from complexity is itself a grave source of inequality, since the capacity of people (and firms) to understand or pay for professional advice varies so much.

8 This section on taxation has drawn heavily on BANNOCK & PEACOCK (1989).

9 No one has found a satisfactory way of measuring the incentive effects of taxation, or even of the incidence of tax. It can be argued that people may work harder to compensate for the effects of tax but it is possible that the effects vary with the level of income, particularly where taxes are progressive, so that

beyond a certain point taxes create a real disincentive for further effort. The incidence of business taxation is also uncertain: firms may pass on taxes wholly or partly to their customers. In this case, it is more likely that large firms with greater market power could shift taxes forward to the consumer than small firms. The impact of death taxes on business survival is also uncertain. BOLTON (1971) had many representations about this problem but could not find any cases where firms had ceased business solely as a result of taxes on death. It should be noted that these caveats do not apply to the existence of capital market distortions or compliance burdens resulting from taxation, which are a matter of logic and fact. The consequences of these distortions, though, are more controversial.

10 This issue is immensely complicated, since business income tax rates can be lower or higher than corporation tax rates, while the self-employed may pay lower social security contributions. Moreover, the treatment of business expenses may be more generous for the self-employed than for employees in companies. In theory, there should be *tax neutrality* between legal forms; in practice, an individual may pay much more tax as an employee of a large company.

11 In the United States, corporations with 35 or fewer non-corporate shareholders may elect to be subject to income tax instead of corporation tax (Sub-Chapter S). This allows a business to choose whichever tax regime is most favourable to it – for example, where it would be advantageous to offset losses in the company against other personal income while retaining the benefit of limited liability. There are similar provisions in France.

12 The abolition of corporation tax is not as crazy as it sounds. Corporations are owned by individuals who are also taxed under other systems. The MEADE (1978) Committee admitted: 'it is possible that if one were starting from scratch one would wish to avoid any special tax on corporate enterprise'. There would, of course, be transitional and other problems, such as treatment of non-residents, but that is true for all radical reform and the problems are not insuperable.

13 Alternatively, VAT could be replaced by sales taxes, as levied in the United States at both Federal and State level. This would eliminate the compliance burdens for very large numbers of SMEs. Japan has a much simpler form of VAT than the transaction-based system of the European Union, based on value added calculated from company accounts. The Japanese VAT, however, is not suitable for multiple tax rates (BANNOCK 2001a).

14 It might be thought that other types of regulation, such as on the environment, are relatively recent preoccupations, but PEACOCK *et al.* (1984) note that there was an 'Ordinance of 1307 on pollution, and Queen Elizabeth I issued a proclamation prohibiting the burning of sea coal in London while parliament was in session'.

15 These types of advantages of regulation are often very difficult to substantiate empirically. For example, the UK Financial Services Authority (FSA) commissioned a report from EUROPE ECONOMICS (2003). A sample of financial service providers were asked if they would spend the same, more, or less on reputation in the absence of regulation: 82 per cent would spend the same, 12 per cent more and only 6 per cent less. On a different point, SYKES (2002), on behalf of the FSA, had earlier argued that 'In an assessment of the overall costs of regulation, one would ideally estimate the difference between the total costs of regulation and the costs that a well-run firm would incur in an unregulated but well-functioning market. Well-run firms should find that properly founded regulatory requirements can be close to the steps that they would take to ensure that their business is run in a suitably prudent manner and that their customers get the service they require. Thus the incremental costs of properly founded regulations should be lower for well-run firms compared to those less well run.'

The UK HM Customs and Excise have made similar claims in relation to the costs of VAT compliance (NAO 1994); see below.

16 Where regulations increase market distortions, then costs (in addition to compliance costs) are incurred in the economy. These costs are known as 'excess burdens', 'efficiency costs' or 'deadweight losses'. Excess burdens are difficult to assess but are thought in some cases to be a multiple of compliance costs. For an example in the case of taxis, see Chapter 10.

17 See SLADE (1998). The 1989 Beer Orders forced brewers to divest estates of in excess of 2,000 pubs and imposed other regulations on the industry. There are SME issues here because although some tied houses are managed directly by brewers, others are tenanted by small firms. These tenants do not appear to have benefited from the freeing of the ties, which have simply been replaced by similar arrangements with independent pub companies.

18 Labour legislation, and specifically employment protection, affects both small and large firms. High payroll taxes certainly bear more heavily on small firms, but there is not much evidence that employment protection laws have particularly adverse effects on SMEs (see Ava Westrip, 'Effects of employment legislation on small firms', in WATKINS *et al.* 1982 and Graham Bannock, 'Social legislation and its impact on employment in SMEs', in BANNOCK & PEACOCK 1989). EDWARDS (2003) establishes that many aspects of employment legislation (for example, parental leave) are tied to specific events that in a very small firm may never occur. This explains why large firms, which experience more such events, find this type of legislation more onerous.

19 Direct costs can include more than the costs of physical equipment. For example, we could include the cost of delays or lost production while necessary permissions are awaited, or the loss of competitive advantage through enforced disclosure of information. This reminds us that we are considering private costs to producers of direct and administrative compliance: excess burdens are costs to society as a whole and might result, for example, from the effects of rules in constraining innovation or the effect of regulatory costs in forcing some suppliers to withdraw from the market. It is usual to analyse compliance costs on a *partial equilibrium* basis – in other words, to assume that producers continue with their existing product portfolios and operations and that demand is not affected as costs are shifted. Under a general equilibrium analysis everything might change, including the incidence of the compliance costs. In practice, the necessary information to conduct general equilibrium analysis is rarely available (see PEACOCK *et al.* 1984).

20 SANDFORD *et al.* (1981), in their estimates of the compliance costs of VAT, made a small allowance for 'management benefits', by which they meant that improved record-keeping and control of debtors by registered traders, in some cases at least, should follow from the adoption of the systems necessary for the administration of VAT. The researchers had some empirical basis for this from their questionnaire survey, which included questions about such benefits. Other researchers do not seem to have made an allowance for these benefits.

21 Detailed regulatory cost surveys usually ask respondents how much staff/owner time is spent on regulatory-induced tasks as well as an estimate of paid-out costs. The valuation of this time is normally reserved for the researcher, though respondents may be asked for information on pay rates. Issues raised in the valuation process include: Should overheads be allowed for? How should the owner's time and unpaid help be costed? It can be argued that time spent at evenings and weekends by the owner or spouse is costless but, given the alternative uses of this time, that seems invalid. HM Customs argued, in relation to VAT compliance, that 'professional fees incurred by traders are optional' (NAO 1994). This, too, is an invalid argument, since the use of professional

support clearly reflects the complexity of the tax regulations and the economies of scale that exist in dealing with them. It has also been argued that surveys may exaggerate the costs of regulation, either through non-response bias or because of general hostility among business people to the burdens imposed. In fact, the limited evidence is to the contrary. For a review of a range of other issues in tax compliance cost research, including the tax deductibility of some compliance costs and 'psychic costs' (stress and anxiety on the part of the regulated), see EVANS (2001).

22 Many regulatory agencies have the power to levy fines where their rules are not correctly interpreted: for example, in the United Kingdom, the FSA has levied fines totalling many millions of pounds on financial institutions. The convention is that these fines are not included in calculation of compliance costs, although it could be argued that the costs of non-compliance have the same economic significance as those of compliance. This is an important issue in developing countries, where the payment of bribes is often an alternative to compliance (see Chapter 9). In developed countries, where there is little corruption of this sort, SME owners complain that they can be penalised for not complying with a vast range of near-incomprehensible regulations. Ironically, one of the arguments against the introduction of single inspectorates to enforce all regulation, as against specialist departmental inspectorates, is that single inspectorates could not have the necessary knowledge of the whole of regulation – yet the lone SME owner is expected to have this knowledge. In practice, of course, the whole body of regulation is not, and could not be, enforced.

23 This estimate is based on data from the government's own regulatory impact assessments (RIAs, see below). The data used by BCC cover only new regulations, not any increases in costs of administering existing regulations.

24 It should be noted that sample sizes are small and that cashflow benefits are not allowed for. These data have been used because the research was carried out on a comparable basis. The source explains the differences between the two countries as attributable partly to the greater simplicity of the VAT system in Germany (fewer exclusions, no voluntary registration and lower thresholds). Disregarding the lowest sizeband, one or two per cent of turnover may not seem very much but it is large in relation to the net profit margins earned by SMEs, which might not be more than 4 or 5 per cent. Moreover, VAT compliance costs are only part of the total. FLETCHER (2001) cites an Inland Revenue sponsored study by the Centre for Fiscal Studies at Bath University (1998) which estimated that the annual compliance costs of administering PAYE, National Insurance and Statutory Sick and Maternity pay were £288 per employee for employers of 1–4 staff, but £5 for employers of 5,000 plus.

25 Cited in Graham Bannock, 'Can small-scale surveys of compliance costs work?', in EVANS *et al.* (2001).

26 Cesar Cordova-Novion and Cassandra De Young, 'The OECD public management service multi-country business survey – benchmarking regulatory and administrative business environments in small and medium enterprises', in EVANS *et al.* (2001). The surveys were carried out in 11 countries, eight in Europe plus Australia, Mexico and New Zealand. Only firms with fewer than 500 employees were included, in all sectors except farming and mining, and three groups of regulation covered (employment, the environment and taxation, covering a large proportion of total costs). Most countries were surveyed by mail, but in Spain and Mexico telephone surveys were used. The source lists a number of qualifications affecting comparability including sample sizes and the impact of cyclical and cultural factors. For example, the source states: 'it is more acceptable to be critical of governments and people in authority in some countries than in others'.

27 The administrative costs of social security contributions were included under employment.

28 Our calculation for the United States assumes that 60 per cent of total administrative compliance costs are borne by SMEs. The US data relate to Federal regulation only, but also seem to include some allowance for efficiency costs.

29 For example, some have pointed out that compliance costs are, in principle, tax deductible. However, the issue of tax deductibility is irrelevant to a consideration of the total real resources absorbed by regulation, since in this context taxation is simply a transfer of resources between the private sector and government.

30 It will be recalled from Chapter 1 that, although SMEs generally account for about 60 per cent of private sector employment, their share of private sector GDP, which is what is relevant here, is much less and of the order of 20–30 per cent. The SMEs' share of administrative compliance costs, we have assumed, is about 60–70 per cent – more than twice their share of value added.

31 OLSON (1982) theorises that stable societies develop intense networks of special-interest organisations and collusions which on balance 'reduce efficiency and aggregate income in the societies in which they operate, and make political life more divisive'. The longer the society goes without upheaval, the worse these consequences become. War or revolution destroys these networks and allows greater gains in economic growth, as in Germany and Japan after the Second World War. The late Mancur Olson does not explicitly discuss regulatory compliance costs, but they are clearly one of the consequences of the forces he identifies. His thesis is not, he emphasises, an argument for *laissez-faire*; on the contrary good institutions, which governments must encourage or put in place, are essential for economic development (see also Chapter 9).

32 If you are living at bare subsistence levels you are not going to worry about the employment of your own or other people's children, for example, whose labour can boost scarce family resources. If you have no job and there is no social safety net you are not going to worry too much about employment conditions. It is, of course, people in developed countries who complain most about these issues in the Third World because they see their jobs being exported to low-wage countries. These are important issues to which we return in Chapter 9.

33 It is important to recognise that although regulation has its basis in legislation, its detailed implementation is left to government departments or agencies. The embodiment of laws into rules for business has implications for the level of compliance costs they generate. The detailed rules, which have the force of law, are not debated in public, although there may be consultation about them.

34 In Britain, recent governments elected on a platform of no increases in income tax have had to increase revenue by raising other taxes, particularly those not immediately visible to the public such as the abolition of tax rebates for pension funds (a procedures not unique to Britain) and which are now referred to as 'stealth taxes'. The imposition of regulatory costs is the ultimate form of stealth tax.

35 Denmark and, to a lesser extent, New Zealand, have very straightforward VAT systems. However, Denmark is being forced to complicate its system in the interests of European tax harmonisation.

36 The late John Bolton, a successful businessman and chairman of the Committee of Inquiry on Small Firms (BOLTON 1971) loved a cartoon representing small business as a donkey overloaded with boxes of legislation, with a government official brandishing a whip and crying 'faster, faster!'.

37 The EDU's name was later changed to the Better Regulation Unit and is now the Regulatory Impact Unit (RIU). The name changes perhaps reflect a growing appreciation of the size and difficulty of the problem.

38 The International Labour Organisation (ILO) commissioned a study which brought out the links between small firms, employment and regulation in Kenya as long ago as 1972.

39 RIAs were first used in the United States, but are now applied by the European Commission and many countries around the world. For details of the UK system, see NAO (2001). The weakness of RIA systems is that they are applied only to *forthcoming* regulation. There is no reason why they should not be used retrospectively.

40 The BRTF is composed of unpaid members from large and small businesses as well as citizens, consumer and other groups. With the RIU it acts as a pressure group for reform and has produced a number of excellent reports. The BRTF has laid down that regulation and its enforcement should be: proportionate, accountable, consistent, transparent and targeted. In commenting upon the quality of regulation, the BRTF asks: is the regulation necessary, is it fair, is it simple to understand and easy to administer, is it affordable, is it effective and does it command public support? (BRTF 2003). Where it is not satisfied with the quality of an RIA, the BRTF now has the authority to refer it to the NAO. The United Kingdom also has a 'Star Chamber', a Cabinet Office committee to review legislation.

41 This is a case where information technology (IT) can help ease compliance burdens. It has been argued by some that the whole compliance burden problem will be eased in the future by greater use of electronic media. Already in many countries tax returns can be submitted on line, for example. However, it is a common characteristic of the new technologies that work burdens are shifted from the government or producer to the consumer: witness the menu-driven system approach increasingly used by call centres. There are also other difficulties: the author was recently told by a specialist accountant that 'the tax system is too complicated to be fully computerised'. FLETCHER (2001) opines that the new technologies may encourage governments to pass more burdens on.

6   Entrepreneurs and managers

What is an entrepreneur?

Entrepreneurs are, like elephants, easier to recognise than to define. They are the prime motors of economic activity: it is the entrepreneur who recognises opportunities and assembles the resources, people, capital and premises, to exploit them in a firm. That is clear enough; in fact it is the popular understanding of the term. The difficulties arise when we try to put the entrepreneur under the economist's microscope to analyse her precise functions and separate them out from those of the owners of capital, the sources of invention, the managers of the firm and all the other elements of business activity. When you do this you are left with an abstraction – yet a vital one, the 'soul in the machine', as it were.

Joseph SCHUMPETER (1934), who emphasised the role of entrepreneurs in innovation, wrote that 'The entrepreneur is never the risk-bearer'. He meant by this that where the entrepreneur is using her own money, she is not acting as an entrepreneur as such but as a *capitalist* – it is the lenders who take the risk. Edith PENROSE (1959) also regarded entrepreneurship as a function relating to the introduction of change, and distinguished between 'entrepreneurial services' and 'managerial services', which have to do with the execution of entrepreneurial ideas. The functions of entrepreneurship may be split among several people, particularly in large firms.

Some economists have taken entrepreneurship to be a fourth input to the process of production, in addition to land, labour and capital: and, conceptually, for it to be remunerated separately by a supernormal profit which will be competed away as others enter the entrepreneur's new field. This is the link with the neo-classical theory of the firm and market equilibrium, which is static in nature and assumes perfect information and mobility of the factors of production. That theory has no place for the entrepreneur because it assumes that all firms adjust immediately and continuously to new market opportunities and the technological means of supply. In the real world, of course, information is imperfect and it is the entrepreneur who is alert to new opportunities and who, in setting up in business, takes the risk that he has identified these correctly.[1]

We use the terms 'small business owner' and 'entrepreneur' as alternatives in this book, in line with common parlance. Small business owners are 'entrepreneurs' in the sense that they assemble resources to pursue opportunities, but only very few are entrepreneurs in the Schumpeterian sense of launching 'gales of creative destruction' through innovations that will bring down large incumbents. The mass of small businesses are not engaged in spectacular innovations nor are they potential growth businesses, nor do they even aspire to be either of these things.

The SBRT *Quarterly Survey of Small Firms in Britain* found a wide range of business growth targets (SBRT 12/99). While many small firms have growth ambitions, the largest group (25.1 per cent) were those that wanted to 'grow to a certain size': in other words, a limit was placed on expansion, either out of realism or perhaps a desire to avoid too much stress and hassle. The next largest group were those who wanted to remain at their present size (20.7 per cent). Only 15.8 per cent wanted to 'expand indefinitely', and 2.1 per cent wanted to 'contract to a certain size', while 6.5 per cent had no growth targets. Most of the remainder wanted to sell or merge their business (22.2 per cent). Owners under 40 years of age were more likely to want to grow to a certain size (44.0 per cent) or to expand indefinitely (25.7 per cent). On average, therefore, only a small minority are aiming at indefinite growth – and, as we shall see, many fewer firms than this actually do achieve long-run growth.

Are entrepreneurs an identifiable group?

Many writers on entrepreneurship, and particularly the authors of texts used in business schools, reserve that term for the entrepreneurial functions in a growth business. Much of the rest of this chapter is devoted to this minority of high flyers and the implications for management and finance. First, however, we look a little more deeply at the majority of owner-managers and try to answer the question: are they a seedbed for entrepreneurial growth companies, or are the high flyers a quite distinctive breed of owner-manager? This is seen by some as an important question because if growth entrepreneurs are an identifiable and distinctive group, then there are policy implications – we should not have to bother about encouraging owner-management overall, but merely restrict our attention to the growth businesses. The importance of the tiny minority of growth businesses is that they account for a large proportion of employment creation (STOREY 1994) and also for the diffusion of new technologies.

The trouble with selective policies towards SMEs is that there is no reliable basis for selection. Many researchers have tried to identify the prior characteristics of successful entrepreneurs and fast-growth firms. STOREY (1994) reviews 18 studies of characteristics of entrepreneurs that could in principle be identified prior to start-up, and their relationship to growth performance. Although higher levels of education, prior managerial experience and middle age are more likely among founders of fast-growing firms and such firms are more likely to be founded by groups rather than single individuals, Storey found that the patterns were not strong. He concludes that 'Prior to start-up, the identikit picture of the entrepreneur whose business is likely to grow is extremely fuzzy'. A similar review was carried out by Storey of research on the strategies adopted by firms. This revealed only a tendency for rapidly growing firms to be more likely to have introduced new products, to have made a conscious decision on market positioning, and to be willing to share equity with external organisations or individuals. This last might merely reflect necessity rather than a positive attitude to collaborative equity, or it might suggest that multiple investors bring a wider range of skills and contacts to the firm.

The view that policies for SMEs should be targeted at potential entrepreneurs and growth firms not only has to confront the practical impossibility of identifying them at an early stage, but also the difficulties of selecting and implementing measures that can actually make a significant difference (we discuss this in Chapter 8). The more one looks at the research on business success, and the more one reviews the life stories of outstandingly successful entrepreneurs, the more one realises that, with present knowledge, the whole process is somewhat mysterious. Some of the factors which qualitative research suggests are important, such as the notion of 'social marginality' introduced in Chapter 2, are very difficult to measure and research.[2] Certainly many highly successful businessmen started in unprepossessing circumstances. To take some well-known UK companies, Sir Alan Sugar of the electronics manufacturer Amstrad started selling radio aerials from the back of a van. Interestingly, Marks and Spencer (M&S), David Whelan of the retail chain JJB Sports, and Tesco, all started as market stalls. David Tripp, founder of Spectrum Projects (a company that fits out office buildings and has a turnover of about £60 million) left school at 15 and started as an apprentice carpenter in a small building company. Finally, it might be added that many successful businesspeople have only the most elementary knowledge of what might be regarded as the basics of 'business management' (you can always hire people who have these skills at a later stage, and at an early stage they may not matter much). The enormously successful entrepreneur Richard Branson was quoted in the press as saying that he had not been aware of the difference between gross and net profit until a few weeks before![3]

Clearly, some people have both the desire and talent to build a large business and some do not. Some people, classified as artisan-entrepreneurs by STANWORTH & CURRAN (1973),[4] start a business for the independent exercise of a trade such as a joiner, metalworker or electrician: for them, job satisfaction rather than purely making money or business-building may be the prime motive.[5] For others, it is not the trade so much as the lifestyle they seek, as with people who sell up a now-expensive house in London, after years in employment, to open an hotel or restaurant in the country (or abroad). Some, inventors and technicians, may be driven by a desire to exploit an original idea – a hard route, this, which more often than not founders on lack of capital or lack of managerial talent, or both. For yet others, some just want to work for themselves or are pushed into it through lack of suitable employment opportunities, and some of these have no fixed ideas on the type of business they want. (Business advisers and support agencies get lots of enquiries from people who want to go into business but lack a specific business idea.) Others might take a business franchise[6] or, if they have capital, buy a shop or some other existing business, perhaps from an entrepreneur on the point of retirement.

Some entrepreneurs (we do not know how many; perhaps a minority of the minority) want and expect a growth business from the start. Entrepreneurs of this kind are more likely to be of 'middle-class' than 'working-class' origins. They may be inspired by, and learn from, a parent in business on their own account; or they may be imbued with, or have ambition and talent reinforced by, a business school education. Other successful entrepreneurs fall into a growth path, surprising themselves as they realise they have a latent talent for it. In other words, these entrepreneurs learn and develop their talent on the job. It is not likely that the market stallholders who ended up with large retail chains anticipated that result at the outset. Most successful entrepreneurs emphasise their hard work, but also an element of luck or chance is no doubt important, provided the basic talent is there.[7] Our examination of categories of entrepreneurs and types of business has revealed only one common factor – a stronger desire for independence - and little guidance on the traits that determine successful growth, though energy and drive are obviously essential.

Several writers, including Schumpeter, FOREMAN-PECK (1985) and BAUMOL (2002) have concluded that there is no fixed supply of entrepreneurs: they seem to emerge when circumstances require it – that is, when the opportunities and the business environment are favourable. Government attempts to promote 'the spirit of enterprise' or an 'enterprise culture' are probably ineffectual. The reason why the supply of entre-preneurs appears to be larger in some countries than others is probably attributable to constraints on enterprise and shortcomings in the business environment, not to a lack of people with a desire for independence and self-expression or for better material conditions. These seem to be universal human characteristics.

We conclude that the mass of small firms are a seedbed for growth entrepreneurs in the sense that the few who have talent can recognise and develop that talent by working in or starting up a small business. There used to be a saying that 'every soldier carries a field-marshal's baton in his knapsack' – but in fact not every soldier has the capacity to be a senior officer, nor does every small business owner have the capacity to be a growth entrepreneur. Business is a creative activity, and building a business of any scale is a work of art that not all have sufficient talent to achieve. Does this necessarily mean that the more small businesses there are, the more growth entrepreneurs there will be? Probably not, because there are other routes to learning and discovering latent talent (education and parental experience, perhaps) and because the number of entrepreneurs is not fixed but depends on the opportunities available and the environment they face. For instance, a surprisingly large number of entrepreneurs popped out of the woodwork in the dot.com boom of 2000–1.

Not only is the presence of entrepreneurial talent impossible to identify a priori, but it is difficult to say what the essential elements of this creative talent actually are. One can speculate that alertness to new opportunities, an ability to select and motivate able colleagues, a strong sense of direction, focus and time management all feature among them. We know more about what helps small companies survive in the long term. One study found that chief executives rated customer service, product quality, good control of cashflow and staff loyalty and retention as the top four reasons for corporate longevity. The same study by FDS International, a market research firm itself 30 years old, concluded that the biggest similarity between heads of longstanding businesses in service and manufacturing sectors was their desire to run their own show with minimum interference, and an acute impatience with prolonged decisionmaking – qualities that make many SME bosses 'psychologically unsuited to mainstream corporate life'.[8]

The stages of growth

STOREY (1994) calculates that only some 4 per cent of small firm start-ups create 50 per cent of employment generated over a 10-year period. He points out that over shorter periods, many more firms are involved in employment generation.[9] This is because, as shown in Chapter 2, small firms are especially vulnerable to failure, and although in aggregate they create jobs, small firms also destroy many. Colin Gallagher and his colleagues, for example, estimated that in the United Kingdom, between 1987 and 1989 firms in the 1–4 employee size band created, net, 356,000 jobs, made up as follows (000):[10]

Births	+323
Deaths	−228
Contractions	− 29
Expansions	+290
Net job generation	356

In fact, the *net fertility index* (job gains divided by job losses) is highest for the 1–4 employee size band. In the study cited, however, and in studies for most previous periods, net job creation dips, reaching bottom in the 10–19 size band and then rising gently up to the 50–99 size band. This suggests that firms on the growth path may be especially vulnerable at around the

20-employee band. This is interesting because anecdotally in small business circles, 20 employees is often cited as the sort of level at which the owner-manager becomes unable to supervise all staff and operations directly and has to introduce some form of decentralised structure.

This trigger point naturally varies with the capacity of the entrepreneur and the type of business, among other things. For example, in clothing manufacturing the owner might fairly easily supervise 15 or more cutters and sewing machine operators, perhaps with a couple of foremen. In retailing, this sort of number of people would be a relatively large operation, probably split over two or three sites. In a building firm an owner might, with chargehands, fairly easily supervise three teams of, say, six tradesmen (bricklayers, carpenters and labourers) working at different sites, and buying in the services of plumbers and electricians. In a consultancy firm, however, one owner would probably find it impracticable to manage that number of people, market the business and supervise quality without appointing section heads or client-managers. In all cases, book-keeping, reception and other staff would be necessary. Far more people could be managed directly if there were two or more working proprietors, but at some point organisational changes would be required.

Many attempts have been made to generalise about the way management styles, structures and systems change as a firm expands.[11] Our purpose is simply to emphasise the thesis of PENROSE (1959) that, although performing similar functions, the management of small and large firms is utterly different. In a much-quoted passage, Penrose writes that the organisation of small and large firms 'becomes so different that we must look on them differently; we cannot define a caterpillar and then use the same definition for a butterfly'.

The differences between large and small firm management include the greater use of rules and systems, which are made necessary by delegation; that is, to replace what MARSHALL (1919) called the 'watchful eye of the master'. In a very small firm, for example, there is no need for: budgets (spend as little as possible); monthly or even quarterly management accounts (the owner roughly knows his sales figures, margins and costs and can virtually monitor things by watching the bank account); regular meetings (she knows what is going on), or written business plans (unless external lenders want them). As the business grows, and particularly as the number of people involved expands, the owner will need to have people responsible for functions such as sales or production, although she will still supervise and co-ordinate them directly and take the decisions. From this point on, the owner will need to delegate more decision-taking and insert more systems to keep her informed of what is going on. Somewhere around this point, too, if the business is successful, it assumes the characteristics of a large firm and continued growth requires further organisational change – and ultimately, probably, the adoption of divisional structure, and later still, staff and line arrangements to achieve co-ordination.

The necessity to shift management style from 'got it all in my head', and intuitive flair, to paperwork and control systems as a business grows explains the strong feelings that business owners have about unnecessary and time-consuming regulation. Regulation inserts a necessity for *systems* at an early stage in business, which eat into the owner-manager's time and conflict with her sense of control and need for freedom and flexibility. Large firms increasingly also complain about regulation, but their focus is more upon the compliance costs incurred; the CEO of a large firm has the comfort of knowing that specialised departments are there to deal with the detail.

Even with success, some owners will want to call a halt to the process of change and arrest further growth that would erode their sense of control and probably lead to increased risks. Or if the business falters, the owner might reverse the process to restore control and personal involvement. Whether the owner does this or not will depend upon her taste for managing others as opposed to personal activity. All this is a very simplified description of the growth process and many complications can arise: the failure of senior appointments; a need for more capital and thus the addition of other stakeholders; or a change in the direction of the business through the gain (or loss) of a big contract. The vast majority of small businesses stay, and are content to stay at the early stages of the growth process: they remain focused on survival and on more efficiency to secure what they have. What they may have is not merely a reasonable living, but the satisfaction of running a business that is an expression of their own personality.

Small business management

Acceptance of the notion that management in the small business is quite different from management in the large firm is central to the thrust of this book. The small business owner has to be a generalist. She may come to the business with a particular functional speciality – it might be production, or sales, though rarely finance – but has to acquire or recruit other skills quickly if the business is to survive.[12] It is no exaggeration to say that for most start-ups, management is a race against time, in which the fast learners and the best financed are most likely to survive, though having an immediately marketable product or service is also important. There are several danger periods in the life of a business and the first three years, for that reason, are certainly the most crucial, since that is when failure rates are highest.

The biggest constraint any small business owner faces is usually the limitation of her own time and energy. There are several reasons why multiple business ownership is an advantage: one is that the functional load can be split; another is that a broader range of skills will be available, and more owner capital too. (Against this, though, damaging conflicts can often arise between partners.) The singleton owner cannot do everything she might be expected to do: she has to take risks and concentrate only on what is crucial for the business – cashflow management, product quality and selling, for example – and not worry too much about textbook tidiness. Innumerable things compete for the business owner's attention, many of them things which only experience will enable her to understand and some of which can cause the death of the firm, and possibly personal ruin, if neglected. If care is not taken, business education can burden the potential entrepreneur with a knowledge of all the things she should be doing if this were a larger firm without giving her guidance on how she should allocate her limited time.[13]

Stan Mendham, the founder of The Forum of Private Business in the United Kingdom, compares the small business owner to the entertainer spinning plates on the end of sticks: if one comes down, or she tries to keep too many going, the lot may come down. By contrast, the CEO of a large firm is conducting an orchestra – if her attention wanders momentarily there may be a false note but the orchestra will keep on playing.[14]

The founder(s) of a growth business have to be able to achieve the difficult transition between spinning plates and conducting an orchestra. Given the will to grow, the entrepreneur has initially to be able to manage the operations of the firm and then later to delegate and devolve responsibility to others. She also has to be able to conceive a strategy for *future growth* that can be communicated to her colleagues. Frequently the founder cannot achieve these transitions; she becomes either an obstacle or drops away like a stage rocket on a space launch from Cape Canaveral, her purpose of getting the business into orbit having been realised. Some founders evolve and develop, of course, because they possess multi-level talents; others stay too long, keep too tight a control, become inflexible and eventually destroy what they have created. *Succession* has to be prepared for, and many fail to ensure the longevity of their business through an understandable reluctance to plan for their own obsolescence.

The quality and skills of the people to whom founder-entrepreneurs delegate functions are obviously important. One study of non-owner managers took a sample of fast-growing UK companies quoted on the Unlisted Securities Market (USM) and matched it with similar unquoted, slower-growing companies (Chapter 10 in STANWORTH & GRAY 1991). The study found that financial expertise was more often recruited outside than developed by the founders or promoted in-house, confirming the view that this expertise is not often in place when a company begins. This was true for both slow- and fast-growing companies, which had both tended to be started by people with a production, marketing or general management background. Significantly, the recruited managers of fast-growing firms were much more likely than those in slow growers to have had a large firm background.

Innovation and technology-based firms

Some high-growth firms are founded to develop and produce goods and services that embody a significant element of recent science. 'High-tech' or technology-based firms (TBFs) may be only a minority of growth companies (many of which are in less glamorous fields such as coffee bars, retailing or financial services).[15] But there is intense interest in TBFs for several reasons, and notably because innovation is central to economic growth.[16] TBFs not only contribute to employment and output, but their activities contribute to the competitiveness of other enterprises.

TBFs or new technology-based firms (NTBFs), upon which most interest focuses in this field, do seem to have some distinctive characteristics compared with other SMEs. The founder-entrepreneurs are much more likely to be highly qualified and to have gained experience in a research laboratory or large industrial firm (from which many of these enterprises are 'spin-offs' in some sense), to have a sectoral specialism (such as biotechnology, electronics or software) and to be a member of a team of entrepreneurs rather than singletons (AGF 1998; OAKEY 1995).

There is evidence that not only TBFs, but small surviving innovative firms in general, grow faster than the average. KIRCHHOFF (1994), analysing a cohort of over 800,000 firms in SBA's small business database (SBDB), categorised them into high-, medium- and low-innovation sectors, and low-, medium- and high-growth performance. He found that among the high-innovation group, 16.2 per cent experienced high growth whereas in the medium- and low-innovation group only 9.8 per cent and 9.0 per cent, respectively, experienced high growth.[17]

Interest in TBFs is particularly acute because the scale of their activity in the United States dwarfs that of Europe. This is not an especially recent phenomenon: the large clusters of TBFs in the Boston Route 128 and Silicon Valley areas have developed since the 1950s. Silicon Valley in the late 1990s employed well over 1 million people, many if not most of these in TBFs. Although there have been similar developments in Europe – for example, in the United Kingdom around Cambridge and in the M4 corridor, in Germany in Munich and in France in Sophia Antipolis near Nice – their scale is tiny compared with the US clusters. The existence of large (not long ago small) IT enterprises such as Cisco, Intel and Microsoft, is unique to the United States. The number of IPOs on US securities markets in the late 1990s was three or more times greater than in the European Union (BANNOCK CONSULTING 1998). Of course, on both sides of the Atlantic the ending of the global Internet boom in 2002 resulted in a severe curtailment of activity in this area, but in the United States in particular this is now recovering. There have been boom/bust cycles in venture activity before; indeed, this is a characteristic of the innovation process (*pace* Schumpeter).[18]

We shall show later that there is a considerable amount of evidence that the superior performance of TBFs in the United States compared with Europe is, at least in part, the result of systematic differences in the framework conditions for innovation finance, including government support (though the existence of clusters owes little to government policy as such). This is important because it is at variance with our conclusion in Chapter 4 that, in general, lack of finance for SMEs is not the severe constraint that it is held to be. It is also at variance with our forthcoming argument in Chapter 7 that government support, again in general, is neither needed nor significant in promoting SMEs. Perhaps high-growth, high-tech companies are an exception to these generalisations. We now turn to a brief discussion of the types of finance particularly used by growth companies in the remainder of this chapter, and we return to government policy in Chapter 7.

Sources of finance for growth companies

We looked at the sources of finance for SMEs in general in Chapter 4. Growth companies might be expected to need more capital than slower-growth firms. Whether or not growth leads to greater need or difficulty in raising funds is not clear, since fast-growing firms tend to be more profitable than the average which in turn provides resources for reinvestment and also should make them more attractive to external investors. Technology companies may have several characteristics that could create difficulties in sourcing finance. These companies, or at least some categories of them, are generally perceived – though they may not be in practice – as subject to high risks (technological uncertainty as well as market risk) and, in some fast-moving fields particularly, experience quite short product cycles. This means that if their product development runs into unforeseen difficulties, they may 'miss the boat'. In some fields, notably biotechnology, development times (and regulatory approval delays) may take many years. It has also been argued that financial institutions, especially banks, may lack sufficient expertise to assess prospects adequately; though, by definition, very few people know much about some leading-edge technologies and some financial (especially venture capital) institutions do create advice networks to guide them.

Verification of all these factors is virtually impossible because the necessary data, particularly for unincorporated businesses, are not available. Data limitations are particularly important because fast-growth and technology firms, like all small firms, are not heterogeneous. For example, some TBFs emerge from university or other incubators with well-developed products, but even then unforeseen problems may be encountered in scaling up to commercial quantities. We have already mention Kirchhoff's finding that innovative enterprises tend to grow faster and to have higher survival rates than conventional firms, but there is also evidence that firms derived from incubators have higher survival rates (see BANNOCK CONSULT-ING 1998 for a review of the research on these matters). Higher survival rates, however, need not imply easier financing conditions; it could mean that investors set lower-risk thresholds for TBFs.[19] Barry Moore, 'Financial constraints to the growth and development of small high-technology firms', in HUGHES & STOREY (1994), did not find that high-technology busi-nesses were more likely than conventional firms to encounter difficulties in raising finance. Other studies, however, have reached different results. OAKEY (1994) concludes that high-technology small firms 'often are not viewed as attractive vehicles for safe return on investment . . . thus forcing them to rely on internal resources'. Moore did find that private individuals (business angels) and venture capitalists were somewhat more likely to be investors in TBFs, and particularly young TBFs, than in conventional firms in the United Kingdom.

'Business angels'

'Business angels', or informal venture capital investors, are wealthy private individuals who invest in the equity of SMEs, and sometimes with loan capital. Since, apart from inheritance, building a small firm is the most common means of acquiring wealth, a large proportion of business angels will be current or former small business owners.[20] Comprehensive data on the number of informal investors and the amount they invest is not available, partly because they are difficult to identify and partly because many are reluctant to discuss their investments. What is well established is that the value of their investments is a multiple of that of professional venture capitalists: perhaps more than eight times as much in the United States, though less (perhaps four times as much) in the United Kingdom (MASON & HARRISON 2000).

Business angels invest smaller amounts than formal venture capitalists, and proportionately more in the early stages of company growth. In these ways, they may complement venture capitalists and help to fill the gap (if there is a gap) between founder-investment and formal venture capital, which is now rarely available in amounts of less than £500,000 in the United Kingdom. Other work by Mason and Harrison has found that business angels prefer to invest in firms that are located near where they reside, and that they are more concerned than venture capitalists with personal relationships; indeed they are most likely to have interest and personal involvement in their investees. Business angels, though primarily motivated to make money, make their judgements based more upon their assessment of individuals and the business idea, and rely less than other lenders and investors upon purely financial calculations and paper plans. In other words, they operate in much the same way as owner-managers, which is what they often were or still are.[21]

Colin Mason and Richard Harrison, 'The role of informal and formal sources of venture capital in the financing of technology-based SMEs in the United Kingdom', in OAKEY (1994), concluded that in the United Kingdom, in contrast to the United States, informal investors were very much in a minority as far as high-tech businesses were concerned. They were supplanted by, rather than complementing, formal venture capital, which was involved in all stages of the growth of TBFs.

Venture capital

Much more is known about formal venture capital investment than about business angels; indeed, venture capital can probably be described as an overresearched industry. In a broad sense, the term 'venture capital' covers external investment by venture capital companies in the equity of unquoted enterprises. In a narrow sense of 'risk' or 'classical' venture capital, the term is reserved for investment in new or growing (or turnaround) ventures only – that is, including capital for expansion but excluding investment in management buy-outs or buy-ins, secondary purchases of shares and replacement capital or the re-financing of debt.[22] In the narrow sense, venture capital is, or is intended to be, all invested in growth companies (which are predominantly SMEs) and time horizons are normally short, so that investment realisations (exits) are expected to be achieved in 3–5 years with sufficient appreciation to reward the investors and return capital for further investment.[23] Investors in venture capital funds managed by venture capital companies include pension funds and insurance companies, banks and funds of funds (vehicles investing in several funds for retail and other investors). The venture capital managers receive fees and a proportion of the fund appreciation (carried interest).

The venture capital industry, which is generally taken to have started in the United States in the 1940s, is now very large in Europe. There are about 1,500 private equity companies in Europe, which in 2001 invested over €24 billion in over 8,000 companies (see Box 6.1). There are large differences in the development of the industry in different countries, but there is a substantial amount of cross-border investment that helps to even out the differences in availability of venture funding.

In terms of the amount of capital invested, the US industry is still much larger than the European. One study estimated that, excluding buy-outs, investment in the United States in 1997 was twice that in EU-14 (BANNOCK CONSULTING 1998) and for early-stage investment, four times larger.[24] These differences have led to criticism of the industry in Europe, and particularly in the United Kingdom where the proportion of early-stage investment is somewhat below the European average. It is not clear that these criticisms are justified. The reason why European venture capitalists invest more in buy-outs is that average returns are demonstrably higher than in early-stage investments.[25]

As we argue later, the climate for venture capital is generally more favourable in the United States than in Europe and, historically, returns on early-stage investment have been much higher in the United States even though overall returns are about the same.

Activity in venture capital is highly cyclical, especially in the more mature US industry. As Box 6.1 shows, total investment in Europe fell by 31 per cent in 2001 compared with the previous year, and was in fact somewhat below the 1999 level. Prior to 1999 there had been growth in venture capital investment in every year since 1994, following a downturn in 1993.

Box 6.1 Private equity in Europe

	2000	2001
Total investment, euro, billions	35.0	24.3
Percentage in high-tech	31	28
Number of investments	11,253	10,672
Number of companies	10,440	8,104

	2001	
	Europe	UK
Percentage value of investment, by stage:		
Seed	2.2	1.8
Start-up	15.0	11.6
Expansion	32.9	25.1
Replacement	4.9	5.7
Buy-out	45.0	55.8

Private equity investment as percentage of GDP:	
Sweden	0.87
United Kingdom	0.65
Netherlands	0.44
Europe	0.25
Hungary	0.25
France	0.23
Germany	0.22

Percentage of total investment:	*By country management*	*By country of of destination*
United Kingdom	28.5	17.4
Germany	18.2	13.2
France	13.5	13.0
Sweden	8.4	7.4
Europe	100.0	94.6

Source: EVCA (2002).

Note: 'Europe' includes the EEA plus the Czech Republic, Hungary, Poland and Slovakia.

In the United States, there was a severe downturn in venture capital activity in the early 1970s. This was followed by a boom in the early 1980s, which ended in the late 1980s, triggered by the 1987 stock market crash. Chart 6.1 illustrates the long-term growth in venture capital investment in the United States and the dramatic upsurge and collapse with the IT 'bubble' in the period 1998–2002. Venture capital activity is influenced by

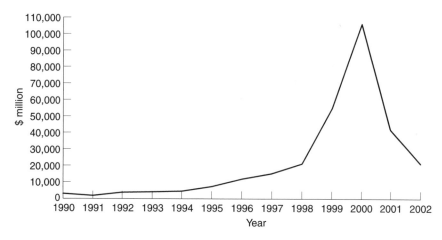

Chart 6.1 Venture capital investment in the United States, 1990–2002

stock market conditions, which largely determine exit values – and, of course, by technological developments.[26]

Corporate venturing

Another source of equity capital for TBFs is corporate venture capital (CVC). CVC may be defined as the acquisition of a minority equity stake by a non-financial enterprise in a smaller unquoted company for strategic or financial reasons. CVC is therefore distinct from both trade investments and acquisitions. There has been much discussion of the motives for CVC investments but, generally, CVC can be a cheap form of R&D by opening windows on new technologies or new markets. There is rarely a conflict between the two motives: if the technology is viable and finds a market, then it is likely to be financially rewarding as well as strategically important.

Corporates may invest *directly*, either through a special fund set up for the purpose or through in-house departments or a special unit; or they may invest *indirectly*, in a fund managed independently by a venture capitalist organisation; or they may do both (McNALLY 1997).[27]

Strategic motives for CVC have been particularly prominent in the 2000–1 Internet boom as an insurance against unforeseen developments that might threaten the established position of the investing company. This has been an important motivation for the engagement of utility companies in CVC – for example, in telecommunications by British Telecom, Deutsche Telekom and AT&T. However, recent CVC has not only, or even mainly, been in telecommunications, software and Internet-related fields. CVC is to be found in other new-technology sectors such as medical equipment and biotechnology, and also in food and drink, construction, water supply and much else (BANNOCK 1999). Nor are the motives for CVC confined to the strategic and financial. Some corporates fund new ventures started by employees, either to help change the culture of the business (fostering 'intrapreneurship') or to ensure that benefit is gained from in-house inventions or ideas that are not relevant to the core activity of the firm. Corporates also make investments in SMEs for reasons of social responsibility – for example, to create employment in regions where the parent company has downsized or closed plants. Finally, SMEs often invest in other SMEs (portfolio entrepreneurship, see Chapter 2), though neither this nor social responsibility investment is conventionally regarded as CVC.

The volume of CVC, like that of venture capital, seems to have fluctuated around a long-term upward trend. According to GOMPERS & LERNER (1999), it was the success in the United States of the first independent organised venture capital funds, which invested in such firms as Digital Equipment Corporation (DEC) and Scientific Data Systems (SDS), that prompted industrial companies to set up their own CVC divisions from the 1960s onwards. By the 1970s, more than 25 per cent of the *Fortune 500* firms had attempted CVC programmes.

CVC activity seems to experience a more pronounced version of the venture capital cycle. Corporates have more freedom to reduce or shut down CVC activities when times are bad than conventional venture capitalists, who are locked into long-term funds for their investors. There are no comprehensive and regular figures on CVC, particularly for Europe. Some heroic estimates in BANNOCK (1999) put the annual average of direct CVC over the period 1994–8 at €1.2 billion in Europe and $5.0 billion in the United States. Since CVC investors focus heavily on early stage and technology situations, it could be argued that the importance of direct CVC (less than 10 per cent of European venture capital investment in 2000, excluding buy-outs) is much greater than it appears.[28]

There is a large literature on the management of CVC – vastly larger than on the economics and statistics of the subject. Early attempts at CVC were weakened by incompatible objectives: lack of insulation of the CVC activity from corporate management, lack of commitment among senior management; and inadequate compensation for CVC executives.[29] The general trend has been for CVC managers to adopt the practice of traditional venture capitalists. Direct CVC does have an advantage over conventional venture capital, however, in that the parent company can confer prestige on its investee companies (the so-called 'certification effect') and also provide R&D and marketing support. Perhaps because of this, MAULA & MURRAY (2000) found, in terms of IPO valuations, that enterprises co-financed by multiple large corporations did better than comparable firms supported by conventional venture capitalists. Multiple co-financers did better than single corporates investing alone, which the authors attribute to a reduced incidence of conflicts between investees and investors.

There are few studies of CVC investees (CBI/NATWEST 1999 is an exception), so that little is known about conflicts of interest between investors and investees. Clearly there is a potential for such conflicts. There is the risk that the small firm may be swamped by the bureaucracy of a large investor and that it may lose its intellectual property rights (IPRs), or even its cherished independence and freedom of action. There is little evidence either way that these risks materialise in practice. MAULA & MURRAY (2001) found that, in the United States, the subsequent acquisition of portfolio companies by one of the original corporate investors is extremely rare. This may be a by-product of the existence of multiple corporate investors and also because strategic learning and other benefits can be gained without control.

Is there a financing gap for technology firms?

We have not so far mentioned the role of banks in financing TBFs. Given the risks involved, the need for specialist expertise and the frequent lack of fixed assets to provide a basis for collateral, one would expect the role of bank lending to be minimal compared with external equity sources of capital for TBFs. In fact, banks do lend to TBFs, according to many commentators (though reliable data are sparse), and there has been a considerable volume of criticism suggesting that they should do more (AGF 1988; OAKEY 1994). UK banks have been a particular target for criticism in this respect, but the apparently smaller role of bank lending to TBFs in the United Kingdom compared with continental European countries may be a reflection of the relatively greater development of venture capital, formal and informal, and CVC in the United Kingdom.[30] Certainly, surveys have indicated that managers of TBFs seek more bank finance than they can find, perhaps partly because they are reluctant to cede equity even though equity, rather than debt, may be a more appropriate source of funding.

Many authorities have concluded that there are deficiencies in the availability of finance for TBFs. Certainly most governments think there is a financing gap of this sort and have mounted a range of measures to close it, as will be shown in Chapter 7. Earlier we showed that the evidence for a gap is conflicting and cannot, as with the argument for a more general financing gap (which we rejected in Chapter 4) be conclusive. There are certainly grounds for scepticism. The tremendous global upsurge in the supply of capital for TBFs in the 2000–1 boom shows that finance is forthcoming when investors believe the opportunities are there. Clearly venture capitalists and stock market investors overinvested rather than underinvested in that period.

The one thing that casts doubt on the negative conclusion about the financing gap and suggests that, in Europe at least, there may be deficiencies in capital markets for TBFs, is the clear superiority of the system for innovation finance in the United States. This is not merely a phenomenon of the Millennium boom; the differences between the United States and

Europe go back a very long time, certainly to the 1960s and before. We have earlier shown the striking difference in numbers of TBF flotations and the greater availability of both informal and formal venture capital between the United States and Europe, especially for early-stage and technology-based enterprises. The US superiority manifests itself in comparison both with the European Union as a whole and with countries individually, though the gap is much smaller than the European average for the United Kingdom and some smaller states, notably the Netherlands, Sweden and Finland (BANNOCK CONSULTING 1998).

Behind the relatively greater supply of innovation finance in the United States lies more favourable conditions for exits by investors, which in turn are related to the size of stock market activity (including that in second-tier markets).[31] BANNOCK CONSULTING (1998) found that, in many other respects, conditions were more favourable to innovation finance in the United States than in Europe. Moreover, the US government has supported innovation finance over a long period of time by deregulation (such as the revisions to the 'prudent man' rules under ERISA mentioned above) and by measures to leverage private sector activity using limited amounts of public funding (see Chapter 7). By contrast, in Europe there are many regulations which affect the freedom of institutional investors; stock markets are fragmented; and the tax environment, including that for capital gains, is generally more hostile. These framework conditions are improving in Europe and are set to improve further, but the differences remain considerable.[32]

Our conclusion is that there are problems in the financing of innovative enterprises in Europe, but these problems are deeply embedded in the institutional framework. It is not simply a question of changing the attitudes of banks, venture investors and other players, as is often suggested, but of improving the *general framework conditions for innovation* across society and its institutions as a whole.

Notes

1 There is quite a large literature on entrepreneurship, going back to Richard Cantillon and Jean-Baptiste Say in the seventeenth and eighteenth centuries. In addition to Schumpeter, most accounts cover Frank Knight, J. M. Kirzner and, more recently, Mark Casson. For an excellent short review, see RICKETTS (2002).
2 David STOREY (1994) mentions that the more sophisticated versions of the social marginality theory are difficult to test.
3 *Sunday Times*, 5 October 2003.
4 Stanworth & Curran's account of the patterns of motivation and change, which cover a hierarchy of latent identities – artisan-entrepreneurs, classical entrepreneurs and manager-entrepreneurs – is a very plausible description of the various stages through which an entrepreneur might pass *en route* to achieving a growth business. Some entrepreneurs stop at one stage. Stanworth & Curran also acknowledge that all growth businesses do not necessarily pass through all these stages; some might start at the last, managerial, stage.

5 Artisan-entrepreneurs are a large, and in a broad sense by far the largest, group of small business people. The EUROPEAN COMMISSION (1997), using the narrower definition of 'craft enterprises' in manufacturing and repairs, which have a special legal status in some countries, puts the number at 600,000 (employing 6 million persons) in Germany, over 800,000 in France employing 2.1 million, and 1.3 million in Italy employing 3.1 million. These figures are not closely comparable because of differences in definition. There is no equivalent concept of 'craft enterprises' in Britain or the United States, though there are enterprises doing similar things. See DORAN (1984).

6 Franchising is a contractual arrangement under which the franchisee pays a royalty to the franchisor for the use of a brand name, and often the technology and supplies required for a product or service. Hotels and fast foods, as well as services such as Dynorod, are often franchised. The franchisee retains a measure of independence and does not have to worry about developing an idea or a brand, or indeed any marketing strategy. See HOY & STANWORTH (2003).

7 Empirical support for the role of chance in determining growth would be established if GIBRAT's (1931) law operated. This *law of proportionate effect* states, in effect, that the possibility of a given percentage increase in firm size in a period is independent of firm size at the beginning of that period. Gibrat's law has been much tested, with varying results, largely attributable to data coverage. In general it has been found that growth is negatively correlated with size, with greater variability for small than for large firms. This result, however, is obtained for data on *survivors*; if exits are included, the law is borne out. In other words, failure rates are not independent of firm size: small firms have higher failure rates.

8 Source: *The Business*, 8 December 2002, quoting Janet Weitz, Chairman and CEO of FDS International, the authors of the study.

9 There are thus very few long-term small growth businesses: in some cases, growth fizzles out; in others, businesses get acquired or just fail, some in the 'valley of death' that we identify here, of around 10–30 employees. There is, however, another group: portfolio entrepreneurs, who may diversify across several businesses (see Chapter 2).

10 Source: Michael Daly, Martin Campbell, Geoffrey Robson and Colin Gallagher, 'Job creation 1987–9: the contributions of small and large firms', *Employment Gazette*, November 1991, reproduced in BANNOCK & DALY (1994).

11 The most frequently cited models of stages of growth are probably those of GREINER (1972) and CHURCHILL & LEWIS (1983), but see M. J. K. Stanworth and J. Curran, 'Growth and the small firm: the alternative view', *Journal of Management Studies*, 13, 1976, reproduced in STOREY (2000).

12 DEEKS (1976) found that more owner-managers were generalists rather than having a technical specialism, but that most of their subordinate managers were specialists.

13 Thanks to Sharon GIFFORD (1998, later expanded into a book) there is now a growing theoretical interest in what she calls 'limited entrepreneurial attention'. Her interest seems to focus upon the trade-off between time devoted to managing the existing business and time devoted to issues of technological development and growth, but the theory has wide-ranging implications for management education as well as economics.

14 GALBRAITH (1967) noted that when the CEO of a multinational corporation (MNC) changes, the share price is unaffected. This may be less true now than it was, especially where companies are in a turnaround situation, but it is clear that the departure of a founder entrepreneur is likely to have a profound effect – for better or worse – on a small firm.

15 BANNOCK CONSULTING (1998) estimated that only 21 per cent of initial public offerings (IPOs) in Europe (EU-14) were technology companies in 1994–7 compared with 52 per cent in the United States.

16 This is not a recent idea. Adam SMITH (1776) showed how the division of labour through specialisation stimulates technological invention. MARX (1867) emphasised the embodiment of technological innovation in capital goods, and analysed the way in which 'the instruments of labour are transformed from tools into machinery'. SCHUMPETER (1943) saw the role of technological innovation in sending 'gales of creative destruction' through the economic system. Modern theories of growth took technology as exogenously determined (that is, given, and not explainable within growth models). More recently, endogenous growth models have emphasised the role of institutions and investment in research and education. These views are associated with ROMER (1986) and their root is the finding that only half, or less, of the expansion of national income can be explained by the growth of inputs of labour and capital (DENISON 1974). For a more recent review of the economic importance of innovation, with further references, see BAUMOL (2002).

17 Kirchhoff's high-innovation sectors were SIC groups, with above-average employment of engineers and scientists and expenditure on R&D. This is a broader definition than that used for TBFs above. Growth rates were classified by deciles of employment growth. Kirchhoff also found that the average survival rates of firms in the high- and low-innovation sectors were very similar, from which he concluded that innovative firms were not high-risk as was generally supposed.

18 There were surges of employment growth in Silicon Valley, followed by downturns in the 1960s (integrated circuits), the 1970s (personal computers), the 1980s (workstations) and the 1990s (the Internet), as was pointed out by Doug Henton, President of Collaborative Economics in a letter to the *Financial Times* (22 December 2002). He wrote: 'Dotcoms never represented a large part of the region's economy. Today, software and computer industries are moving towards higher-value applications such as mobile wireless networks, while a convergence of information and biotechnologies is leading to a growth of new companies and jobs in emerging fields such as bioinformatics and genomics.'

19 It has been frequently noted that manufacturing businesses tend to have lower failure rates than less capital-intensive firms, probably because investment propositions in these companies are more thoroughly examined both within and outside the company.

20 It was noted in Chapter 2 that many SME owners are portfolio entrepreneurs. This is another reason why SMEs breed other small firms, yet another being the greater propensity of people working in small firms, or having a parent in small business, to set up on their own.

21 There has been much speculation as to why business angels are more prominent in the United States than in Europe, and what policies could be pursued to enhance their role. Mason and Harrison point out that the smaller number of successful entrepreneurs in technology fields limits the pool of informal investors with the necessary understanding, but also place emphasis upon the greater role of networks in the United States. As we show below, there are many reasons why the business climate for TBFs is superior in the United States to that of Europe.

22 EVCA (2002) provides definitions of these various categories. To get over the ambiguities, the industry recently has preferred to use the term 'private equity' to cover venture capital in the broad sense. In practice, some loan capital (e.g. subordinated debt) is included.

23 According to EVCA (2002), in Europe 81 per cent of the number of investments

by venture capitalists were in companies employing fewer than 100 people, which accounted for 34 per cent of total investment. Venture capitalists aim for annual compound returns (measured as an internal rate of return (IRR) of around 40 per cent or more on individual investments (much more for high-tech) but achieve less than this overall, on average, because of company failures or slower than expected growth.

24 For seed capital (i.e. pre-start-up funding), the US investment was over seven times higher. Comparisons are difficult because of differences in coverage. National Venture Capital Association (NVCA) data used for the United States, for example, does not include many smaller venture capital companies that are not NVCA members. Deal sizes are also higher in the United States (BANNOCK CONSULTING 2001c).

25 The average (median) cumulative annualised IRR in Europe for 1980–99 was 10.2 per cent for buy-outs against 5.4 per cent for early-stage investments. However, the best venture capitalists (upper quartile) got 19.8 per cent for buy-outs against 15.7 per cent for early-stage investments. The median return for all venture capital was 5.4 and for all private equity, 6.6 (EVCA, *Network News*, August 2002).

26 See BYGRAVE & TIMMONS (1992) and GOMPERS & LERNER (1999). As mentioned in Chapter 5, capital gains taxation influences the supply of venture capital. The cited studies find that this connection operates mainly through its effects on the demand for funding by entrepreneurs, rather than through the flow of funds from investors, many of which are tax-exempt. They also found that the 1979 clarification of the 'prudent man' rule in the US Employee Retirement Income Security Act 1974 (ERISA) led to the acceptance that the allocation of a small fraction of a portfolio to high-risk, high-return investments such as venture capital was prudent and necessary. The supply of informal venture capital is probably more directly influenced by tax rates.

27 Indirect CVC may suffer from loss of direct contact with the investee company, but it helps to insulate the activity from the commercial pressures arising in the corporation – which can be damaging where, as is often the case, a long-term commitment is most beneficial. The distinctions between direct and indirect CVC are blurred by the fact that a large proportion of CVC vehicles attract funds from other corporates: in other words, direct investment is often *co-investment*.

28 A significant proportion of European CVC is actually invested in the United States, and vice versa. The estimates in EVCA (2000) are similar to those quoted above, although methods and coverage were very different. Both surveys showed that the majority of CVC players are located in the United Kingdom, France, Germany, Sweden and Italy.

29 If internal CVC managers, like conventional venture fund managers, get a percentage of the returns, then if they are successful they may earn very substantially more than their colleagues in other branches of the firm, creating tensions. If the managers are not incentivised in this way, it may impact adversely on their performance.

30 As an example, see Annareelta Lume, Ilka Kauranen and Erkko Autio, 'The growth and the funding mechanisms of new technology-based firms: a comparative study between the United Kingdom and Finland', in OAKEY (1994). This study showed that in a sample of NTBFs there was considerably more use of venture capital and CVC by UK firms than by those in Finland.

31 The main reason why the United Kingdom has a more developed venture capital industry than the rest of Europe is that it has stock market- rather than bank-based capital markets, and also a relatively large volume of institutional investment, as do Sweden and the Netherlands. In the United States, NASDAQ is not a second-tier stock market but an alternative market specialising in

smaller growth companies. The key to success in second-tier (and alternative) stock markets is tight regulation to give investors confidence: NASDAQ has standards which are as stringent as those on the main market, the New York Stock Exchange (NYSE). Early attempts to create European stock markets for emerging growth companies to rival NASDAQ failed, primarily because of a lack of differentiation from the main stock exchange segments and lack of interest from institutional investors. See BANNOCK (1994b).

32 The study found numerous other differences which contribute to US superiority, including closer university–industry relations, the tax treatment of intangibles (i.e. revenue expenditure on R&D) and the available facilities for innovation risk assessment. A series of European Council Directives, for example the *Investment Services Directive*, the *Prospectus Directive* and the *Listings Particulars Directive*, have aimed to promote cross-border investment and stock exchange activity. The improvement of framework conditions in Europe is proceeding, but with difficulties. The deregulation of the London Stock Exchange in 1986, which followed similar moves on the NYSE in 1975, eventually stimulated competition among European stock markets. Euro.NM, an alliance of Belgian, French and German stock exchanges, was formed in 1996. The European Association of Securities Dealers Automated Quotation System (EASDAQ), a pan-European stock exchange for growth companies modelled on NASDAQ, also opened in 1996. The Alternative Investment Market (AIM) was introduced in London in 1995, and the *Neuer Markt* launched in Germany in 1997, both second-tier markets for small companies. The *Neuer Markt* proved to be a victim of inadequate regulation (and the puncturing of the dot.com bubble), and EASDAQ was absorbed by NASDAQ in 2000. AIM has done well, and early in 2003 listed 653 companies, 50 of them from abroad – a record, though inevitably market capitalisation has fallen 35 per cent from 2000 levels. The European Union has not yet been able to reach agreement on a Pensions Directive that would have removed many of the restrictions on the investment freedom of pension funds and insurance companies.

7 Government policies on small firms

A universal official preoccupation

Virtually all governments now have specific policies for the promotion of small business and dedicated machinery for implementing them. This is not a recent development, though interest in the subject increased after the Second World War. This interest increased further from the 1980s, stimulated by rising unemployment and the results of research on the employment creation role of SMEs mentioned in Chapter 2. The Netherlands set up the RND Consultancy Service as long ago as 1910, while Japan introduced a special programme to provide financial assistance for Farms and Small and Medium Industry in 1912. AOYAMA (1999) traces the origins of comprehensive small business policies in Japan to the 1930s. By 1937, the Ministry of Commerce and Industry, the predecessor of Japan's MITI, initiated programmes which included assistance in financing, technical and management support aimed at promoting rapid industrialisation in the peripheral areas. US policies, and indeed those of other countries, also have their roots in the 1930s Depression era, particularly in support for farming.[1] Another root of small business policy, in Europe especially, is the regulation of an artisanal sector that goes back to the trade guilds of the Middle Ages.

We begin by reviewing the underlying rationale for present-day small business policies, the (relatively slight) differences between that rationale in different countries, the various organisational forms adopted for implementation, and the resources employed. We then review briefly the types of policy measures taken (but not discussing training and support in detail; this requires a chapter in itself, Chapter 8). We then return to the theme raised in Chapter 5, that of the mismatch between what governments offer and what small firms really want and need. This concluding section also discusses the overall effectiveness of small business policies and the principles that we think should ideally underlie them.

The rationale of SME policy

Policy statements

Statements of the reasons for, and objectives of, small business policy can be found in reports of responsible government agencies or departments and in legislation, as well as in speeches and other declarations by ministers. Some examples are given in Boxes 7.1–7.3.

Common themes of SME policy statements, whether explicit or implied, are that small firms are a vital component of the economy and that without government intervention their role will be less than optimal. For the United States, at least in its pioneering 1953 Small Business Act , there is an emphasis on the role of SMEs in promoting competition. This does not mean, however, that the role of small firms is seen as purely economic, as the excerpt from the Act in Box 7.1 makes clear (the phrase 'the security of this Nation' is a reference to the advantages of dispersal of power).[2]

Box 7.1 Statements of SME policy: United States and United Kingdom

---

United States

Only through full and free competition can free markets, free entry into business, and opportunities for the expression and growth of personal initiative and individual judgement be assured. The preservation and expansion of such competition is basic not only to the economic well being but also the security of this Nation. Such security and well being cannot be realised unless the actual and potential capacity of small business is encouraged and developed. It is the declared policy of the Congress that the Government should aid, counsel, assist, and protect, insofar as is possible, the interests of small-business concerns.

(The preamble (Section 2) of the US 1953 *Small Business Act*)

United Kingdom

Small businesses account for 99% of all UK firms, employing over half of our private sector workforce. They are vital to a modern economy, and major drivers of productivity, bringing innovation, challenge and competition, and the productive 'churn' which is a feature of a dynamic business sector.

The Small Business Service now has a simple ambition. We want the UK to be the best place in the world to start and grow a business. That means championing a culture which prizes and fosters enterprise, helping businesses start and then develop their capabilities to grow. It means making sure that government support services, including access to finance, are accessible, relevant and of high quality. And it means special efforts to release the enterprise of ethnic minority groups, women entrepreneurs and others who have such potential to contribute to UK business.

Above all perhaps, it also means a challenge to government to understand better the impact, positive and negative, that it can have on small business. Better regulation, alternatives to regulation, and other policymaking initiatives, can make a real contribution to the needs of small business.

(Foreword to SBS 2003)

There are three strands in the Government's approach to small firms.

First, and of most importance, the role of Government is to ensure that small firms can flourish in conditions of fair competition and to create space and incentives for enterprise by minimising taxation, regulation, and red tape.

Second, the Government strongly supports and reinforces the change to more positive social attitudes towards the small business sector.

Third, the Government helps to fill gaps in the supply side by providing commercial services for small firms, largely to improve their access to finance, information, professional advice and training. Wherever possible, the Government's support is provided in partnership with the private sector.

(UK Department of Employment, *Small Firms in Britain*, 1989)

US policy on small business has evolved over time: the 1953 Act has been amended, and other legislation enacted. Subsequent legislation acknowledges the tensions that may exist between central government policies and actions and the objectives of small business policy. Most important – and, as far as we know, unique to the United States – was the addition in 1976 of an Office of Advocacy in the Small Business Administration (SBA), which was established under the original Act. The task of the Chief Counsel for Advocacy who, like the Administrator of the SBA, reports directly to the President, is to represent small business interests and, effectively, to defend these interests where necessary against the Administration. Subsequently the United States enacted other legislation intended to control the growth of administrative burdens, such as the 1980 Regulatory Flexibility Act.[3] Finally, as AOYAMA (1999) points out, since the late 1960s, small business policies in the United States have begun to serve as a redistributive instrument – for example, in granting equal access to capital for economically disadvantaged sectors of the population.

Box 7.2 Statements of SME policy: Germany and Japan

Germany

(1) The law aims at ensuring a balanced economic structure of the country by:
   (a) maintaining and strengthening the productivity of small and medium-sized businesses as well as independent professions, and particularly by compensating for disadvantages in competition, by improving the provision of capital and by promoting the timely adjustment to economic and technological change;
   (b) facilitating the start-up and development of new businesses in the small and medium-sized economy;
   (c) securing and increasing jobs and training opportunities in the small business sector.
(2) To achieve this objective the *Land* will make available trade and industrial promotion resources at its disposal as well as funds from the *Land* budget.

Self-help has precedence over state promotion. Official assistance according to this law usually presupposes that the receiver of the assistance is providing an adequate counterpart and offers the guarantee of successful execution of the project.

(*1975 Law to Promote Small and Medium-Sized Firms*, Baden-Wurttemberg, translated in GIBB 1980)

Japan

Considering the important role that SMEs play in the national economy, it is therefore the purpose of state policy regarding SMEs to attempt to encourage the growth and development of SMEs and contribute to the economic and social status of the employees of SMEs so as to allow them to fulfil their important role in the national economy through responding to the growth and development of the national economy and rectifying the disadvantages of SMEs caused by economic and social restraints.

(*1963 Small and Medium Enterprise Basic Law*, quoted in TERAOKA 1996)

With these developments, some of the clarity and intellectual coherence of the original US approach to small business policy has been muddied and brought closer to that of other governments. However, the US government remains more willing to accept restraints on the impact of its own actions in regulatory issues than do other countries. The policy statements of these

Box 7.3 Statement of policy: European Union

> The European Council emphasises that small and medium enterprises (SMEs) play a decisive role in job creation and, more generally, act as a factor of social stability and economic drive.
>
> It likewise emphasises that in order to stimulate employment, competitiveness and innovation, it is important to combat excessive regulation where simplification is justified, without jeopardising what has been achieved.
>
> (*Presidency Conclusions*, Council of Ministers, Cannes,
> 26–7 June 1995)

latter tend to place greater emphasis upon the disadvantages which SMEs suffer, and on related support measures, rather than on issues of principle (for example, no other country mentions dispersal of power).[4]

The UK and German statements do include references to competition (though they are weak compared with the US ones) but these are conspicuously absent in the excerpt from the Japanese Basic Law (see Box 7.2). However, according to AOYAMA (1999), later policy statements are moving away from the traditional Japanese emphasis on co-operation between large and small firms and dualism, and towards encouragement of independence of SMEs. Two things are of particular interest in the two successive statements of UK policy in Box 7.1. One is a continuity: the need for more positive attitudes to enterprise, and the fostering of an 'enterprise culture'.[5] The second is a change: a modification of an earlier insistence on 'minimising taxation, regulation and red tape' to an emphasis on 'better regulation'. These references reflect differences in the political priorities of successive governments.

As we shall see, differences in the policy statements (and, one might also say, the rhetoric) of different countries do not translate into vastly different policies or degrees of intervention in practice. These policies are basically similar though, as mentioned, the United States does have a somewhat more aggressive approach to resolving the tensions between SMEs and government.

The Council of the European Union has not found it necessary to issue Directives for a Small Business Act; however, it has issued decisions on the Commission's small business policy programmes which contain most of the elements of a Small Business Act. The extracts from the Cannes declarations of the Council of Ministers in Box 7.3 (above) express similar sentiments to those of individual member states. European Commission documents generally recognise the disadvantages that SMEs suffer, including those of dealing with regulation, though the reference to simplifying regulations in the Cannes declaration is less than forthright.[6]

Institutional arrangements

Governments have found it necessary to have a central department or some other institution to give focus and impetus to SME policy. These units are necessary to formulate and evaluate policy, administer programmes, consult constituents and advocate and co-ordinate policies within government. More often than not, SME units are located in departments for trade and industry, as in Japan, the United Kingdom and Scandinavian countries; or Ministries of Economy, as in Austria, Germany and the Netherlands.[7] Some countries also have a specialised agency, as in the United Kingdom (SBS), Japan (Small and Medium Enterprise Agency, SMEA), United States Small Business Agency (SBA), Poland (Polish Agency for Enterprise Development, PAED), Portugal (The Institute for the Support of Small and Medium-sized Enterprises, IAPMEI), Spain (Institute of Small & Medium-sized Industrial Enterprises, IMPI), Greece (Hellenic Organization of Small and Medium sized Enterprises and Handicraft SA, EOMMEX) and Hungary (Hungarian Small Business Association, SBA).[8] Belgium has a separate ministry (Ministère des Classes Moyennes) and most countries now have some sort of separate machinery for tackling administrative burdens, as this has become recognised as a major issue for SMEs.[9]

There are therefore a wide variety of institutional arrangements for dealing with SME policy issues. The central difficulty for these arrangements, whatever their principal location, is that the policies of all arms of central (and local) government, including revenue and other agencies, affect SMEs. While a department of trade and industry may be responsible for SME policy, it has no direct control of the levers of power to affect change in most of the relations between government and SMEs. These levers are located elsewhere – for example, in ministries of finance or local government – and are in fact dispersed throughout the government administration. This means that the responsible ministry has responsibility without power, and has to work through other ministries whose crucial interests lie elsewhere. The addition of separate SME agencies, while providing a clear point of contact for SMEs, is not a solution since the agencies generally have even less power than their responsible ministries and are driven to focus mainly on costly programmes, which they can directly control, to 'support' SMEs. The best that can be done to enhance the impact of the small business agency is to sever direct links with a ministry and, as in the United States, to have it reporting directly to the head of state.[10]

Another difficulty with the institutional arrangements for SME policy is how to ensure adequate consultation with the mass of small firms, which are not, like large employers, centrally and comprehensively organised. Consultation is important: it helps to avoid error on the part of officials, who are often distanced from the everyday experience of small business; and it can help relationships with the SME sector, which believes – with some justification – that its interests are often neglected in favour of unions and big business.

We have already noted in Chapter 5 that membership of multi-sector SME representative bodies is limited and that few owner-managers have the time or the inclination to engage in lobbying government. While regular questionnaire surveys pick up broad trends in owner-manager opinion, it is more difficult for governments to get guidance on the nuts and bolts of specific issues, especially since the diversity of the SME sector is such that on some matters the numerous trade associations may, on occasion, voice conflicting views.[11]

There are various approaches to consultation (GAMSER 1998). One is simply to rely mainly upon dialogue with representative bodies, as in France and, until recently, the United Kingdom. Another approach is to set up formal mechanisms for public hearings on proposed new legislation, as in Austria and Denmark. A few countries (for example Germany, the United Kingdom, the Netherlands and Hungary) have permanent SME councils, including independent entrepreneurs and representative bodies. Most countries also use *ad hoc* committees or task forces, occasional commissions of inquiry and legislative committees which hold hearings. The United States, every four years or so, convenes the White House Conference on Small Business, a major event which begins with meetings at state and regional levels that elect delegates to the national conference. The national conference submits resolutions to the President of the United States (who also attends the conference for part of the time). Many of these resolutions are acted on by the legislative or executive branches of the government. The unique White House Conferences apart, *ad hoc* arrangements seem to work best; the vitality and effectiveness of councils in particular seem to be hard to maintain, although the new UK Small Firms Council has made a good start.

Resources

Very little published analysis is available on the resources devoted to small business policy around the world. The amounts spent do not seem to be very large relative to other expenditures by governments, but the size of budgets is not necessarily evidence of either commitment or effectiveness. The composition of these expenditures is, however, of some interest.

Table 7.1 compares expenditure by the SBA in the United States and the SBS in the United Kingdom. The SBS expenditure is of the same order of magnitude as that of the SBA in sterling terms, but is of course larger as a percentage of GDP. This is, however, misleading because the SBA is a Federal agency and the individual states also spend large amounts on SME policies.[12] The United Kingdom also probably 'spends' more on tax reliefs for SMEs, which are not included in figures for either country (see under Taxation below). Certainly the SBA employs many more people: some 2,800, excluding those administering disaster relief, compared with 500 in the SBS.[13]

Table 7.1 Expenditure by US SBA and UK SBS compared

	SBA (FY2003)[e] ($000)	(%)		SBS 2002–3[c] (£ million)	(%)
Advocacy[a]	12,137	2.0	–		
Finance[b]	361,001	59.4	Finance[a]	116	32.8
Advisory & information[c]	136,157	22.4	Advisory & information[b]	172	48.6
Other, incl. admin.	98,669	16.2	Other, incl. admin.	66	18.6
Total[d]	607,964	100.0	Total	354	100.0
Percentage of GDP = 0.01			Percentage of GDP = 0.03		

Source: SBA Budget Request and Performance Plan.

Notes
a Includes White House and State Conferences.
b Includes SBIC securities, loans, securitisation and risk management.
c Includes SCORE, SBDBs and BICs.
d Excludes Disaster Assistance, which amounted to over $233 million.
e The SBA expenditure covers a wider range of responsibilities than that of the SBS, while neither includes all spending on small business by the respective governments.
FY = fiscal year.

Source: SBS, *Annual Report*, 2003.

Notes
a Includes Small Firm Loan Guarantees, and SMART, Phoenix Fund and Enterprise Grants.
b Includes Business Link and Farm Advisory Services.
c The SBA expenditure covers a wider range of responsibilities than that of the SBS, while neither includes all spending on small business by the respective governments.

Both organisations spend a remarkably similar proportion of their total resources on support for finance and advisory services (81.8 and 81.4 per cent for the SBA and SBS, respectively) but the relative importance of these activities is reversed, with the SBS spending almost half its budget on advisory services and the SBA more than half on finance. In fact the SBS spends more than the SBA on advisory services in absolute terms.[14]

A now dated (1988) but more comprehensive comparison of government support for SMEs in Britain and Germany found that almost 63 per cent of German expenditure was on finance, compared to 40 per cent in Britain. The largest item in Britain at that time was on start-up assistance in the form of the Enterprise Allowance Scheme (EAS). Information and advisory services absorbed only just over 15 per cent of spending in Britain and 3.5 per cent in Germany, where these services are mainly provided by the private sector (BANNOCK & ALBACH 1991).[15]

Table 7.2 gives some data on central government expenditure on SMEs in Japan. As in the United Kingdom and the United States, a large proportion of expenditure (86.5 per cent) is spent on finance and advisory services. Japan spends proportionately more on finance in the most recent period than even the United States, presumably because more support was needed to help SMEs to adjust to the country's economic troubles. Japan spends relatively little on advisory services, certainly when compared with the United Kingdom but, as with Germany, this is probably attributable to the

Table 7.2 Central government expenditure[a] on SMEs, Japan, 1990, 1993

Item	1990 (%)	1993 (%)
Finance[b]	58.6	66.2
Advisory and information	20.9	18.3
Other, including admin.	20.5	15.5
Total	100.0	100.0
Yen (billion)	255.9	416.4
Percentage of GDP	0.06	0.09

Source: TERAOKA (1996).

Notes

a Includes expenditure by MITI (51.6 per cent in 1990), Ministry of Finance (30.1), Ministry of Labour (1.6) and Treasury Investment Account (5.9); excludes prefectural and city governments.

b Includes grants/investment in Credit Guarantee Associations Fund, SME Finance Corporation and SME Retirement Allowance Mutual.

greater role of mutual and trade organisations. Overall, it is difficult to draw firm conclusions about the total level of expenditure given the multitude of qualifications attaching to the data. On the face of it, the United Kingdom now spends more on SME policy in relation to GDP than the United States, but less than Germany or Japan.

SME policy instruments

Introduction

Governments use a wide range of specific measures to assist or promote SMEs, as shown in Table 7.3. The most widespread of these measures are information and employer training services, schemes to assist start-ups, bank guarantees and subsidised lending, technology transfer, and the encouragement of co-operation amongst small firms. These measures in some form are used by virtually all European governments, and indeed by governments in Japan, the United States and also often, with donor assistance, in the developing world.[16] As already discussed, many countries also have special measures to control administrative burdens. The figures in Table 7.3, which relate to 1994, do not entirely reflect the current situation. In particular, the number of countries using *fiscal measures* of various kinds has increased, while subsidised lending and the promotion of start-ups (at least by financial assistance) have fallen out of fashion.

In what follows we do not discuss the whole range of measures (not all of which are mentioned in Table 7.3). To discuss all of them in detail would require a separate book. Our account is very selective, focusing on difficulties and effectiveness and a few instances of better practice (there is no

Table 7.3 European countries adopting measures for the promotion of SMEs, 1994.

Measure	Number of countries
Information and Training	
Subsidised information services	18
Subsidised employer training	13
Finance	
Bank loan guarantees	16
Subsidised loans, grants	14
Taxation	
Graduated corporation tax or other SME reliefs	8
Relief for SMEs for local taxation	4
Income tax relief for investment in SMEs by third parties	6
Measures to promote venture capital	4
Other	
Measures to promote public purchasing	4
Measures to promote co-operation among SMEs	14
Exemptions for SMEs from social legislation	9
Measures to promote technology transfer	14
Promotion of start-ups	16
Total	21

Source: BANNOCK (1994a).

universally applicable *best* practice: circumstances differ from country to country).

Our focus on difficulties and effectiveness does not reflect a negative or defeatist attitude, but simply leads up to our conclusion in this chapter: that the right approach to promoting SMEs is to concentrate on getting the *framework conditions* for all forms of enterprise as favourable as possible, even though a few measures specifically to promote SMEs may be necessary. The most widespread form of SME promotion, information and employer training is a big subject, riddled with misconceptions, and deserves a whole chapter to itself (Chapter 8). We start here with finance, also a large subject and one with a vast literature that we largely leave aside here, although some of the ground has already been covered in Chapters 4 and 6.

Finance

Many governments, directly or indirectly, make loans and grants to SMEs or take other measures to help reduce their perceived difficulty in raising finance. The obvious difficulty with measures of this sort is that demand may exceed supply. Judgements will then have to be made by officials on what are the deserving cases, though to some extent demand will be curtailed by the paperwork and conditions that are felt to be necessary to safeguard the use of public funds. There are other difficulties. Public intervention may crowd out private sources of finance, or stimulate imprudent investment at government expense (moral hazard). Perhaps the greatest problem, and one that bedevils all SME policies, is that however well-designed the scheme, it is not likely to make a significant difference in the small firm scene without incurring very substantial government expenditure.

There are two basic approaches to public financing interventions. The first is to finance individual firms directly, either by providing 'soft' loans or grants or by setting up fund structures to make loans and invest in equity. In the United Kingdom, soft loans and grants are not used much except in disadvantaged regions, or in support of technological innovation as in the SMART programme. In many European countries, 'soft' loans are available on a wider scale. The second approach is to provide funds for private financial institutions to invest in target groups of SMEs. There is much more interest in this approach now that 'picking winners' is discredited and it has been appreciated that relatively small amounts of public funds can be leveraged for greater impact by boosting private sector activity.[17] Finally, tax or other incentives can be made available to private individuals or financial institutions to encourage small firm investment (see also under Taxation below).

To illustrate the variety of approaches to encouraging private sector investment in SMEs, we describe briefly four types of schemes from different countries, which go some way to overcoming the difficulties mentioned above.

By far the largest programme for 'soft' lending in Europe is that of Germany, administered by the public banks.[18] These banks, being guaranteed by the state, can borrow and lend at below market rates.[19] Picking winners and moral hazard are avoided because loans are assessed and made by the commercial banks, who assume the whole of the risk and in each case make advances in parallel using their own funds.[20] The scheme therefore encourages banks to make long-term loans, for up to 10 years, everywhere difficult to obtain, as well as reducing the costs for borrowers. Loans are made for investment not only in fixed assets but also for research, production and marketing; there are no sectoral or regional limitations (BANNOCK & ALBACH 1991). The programme is very large, and in the late 1990s it was estimated that 'soft' loans accounted for 4 per cent of all commercial bank lending in Germany.

The United States, Japan and most European countries have state-supported schemes for guaranteeing bank loans to SMEs.[21] The objective is to facilitate lending, particularly for otherwise sound borrowers who do not have the necessary collateral. In most cases, the borrower or the bank pays an insurance premium and to avoid moral hazard, a substantial proportion of the risk (50–80 per cent) remains with the bank, which in case of default can claim reimbursement of the loan. Some of these schemes (for example in Denmark, France and Spain) are private sector mutual organisations, but they generally receive some support from the state. There are two types of guarantee schemes, funded and unfunded. In Germany, which has schemes of the first type for example, there are several guarantee associations in each of the *Länder*, formed by financial institutions, local authorities and trade associations. These associations operate funds out of which claims are met. The guarantee funds were created by capital contributions from the founders and by the Federal and *Land* governments, who also provide counter-guarantees. The funds receive income from guarantee premia paid by borrowers and from investments. *Credit assessment* is an important element of the system and is carried out by the lending banks and by chambers of commerce and trade associations.

Unfunded bank guarantee schemes also operate on the insurance principle, but claims are met directly out of state budgets. The principal SBA scheme, the 7a Loan Guarantee Program, is very large and in 1999 guaranteed 39,000 bank loans totalling $9 billion (4.6 per cent of total commercial bank loans of less than $1 million to non-farm businesses). Guarantees are given (no premia are charged) at the rate of 80 per cent for smaller loans, and maturities may be up to 25 years for fixed assets. There are restrictions on the interest rates that may be charged by the guaranteed banks. A special feature of the US system is that the guaranteed portions of the loans are pooled and sold to investors (*securitised*), which allows some of the bank advances to be recycled for further lending. These securitised issues, being guaranteed by the Federal Government, are attractive to the banks, issuing brokers and investors such as insurance companies, alike.

On a much smaller scale, the UK Small Firms Loan Guarantee Scheme (SFLGS) is also an unfunded scheme. It is intended to guarantee bank loans for SMEs with 'viable business proposals' who have tried and failed to get a conventional loan because of lack of suitable security. Borrowers pay 2 per cent per annum on the outstanding balance, and 75 per cent of the loan is guaranteed. In 2001–2, 4,269 loans were guaranteed for an average loan size of £59,660, amounting to less than 1 per cent of total term lending to firms with a turnover of less than £1 million. The SFLGS probably did encourage banks to extend the frontiers of their lending to SMEs when it was introduced in the early 1980s, but it is now of only marginal importance.

The US Small Business Investment Companies (SBIC) scheme also makes use of loan and equity investment in small businesses. SBICs, first launched in 1959, are private companies rather like venture capital companies, who often are participants, formed to make long-term minority investments in small businesses. The attraction of setting up SBICs is that they can leverage their own funds by borrowing relatively cheaply from investors whose loans are guaranteed by the SBA.[22] The advantage of the system is that for an annual budget allocation of $24 million (which is necessary to cover administrative costs and claims under guarantees), new financing commitments of about 100 times that amount are stimulated, reaching some 4,500 investee companies in 1994/5. In 1999, BANNOCK CONSULTING (2001d) estimated that financings by non-bank-owned

SBICs amounted to about 30 per cent by number and 2 per cent by value of total venture financings by SBICs and NVCA members.[23] SBICs have had problems – for example, through interest rate fluctuations. Between 1986 and 1994, 145 SBICs went into liquidation and there have been a few cases of fraud. Overall, however, the programme is judged a success. According to the SBA, over 100 well-known companies were financed by SBICs during their initial growth, including AOL, Apple, Federal Express, Intel and Sun Microsystems. Of course, as with all state interventions, it is impossible to know how much of the investment covered is additional and how much would have taken place in any event.

Various other approaches have been used to promote venture capital investment. Regional investment vehicles funded wholly or partly by central and regional governments have been used in most EU countries and the United States: however, the amount of investment stimulated by these public initiatives has been very small in relation to commercial venture activity because this route does not allow large leverage of public funds (at most, 4:1 or 5:1). Higher leverage can be achieved by providing risk-sharing arrangements for equity investment by venture capitalists, analogous to the bank loan guarantees described earlier, on either an individual-investment or whole-fund basis. These approaches have been taken in many countries but the scale of the operations is generally quite small (commitments of €200 million or less).

An example is the *Garantie Capital PME* fund operated by SOFARIS in France, part of the BDPME *Banque*, a mixed public–private institution. SOFARIS guarantees up to 50 per cent of the loss incurred on equity investments (70 per cent for start-ups) on investments up to €750,000 per investee. The scheme covers mainly early-stage investments made by a wide variety of regional and national investors, including state or mixed public–private bodies (*Sociétiés mixtes*). SOFARIS charges premia of only 0.30 per cent for individual investments and 0.15 per cent for portfolio insurance. In addition, it takes 10 per cent and 15 per cent, respectively, of gains. In 2000, some 1,400 new commitments were entered into, for a total amount of €120 million. Subsidies are necessary to cover deficits and expand capacity, amounting to €15 million in 1999, though this represents a substantial leverage of public funds. Demand for the guarantees exceeds supply.[24]

Taxation

Like finance, taxation, which is clearly related to it, is a large subject. The workings of tax systems are very complicated and the details change frequently.[25] Some aspects of the way tax systems impact upon SMEs were discussed in Chapter 5. Here we discuss briefly the types of measures governments have taken to ease the tax burden, together with its associated paperwork burden, and to encourage investors in SMEs.

Many countries have introduced an element of *progression* in company taxation as well as personal income tax. Japan levies a lower rate of corporation tax for small companies, while many other countries, including the United Kingdom, United States, Belgium, Italy and Finland, have reduced rates of corporation tax below a fixed threshold. On the whole, the income of unincorporated businesses is treated under income tax schedules in the same way as that of employed persons, though a few countries (for example Germany, the Netherlands and Italy) provide special tax allowances for the self-employed. The self-employed also pay lower social security contributions than the combined employer and employee rates, since they are not eligible for unemployment benefit.

As pointed out in Chapter 5, the different tax treatment of incorporated and unincorporated businesses means that the systems may not be neutral between legal forms. This is a distortion that should be avoided, since it can encourage businesses to incorporate solely to avoid tax.

For example in the United Kingdom in 2002–3, corporation tax was reduced to zero for the first £10,000 of profits and the number of new incorporations jumped by 45 per cent in that year over recent average levels as sole traders rushed to benefit from a major reduction in their tax liability.[26] In the United States certain small firms (S corporations), as mentioned in Chapter 5, may elect to be subject to income tax instead of corporation tax, and it is difficult to see why this alternative has not been more widely adopted.

Various other measures have been taken to ease tax burdens for SMEs, including temporary R&D or depreciation allowances and special treatment for artisans, farmers and other groups. There are also some reliefs from local taxation in several countries. Finally, there are special reliefs for business assets under various forms of inheritance, capital gains and wealth taxes.

Turning now to fiscal measures to promote personal third-party investment in SMEs, we again find a wide range of instruments in use. Prominent among these are differential rates of capital gains taxation for investment in unquoted companies, as in the United States and the United Kingdom. Other examples are Venture capital trusts (VCTs) which, since 1993 in the United Kingdom, allow private individuals to obtain income tax relief, tax-free dividends and capital gains from pooled investments in qualifying unquoted trading companies. Some £270 million was subscribed to VCTs in 1999–2000, and the UK Inland Revenue estimates the tax forgone at £110 million. In France there are similar vehicles (*Fonds Commun Placement pour l'Innovation*, FCPI). The Netherlands allows rollover relief for capital gains tax when an investment profit from any source is reinvested in an unquoted SME. The United Kingdom also has an Enterprise Investment Scheme (EIS), which provides private individuals with up-front income tax relief, capital gains exemption and tax relief on losses.

It is difficult to judge how effective these various forms of fiscal inducement for third-party investment in SMEs have been. The amounts of investment through them are very limited in relation to other forms of external investment in SMEs; nor, on the other hand, have the revenues forgone in tax concessions been very great in most countries. In Europe, the various incentives have been criticised as being insufficiently targeted, or at least ineffective in getting funds into new technology-based enterprises or into depressed regions. There is also the suspicion that much of the resulting savings and investment through tax shelters is simply a diversion of funds that would have been saved or invested in any event (little additionality). Against this, in the United Kingdom (the country in Europe which most favours the use of tax incentives for SMEs),[27] VCTs have had a favourable impact on the success of the AIM.[28] The most fundamental criticism of all the schemes reviewed here is that except for low tax rates, they provide no help to SME owners, who are invariably forced to invest personal funds in their own businesses out of taxed income while receiving full tax relief on savings placed in pension funds and other institutional vehicles which mainly invest in large firms and government securities. The exclusion of the very people – the majority owners in SMEs who are the most likely to be willing to assume the risks – from SME tax investment shelters is a serious omission. This omission is compounded by the fact that under most tax regimes, profits earned and not immediately invested in the business are also taxed. This is to avoid abuse and manipulation of tax relief, but it ought to be possible to devise means for preventing such evasion.

Finally, we come to approaches to minimise the compliance costs of taxation for SMEs, which represent such a large proportion of total regulatory burdens. It was argued in Chapter 5 that the only really effective way of simplifying tax administration would be wholesale reform of tax systems and, in particular, shifting them from an income to a progressive expenditure basis. The various palliatives adopted are of limited effectiveness in practice, and all introduce undesirable economic distortions. VAT is one of the worst culprits in terms of the compliance costs it imposes on business. One approach is simply to have very high thresholds for registration, as in the United Kingdom and Ireland. Firms with a sales turnover below the threshold (£56,000 per annum in the United Kingdom in 2003/4) do not need to register, charge VAT to their customers, keep special records or make returns to the authorities. There are two problems with this approach, the first being that unregistered firms, like ordinary consumers, cannot reclaim the VAT charged to them on their inputs. They may, by not registering for VAT, therefore simply be exchanging a compliance burden for a tax burden. How serious a problem this is will vary with the individual case. For a self-employed person with few tax inputs and basically selling his or her personal services, it will not matter very much; but for a small trader with a large proportion of taxed inputs, it will result in a higher tax penalty. Under European VAT regimes, traders can opt to register even if below the threshold and in countries such as the United Kingdom, with high thresholds, large numbers do so. Voluntary registration, however, not only defeats the purpose of removing compliance burdens but also eliminates the advantage of high thresholds for the authorities – which is that it saves their costs of administering large numbers of traders that yield little or no net tax revenue. The second problem with high thresholds is that they create economic distortions: many unregistered firms will be able to undercut only slightly larger competitors who are registered and have to charge tax, and also successful firms may choose not to grow so as to stay below the threshold.[29] Another, and generally superior method of reducing VAT compliance costs for small firms is to allow registered traders below a certain threshold (£150,000 in the United Kingdom) to opt to pay a net composite VAT rate of turnover to the authorities without the necessity for the detailed recording of inputs. This system, which is attractive only to traders who consistently have to pay over tax under the standard regime, has long been used in continental Europe and has been introduced in the United Kingdom since 2000.[30]

The fact is that VAT is inherently a complicated tax that is costly to administer in business. As mentioned in Chapter 5, the best VAT systems are those with single rates covering virtually the whole of consumer expenditure. Political pressures resulting in multiple rates (e.g. higher rates for luxury items) or exemptions (such as food) create additional compliance costs for firms dealing in goods with different rates, as well as economic distortions. In some countries, these different rates result in absurd anomalies – for example, a sandwich may be free of VAT but a toasted sandwich, classed as cooked food, attracts it. Costly court cases are frequently held over the interpretation of VAT regulations. Another ridiculous example in the United Kingdom was an argument over whether fish bait should attract VAT. The supplier maintained that bait was fresh food and therefore exempt; the court, however, ruled that the purpose of the bait was to catch fish, not provide nourishment, and the claim was disallowed. The European Commission has striven to get member states to agree and implement simpler VAT regimes, particularly the reduction in the number of rates and exemptions, but progress is slow.

Various approaches have been taken to the reduction of compliance costs for business income tax. Most of these are analogous to those for VAT. In some European countries, lighter accounting obligations are required from SMEs to establish business income tax liabilities. In the United Kingdom, for example, three-line accounts (turnover, costs, net income) are sufficient for the smallest firms, though full records have to be kept and may be investigated by the revenue authorities. In continental Europe, and especially countries in transition, various forms of lump sum or 'forfait' taxes are used. These forfait systems are of two kinds, discretionary and non-discretionary. In the first kind, the small firm agrees an annual lump-sum tax with the tax inspector for a short period (two years). These negotiations can be time-consuming. Under the second system, tax is charged as a standard percentage of turnover for each trade, minus certain costs; or for some trades, such as taxi drivers, a lump-sum tax is fixed. In all these cases, taxpayers have the option of submitting full accounts and being taxed in the normal way.[31]

Government purchasing

Outside the United States, government purchasing is probably a neglected aspect of SME policy. Comprehensive data are not available, but some studies have suggested that considerably less than 10 per cent of public purchasing is from SMEs in Europe. Since the SME share of private activity in terms of value added is two to three times as much, public purchasing may be seen to be another factor depressing the size of the SME sector. Of course, some goods and services bought by the government are not available from SMEs (such as high-value defence equipment), though subcontracting to SMEs by large suppliers can go some way towards offsetting the effects of this.

Attempts have been made to counteract what seems to be an inevitable affinity between public purchasing officers and large suppliers. This is not simply a question of restricted large firm sourcing availability but also the perceived lower risk of contracting with well-known large suppliers than with less well-known, and possibly vulnerable, small suppliers (even in the private sector there are 'safe and sure' maxims such as 'no IT manager was ever fired for buying from IBM'!). The UK authorities have tried to simplify public purchasing procedures and make more information available. Local purchasing autonomy has also been increased in the belief that this will lead to more purchasing from SMEs than where national purchasing decisions are concentrated in one place. Bidders for government contracts are also required to state their employment size for statistical purposes, and to ensure that small potential suppliers receive extra-serious consideration. Despite these efforts, SME bidders continue to complain about the difficulties of selling to government. For one thing, local authorities may require certification under often irrelevant quality standard systems such as ISO 9000, statements of policy on health and safety, conformity with equal opportunities legislation, and so on.[32] It is not clear why public purchasing should be used as a means for enforcing social and employment legislation which is already the responsibility of other arms of government.

Germany has guidelines requiring public purchasing organisations to break down their requirements into lots that are within the scope of SMEs to supply. SMEs are also given a second chance, where their bids are close to those of larger suppliers, to match the lowest price. As usual, it is the United States that has been most aggressive in promoting public purchasing from small business. Statutory goals for purchasing from SMEs are set, not only for the award of prime contracts but also for prime contractors in relation to their subcontracting. For the FY1998, the goal for Federal prime contracts awarded to small business was 23.3 per cent of the total (against 23.4 per cent actually achieved); for subcontracts it was 41.0 per cent (40.4 per cent achieved). The percentages for prime contracting were highest for the Department of the Interior (58.0 per cent) and lowest for NASA (10.6 per cent) (SBA 2001).

Competition policy

Competition policy is usually thought of in relation to correcting restrictive practices and preventing collusive action and abuses of market power by large firms. Such policies can benefit small firms (FOER 2001) by easing barriers to entry and helping to keep supply prices down – though, as illustrated in Chapter 5, the actions of competition authorities can also unintentionally harm SME interests. There are, however, other aspects of competition policy that need to be considered. One is that all kinds of measures to promote SMEs can be seen as promoting competition by stimulating innovation and new challenges to monopoly (Schumpeter's 'creative destruction'). Indeed, as shown at the beginning of this chapter, this is the underlying philosophy of US policy. NFIB (2001) states: 'The United States has no small business policy. Rather it has a competition policy of which small business is an essential component.' It is important that regulation that can unintentionally favour large firms against small is informed by the need to maintain freedom of entry and competition. The NFIB mentions that deregulation of interstate trucking by the 1980 Motor Carrier Act, which removed severe constraints on entry, led to a doubling of the number of small truck operators, lowered carriage prices and left safety unaffected. The privatisation of the British telecommunications monopoly in the United Kingdom has had similar results. It is not always easy to achieve such favourable effects: more competition through re-regulation can have perverse consequences. For example, the 2000 UK Financial Services and Markets Act specifically places a duty on the regulator, the Financial Services Authority (FSA), to take competition into account in its regulatory activities, but large numbers of independent financial advisers have been driven out of business by the high compliance costs of the new system.

However, deregulation – provided SMEs have opportunities to compete – is better than protection of small business, which in the long run never seems to work because it arrests change by suppressing competition, creates distortions and is ultimately counter-productive. The United Kingdom introduced 'enterprise zones' (EZs) in 1981, typically in depressed inner-urban areas, in which firms were given favourable tax concessions (such as a 10-year exemption from local taxes) and freedom from certain regulatory constraints. The zones were not a success, partly because they simply attracted activity into the zone from the periphery rather than creating new enterprise, and no new zones were opened after 1989.[33] Other examples of misguided policies are the reservation of particular industries, trades and crafts to small firms (India) and the protection of small retailers by refusing licences or planning permission for large operators (Japan).

A better way of encouraging small retailers is to ensure that manufacturers do not discriminate against them in their pricing policies. Small retailers complain that they often can buy goods for resale from manufacturers and wholesalers only at prices which are the same or higher than those at which the same goods are sold retail by large multiple stores. The UK competition authorities have investigated these claims more than once, but have failed to substantiate them. Yet there remains a suspicion that manufacturers, faced with the enormous buying power of large retailers, do in fact practice differential pricing. One reason for this is the simple observation that small fruit and vegetable retailers seem to be able to compete on price and quality with the multiples. This could be because they can buy from large competitive wholesale markets. In any event, the United States has again adopted a firm approach to this problem. The 1936 Robinson–Patman Act makes it illegal to sell goods to retailers or wholesalers at different prices unless justified by differences in the cost of supply. Apparently few cases have been brought recently under this Act, but it seems possible that its provisions have acted as a deterrent to anti-competitive behaviour (though BLACKFORD 2003 doubts the effectiveness of Robinson–Patman).

Another issue in competition policy as it affects SMEs is that it can (although it is not clear that it does) inhibit kinds of co-operation among small firms that could help them to offset the weaknesses that prevent them from competing with large firms (the European Commission is a proponent of this view). Most SMEs have little market power, by definition (see Chapter 1), and therefore the threat of damaging collusive action is a rare one. In fact, European competition law, which in principle prohibits state aids to industry, can (and has) inhibited some member governments from taking certain measures to promote SMEs.[34]

Beyond competition policy, it is possible that more should be done to encourage SMEs to collaborate in the sharing of large-scale facilities for purchasing, production (where economies of scale are important), marketing and research. There is, of course, already a lot of collaboration of this kind, particularly in continental Europe: SABEL & ZEITLIN (1997) give the example of co-operative use of large centrifuges for separating cream from milk used by Danish dairy farmers; and shared facilities for wine storage and bottling, as another example, are commonplace in France.

PIORE & SABEL (1984), in their original and stimulating book *The Second Industrial Divide*, argue for the possibility that a shift to smaller firms and specialised flexible production is a solution for the economic and social disruption caused by globalisation and the instability of contemporary economic systems. They point to the success of industrial districts in Italy, such as Emilia–Romagna, and emphasise that these and similar districts depend very much on community spirit and institutions that promote efficiency, moderate excessive price competition in favour of competition in quality and modulate the forces for the exploitation of labour. These districts reflect in a contemporary way the traditions of medieval craft activities under the regulated guild system. The argument of *The Second Industrial Divide* is further that the first 'Divide' – which led to the emergence of capital-intensive mass production systems in the nineteenth century, requiring high utilisation rates for viability – has produced a system which cannot cope with the breakdown of post-Second World War macro-economic arrangements for continuously expanding demand and the saturation of core markets for consumer durables. The restoration of a modern system of small-scale flexible specialisation offers a potential solution to these problems.[35]

Technology and innovation

In Chapter 6, we sketched out the centrality of technological development to economic progress, and in Chapter 3, the important role of SMEs in innovation. It is not surprising that governments all have policies to promote technology and innovation and that SMEs are an important element in these policies. There are two approaches to technology policy: the first is to try to enhance national innovation systems – public and private research facilities, universities, government agencies and commercial companies.[36] The second approach is to attempt to remove barriers to the flow of information within the system, by promoting industry–university relationships, for example.

Thinking on innovation has evolved rapidly in the post-Second World War period. In earlier theories the innovation process was taken to be linear: from R&D establishments to innovating firms in the market place ('push') or from the need in which research was stimulated by market demands ('pull'). However, observation revealed that countries and regions with high R&D spending did not necessarily have high rates of innovation and economic growth. It became understood that *diffusion and feedback* were just as important, perhaps more important, than knowledge creation. The latest theories of innovation emphasise a complex pattern of circular relationships between firms and technologies and their sources, and firms and customers and suppliers. The latest theories suggest that it is not enough for governments to promote R&D expenditure: they have to ensure that knowledge and ideas move around and are absorbed by the system.

These theoretical developments have implications for SME policy. The fact that research information moves, and must move freely, around the system makes it important that SMEs should be well plugged into the process. In practice, this is not an easy thing for governments to promote. Efforts to link SMEs into research networks have been frustrated by the lack of time and inclination on the part of many SME owners to participate in government schemes. Happily things are not as difficult as they seem because, as mentioned in Chapter 3, people move from research establishments to join others or set up on their own to exploit research developments, and knowledge moves with them.

Box 7.4 lists some of the measures taken by governments to promote innovation, among both small and large firms. Some of these measures have been discussed already, notably innovation finance in Chapter 6, but it would take too much space to discuss them all, together with their theoretical underpinnings. It is also unnecessary because there is a very large literature on innovation policy.[37] In this chapter, we look briefly at only two of the measures in the box: pre-competitive research and science parks.

Despite our general conclusion that, in most developed countries, SME finance is not a serious constraint, technology finance – and in particular, very early-stage finance for innovation – may well be an exception. An entrepreneur who has an idea for a commercially exploitable product (for example an innovative use for carbon fibres in vehicle design, or a cheap and effective form of solar heating) will almost always find it difficult to raise finance first to develop and prove the technology, and secondly to research how it might be adapted for commercial production. Once the entrepreneur has a working prototype, has done market research and produced it on a pilot basis, then further funding for the innovation may not be too difficult to find. The early stages of R&D, however, are a different matter. Conventional financial institutions are unlikely to be interested; even venture capitalists only rarely fund the initial phase of R&D because the lead times are very often too long and the risks too high. There are often only two alternatives available: to go to a large firm and either sell the idea or propose

Box 7.4 Public policies to promote innovation

- Educating scientists and technologists.
- Encouraging technology transfer through inward and outward FDI.
- Funding or part-funding of research institutes and technology centres.
- Developing government research programmes.
- Awarding grants for pre-competitive research.
- Stimulating R&D by fiscal measures.
- Promoting commercial innovation finance.
- Promoting industry–university linkages.
- Facilitating patent protection.
- Encouraging JVs, especially between large firms and SMEs.
- Promoting science parks, clusters, business incubators and networks.
- Stimulating innovation through public procurement.
- Encouraging academics to exploit scientific developments.

a joint venture, which means losing control, or to apply to a government funding programme.

Most governments have schemes for providing grants for innovative R&D projects, as does the European Commission, which attaches great importance to 'pre-competitive R&D'. A successful example is the US Small Business Innovation Research (SBIR) program. SBIR awards R&D contracts on a competitive basis for innovations that have commercial prospects and are needed by government agencies. The program, which began in 1983, is administered by the SBA and is funded out of a 2.5 per cent set-aside from the R&D budgets of 10 federal agencies, amounting to $1.1 billion in 1999. Phase I awards cover about six months' technical feasibility studies, and winners in that phase can compete for Phase II awards for detailed R&D, often ending with a prototype, at which point the competitors can seek commercial funding for introducing the innovation. In 1999 there were 19,016 Phase I proposals, of which 3,334 were successful, and 2,476 Phase II proposals, of which 1,256 were successful (SBA 2001). About 30 per cent of all projects result in saleable output, and evaluations indicate that the programme achieves additionality in terms of both quality of innovation and providing funding support.[38]

The United Kingdom has a similar, competition-based scheme for providing grants to SMEs for R&D (the SMART programme closed in 2003 but has been replaced by the Grant for Research and Development).[39] Other countries have similar schemes, for example those of the *Agence Nationale pour la Valorisation de la Recherche* (ANVAR) in France.

The need for SMEs to be plugged into national and regional innovation systems, the availability of external economies in agglomerations of small firms, as well as the success of the Silicon Valley and Route 128 clusters, have all pointed to the value of science parks, networks and clusters.[40] Since the 1980s there have been many initiatives to stimulate clustering in Europe. It has been noted that most dynamic clusters include research institutes and universities, industrial research laboratories and access to a highly skilled workforce, all characteristics apparently amenable to public action. Many governments, especially regional ones, have attempted to stimulate clusters. By the early 1990s, for example, there were over 120 technology parks in Germany, 80 per cent of them involving local authorities.[41]

Despite initiatives of these kinds in many countries, there are few cases where dynamic clusters have been initiated by public action. Certainly Silicon Valley and the US Boston cluster (BLACKFORD 2003), the agglomeration of NTBFs in Cambridge (UK) or Grenoble (France), were not planned by governments. There are one or two exceptions: Sophia–Antipolis, near Nice, in France and the North Carolina–Texas clusters do appear to owe their original existence mainly to local public initiatives.

Many, if not most publicly sponsored science parks have remained small, and some purely commercial ones are simply fashionable forms of property development. Indeed, many science parks do not predominantly contain firms that can be described as innovative or high-tech. Some academic studies have been sceptical of the value of science parks, which MASSEY *et al.* (1992) argue are based on the outdated linear theories of innovation and tend to increase social and geographical polarisation. Of course, innovative firms can be found almost everywhere, even in some remote rural areas.[42]

Other SME policies

The foregoing covers all the important areas of SME policy apart from training and support (which is covered in Chapter 8) and, in our view the most important of all, the control of administrative compliance costs, which is discussed in Chapters 5 and 10. We might just emphasise here that the increasingly widespread attempts to control paperwork burdens have yet to bear any fruit in the face of enormous social pressures for more regulation and a lack of real political will to simplify things. The fact is that the mechanisms adopted, such as regulatory impact assessments (RIAs, see Chapter 5), are still not working effectively in government departments despite the best efforts of the staff of the regulatory impact units mentioned at the beginning of this chapter. Research by CHITTENDEN *et al.* (2003) for the United Kingdom, where RIAs are probably taken more seriously than elsewhere in Europe, found that only a minority of regulations are introduced after a proper assessment of the costs and benefits to business, consumers and the environment. In a sample of 200 RIAs studied, the views of small firms were considered in only 11 per cent of cases, and incremental compliance costs borne by small firms were quantified in only 2 per cent of cases. Chittenden and his colleagues concluded that civil servants did not understand the regressive nature of these costs. The European Commission has set up a working party to investigate the reasons why its Business Impact Assessment (BIA) system was ineffective. It concluded that 'BIAs are often carried out as an ex-post "paper exercise" on already finalised proposals . . . As a result many BIAs are perfunctory and incomplete' (EUROPEAN COMMISSION 2002d).

There are, of course, other elements in small business policy which have not been considered here. The promotion of start-ups is one area. The United Kingdom and Germany have provided tax reliefs or loans to encourage executives and others in salaried employment to set up on their own. The scale of such schemes is, however, tiny when compared with the hundreds of thousands of people who start businesses each year. The UK Enterprise Allowance Scheme (EAS), which provided a weekly allowance and some training to unemployed people, did encourage quite large numbers to set up a business but evaluations were not entirely favourable and the scheme was eventually abandoned as unemployment fell.[43]

We give one final example among many possible ones of ineffective SME initiatives. In 1998, the UK government enacted legislation to allow businesses to charge interest on debtors that took longer than 30 days to pay their bills, and laid down reporting requirements on payment delays. Late payment is certainly a problem for many firms, and SMEs in the United Kingdom (where the problem seems more acute than elsewhere) have consistently complained about this impact on cashflow, particularly of late payment by large firms. It was predictable, however, that legislation would have little impact because the problem arises from an imbalance of power between large firms and their small suppliers. In fact, the average payment period for large firms has actually increased from 72.1 days in 1998 to 77.9 days in 2003. Small firms have become marginally faster in paying their bills, but still take an average of 56.4 days.[44]

Re-focusing SME policy

The marginality of present policies

Our review of small business policy instruments, which continues in Chapter 8, indicates that, with a few exceptions, results are unimpressive – and even for the exceptions, they are fairly marginal in their effects. There is no reason to suppose that if most subsidy and assistance programmes were abolished altogether, it would make a significant difference to the shape and prosperity of the SME sector anywhere. This is not to say that positive government measures are totally useless: government action in the United States, taken in the round, has probably made a material contribution to the success of the innovation system and the role of SMEs within it, and there are some good programmes in other countries.

The real problem is that given that selective targeting does not work and the SME sector is so large, any realistic scale of intervention can only be marginal. Not only are there limitations on what governments can do, but existing efforts and resources are too widely dispersed and diluted over a proliferation of small interventions. NFIB (2000) lists some 60 Federal small business economic assistance programmes and individual states have more, many funded from Federal sources. The United Kingdom has about 100 schemes, and in continental Europe the number is apparently even greater.[45] SME owners cannot, of course, be expected to keep track of such a large number of sources of help, especially since many of them have quite a short life.

At several points in this book we draw attention to the mismatch between the constraints that SME owners face and the assistance offered by governments. There has been no strong demand from the small business community for support and assistance: rather than support, they would prefer a reduction in regulatory burdens. NFIB (2000) is worth quoting on this:

> Curiously, small business owners in general have shown little interest in economic assistance (subsidies), e.g. loans, management assistance. Surveys, White House conferences, and other forms of expression to

gauge owner feelings never elevate subsidy programs to the point of government action on their behalf. Most of the interest in such programs seems to come from providers such as 'economic development' officials. This is not to say that small business owners will not take economic assistance – particularly as a last resort – or that individual business owners do not strongly support them.

What is interesting is that the attitudes of governments around the world to SME issues are so similar. Indeed, they seek inspiration from one another in devising assistance programmes. For example, the UK Business Link programme described in Chapter 8 was heavily influenced by the US SBA's Small Business Development Centers (SBDCs). According to NFIB (2000), these were 'instituted with the enthusiastic support of service providers and government officials, but serious reservations from small business owners and their representatives'.[46] It is not difficult to see, however, why governments prefer to provide SME assistance than to tackle the real problems which SME owners complain about – and, in particular, taxation and other regulatory constraints. To deal with these problems is much more difficult and costly in political terms than introducing assistance programmes, which cost little and to which few can object.

Better directions

Most governments are concerned about the high churn rates in the small business sector (as exhibited in the discussion of 'births' and 'deaths' in Chapter 2). Indeed, reducing business failures, which are seen as a 'waste' of resources, is a prime motivation for the provision of training and support services (Chapter 8). This preoccupation with failure is an error, since high rates of 'births' and 'deaths' are in fact a symptom of vitality and competition, and these are part of the learning process. Happily, there is no evidence that government support services have influenced churn rates anywhere.

Rather than focusing so much on specific policies and programmes for SMEs, it would be far more productive to concentrate energies on improving the *framework conditions* for all enterprise. In most cases, measures favouring all enterprise will have a disproportionately beneficial effect upon SMEs. For example, since regulatory burdens bear most heavily on SMEs, reducing them will benefit small firms much more than large ones. Instances where the interests of small and large firms conflict are surprisingly rare, and can be approached via a sensitive and sophisticated competition policy. Moreover, as we have shown, discriminatory programmes for SMEs can introduce undesirable economic distortions – as, for example, in providing exemptions up to thresholds which then form a barrier to growth. General measures are more likely to be well publicised and understood, are administratively easier and require fewer arbitrary judgements on the part of officials. The preference for the general over the specific need not be absolute: some specific measures and programmes may be desirable, but they should be kept to a minimum. This would enable them to be widely known and given sufficient resources for them to make a significant difference.

We reject the widespread assumption that SME owners do not know what is best for them, and believe that wide consultation should precede the introduction of SME programmes. While it is widely recognised that SMEs should be consulted over legislation, in practice they frequently are not, and consultation often stops short of the detail of implementation, which is often critical.

Finally, among the principles for refocusing SME policy advocated here is the desirability of pushing implementation, in the few cases where intervention is justified, down as far as possible through the hierarchy of government. Despite globalisation, most SMEs are single establishments rooted in local areas. Communications with them can be better at local level, and 'one size fits all' policies administered nationally cannot allow for varied regional circumstances.[47]

There have been extensive debates about the appropriateness of any public intervention to promote SMEs. Some have argued against it on grounds of equity, in that SME owners tend to be better off than people on average (this, as indicated in Chapter 2, is doubtful). However, as pointed out in Chapter 5, intervention can be justified only if the benefits exceed the costs. That the benefits exceed the costs is also doubtful, and in this chapter we have argued that, in any event, the effects of present SME policies are overall of little significance.

Notes

1 Today, many large private corporations such as American Express, British Telecom and Barclays Bank have special units for small business affairs. These are companies for which small business is a significant part of their customer base. The units carry out research to ensure that products and marketing operations are adapted to the special needs of small firms. They also, by sponsoring research, publications and other activities such as websites directed at SMEs, promote their corporate image. Finally, large steel, mining and other companies have directly supported new business formation in regions where they have closed or downsized operations.

2 The earliest SME Acts seem to be (in addition to the USA, 1953), Japan (1963) and the German *Länder* (1975), but it is interesting that more recently many countries emerging from Communism, such as Russia, Poland, the Czech Republic, Hungary and Bulgaria, as well as developing countries such as Ghana and South Africa who are transiting from single-party states, have seen fit to enact specific legislation for small business. Most countries do not have general small business acts at all. Both the United Kingdom, which is generally reluctant to legislate on policy and principle (and does not have a written constitution), and France, for example, do not have Small Business Acts as such.

The key elements of Small Business Acts are declarations of a legal commitment to SMEs and the policy criteria to be used in providing them with assistance. Without these general elements there is little to distinguish a Small Business Act from the other numerous acts and regulations affecting SMEs which all countries have. Many of these acts also define SMEs (see Chapter 1) and set out institutional arrangements. In Federal countries, SME Acts may be solely at a regional level, as in Germany, or at both central and regional levels, as in the United States, where individual states also have Small Business Acts.

3   While in most other countries small business agencies and departments defend the interests of small firms in government, in the United States alone the arguments are made in public. The Chief Counsel for Advocacy also has legal powers – for example to bring actions in the courts against government agencies which act in contravention to the Regulatory Flexibility Act.

4   The original US Act did not emphasise the disadvantages of SMEs, although it declares the need to 'assist and protect' them. The 1953 Act did, however, specifically state that small businesses were placed at a disadvantage in gaining access to government-funded R&D programmes. The 1980 Small Business Economic Policy Act later set out these policies in more detail. Wariness of undue concentration of economic power seems to be deeply ingrained in the mind of the US public. Farmers and small business owners strongly supported the introduction of legislation to control the railroad cartels and later anti-trust measures generally introduced by Theodore Roosevelt in the 1880s. Dispersal of economic power is seen to have effects beyond the purely economic. PARRIS (1968), for example, quotes Judge Learned Hand as saying in *United States* v. *Aluminium Company of America*: 'It is possible because of its indirect social or moral effect, to prefer a system of small producers, each dependent for his success upon his own skill and character, to one in which the great mass of those engaged must accept the direction of a few.'

5   This aspect of government policy has attracted much academic criticism (GRAY 1998). It is most unlikely that government exhortation can materially affect the quality or extent of entrepreneurship. We argued in Chapter 6 that the number of entrepreneurs is not fixed but varies in response to the framework conditions for enterprise (prospective rates of return, innovation, obstacles etc.). Governments wishing to promote enterprise should therefore seek to improve these framework conditions rather than to attempt to influence attitudes to enterprise in general. For references to those who argue that 'The rhetoric of the enterprise culture is a post hoc rationalisation of causal influences that are material and structural rather than cultural and ideological in character', see Chapter 7 of STANWORTH & GRAY 1991).

6   EU material on SMEs is very action- and programme-oriented. It tends to emphasise the importance of competitiveness rather than competition, without recognising the role that competition can play in improving competitiveness. The policy commitments of the European Commission on SMEs go back a long way to the Colonna report on industrial policy presented by the Commission to the Council of Ministers in 1970. However, little happened until the establishment of the SME task force in 1986. Later, in 1989, the task force became the nucleus of a separate Directorate (DG-23) with responsibility for enterprise, artisans, the distributive trades, tourism and co-operatives (BANNOCK & ALBACH 1991) which more recently has been absorbed into the Enterprise Directorate. Multilateral institutions such as the World Bank and the OECD also have divisions or units concerned with SME affairs.

7   Many countries have a separate Minister responsible for SMEs within these departments, as in France (Secrétaire d'Etat aux PME) and the United Kingdom (Minister for Small Business).

8   The UK SBS was established as an executive agency of the DTI in April 2000; the others are much older.

9 In a survey of 21 country members of the Council of Europe, BANNOCK (1994a) found that the central government department responsible for SMEs was that for Industry, Trade and Commerce in 14 of the countries, and Economics in four. Seven countries had a special unit charged with reducing government administrative burdens, and eight had special committees or other co-ordinating machinery for that purpose. (Since 1994 the number of countries with RIUs has increased and they now include Denmark, Italy (Regulatory Simplification Unit, Ministry for Public Administration) and Spain (Directorate General of Inspection, Simplification and Quality of Public Services).) These regulatory impact functions are rarely located in the Ministry responsible for SMEs and have high-level access. For example, the RIU in the United Kingdom is in the Cabinet Office and in France the Commission for Administrative Simplification (COSA) reports to the Prime Minister. In a majority of countries (12), local as well as central government had a significant role in promoting SMEs, and in some countries (notably Switzerland) this local role was pre-dominant.

10 The SBS in the United Kingdom, as an executive agency of the DTI, has a strategy Board chaired by the Minister for Small Business.

11 As pointed out in Chapter 5, there is a wide consensus among owner-managers on the broad important issues such as administrative burdens, but on more detailed matters – such as the elements of competition policy, for example – interests do vary.

12 In an earlier study we found that in Germany, another Federal state, local and regional authorities accounted for about one-third of expenditure on SMEs. In Britain, local authorities accounted for only 8.5 per cent of the total (BANNOCK & ALBACH 1991).

13 In case the reader should have any doubts about the complexities of inter-national comparisons of expenditure on SMEs, it should be noted that the SBS data do not include expenditure by other departments, such as the DTI Loan Guarantee Scheme or tax expenditures (estimates of tax revenue forgone through tax concessions for SMEs). HM Treasury (2002) estimated that the UK central and local governments spent £8.0 billion in 2001–2 on 'services to small firms'. However, this is a very broad estimate that includes £2.8 billion of spending on production subsidies to farmers (under the Common Agricultural Policy, CAP) and £2.7 billion on tax expenditures. Even the remaining £2.5 billion includes much that cannot really be counted as SME support in com-parison with figures for other countries.

14 The SBS does spend £6 million a year on the Farm Business Advice Service, but this is only a very small proportion of the total; most goes on grants to operators of Business Links. The US advisory system is quite similar to that in the United Kingdom, but perhaps private companies and educational establishments contribute more to the total cost. The SBA does not seem to concern itself much with farming, which is looked after by the US Department of Agriculture.

15 Unlike Table 7.1, this earlier study included training, and other matters such as local authority expenditure, which are not the responsibility of the SBS. In total, German expenditure on SME support was three-and-a-half times that in Britain (0.25 per cent of GDP against 0.10 per cent). Moreover, in Germany most advisory services for SMEs are provided by chambers of commerce, which are public law bodies. Since membership is mandatory, it could be argued that subscriptions are equivalent to tax revenue.

16 Table 7.3 relates to 21 countries which are members of the Council of Europe. Some smaller countries, such as Denmark, Cyprus and Lichtenstein, do not generally differentiate between measures to promote SMEs and business in general, and therefore do not register in the counts for many of the measures.

17 A wide range of financial instruments have been used under this head to promote professional private investment in SMEs – for example, debt or equity guarantees which amount to risk-sharing with investing institutions; the provision of loans or investment in private investment funds on attractive terms such as subordinated debt; counter-guarantees for private loan guarantee systems (as is done by the European Investment Fund); and grants or loans to investment funds to offset the high costs of investing in small firms.

18 The *Kreditanstalt für Wiederaufbau (KfW)* accounts for a large proportion of the programme; the other banks are the *Industrie Kreditbank*, the *Deutsche Ausgleichsbank (DAB)*, now merged with *KfW*, and the *Berliner Industriebank (JB)*. Federal grants and bond issues make up much of the funds, but a small part is derived from interest retained on repaid loans made by the United States under the Marshall Plan to assist European recovery after the Second World War.

19 There is some controversy about whether the use made of public funds in this way amounts to state aid for industry which is, in principle, contrary to European Commission competition law. The commercial banks may be able to offset some of the risks they bear via the credit guarantee scheme (see below). In part of the programme for technology lending the government bears some of the risk.

20 In general, loans are made for up to only 50 per cent of the cost of investment projects.

21 Many non-OECD countries have similar schemes. A study carried out by Alan Doran and Jake Levitsky (BANNOCK & PARTNERS 1997) counted 37 schemes in Latin America, 32 in Africa and 22 in Asia, out of a world total of 146. Among the larger schemes, the Japanese scheme was established in 1937 and the US and German schemes from the early 1950s.

22 It should be noted that it is the *investors that SBIC borrow from* that are guaranteed, not the SBICs themselves, who remain fully responsible for repaying their loans. SBICs are allowed to leverage up to three times their capital, and a minimum of 20 per cent of invested assets must be in smaller enterprises (less than $6 million net assets). There are two main types of SBIC, bank-owned and non-bank-owned. The former do not typically use SBA leverage; the attraction to them is, or was, that it allowed them to invest in equity which was severely restricted under the Glass–Steagall Act (since amended).

23 There were 246 SBICs and 75 SSBICs (these invest in businesses of disadvantaged owners) in 1999. Total obligations of SBICs and SSBICs in 1999 were about $1,000,000 million.

24 The net deficit on SOFARIS operations was €5 million in 1999 compared to new commitments of €120 million in the following year: that gives leverage of over 120:1, though that is not necessarily the long-term average.

25 For a detailed – though in terms of tax legislation, dated – account, see BANNOCK (1990a), which covers Europe with some comparisons with the United States and Japan. Virtually all equity guarantee schemes are available only for professional investors, not business angels. BANNOCK CONSULTING (2001d) identifies two guarantee schemes from Austria's *BurgesForderungs Bank* that are directed at individual angel investors. One scheme is for equity in unquoted companies, and the other for purchases of publicly issued SME bonds.

26 It will be recalled from Chapter 5 that the ability that small company owners have to draw part of their remuneration in dividends, which are free of National Insurance contributions, also encourages incorporation. As far as the author is aware, only Denmark has integrated social security contributions and income tax, which is a solution to this problem (at the expense of a headline (though not a real) increase in rates of (income) tax).

   The full rate of corporation tax in the United Kingdom is 30 per cent (2003–4).

The small company rate (profits up to £300,000) is 19 per cent, with a starting company rate of 0 per cent (profits up to £10,000). There are also intermediate rates.

27 The United Kingdom has even introduced incentives for corporate venture capital (CVC, see Chapter 6), even though the motives for CVC are often primarily strategic rather than short-term profitability.

28 It is highly desirable to improve price/earnings (P/E) ratios and liquidity in securities markets for SMEs, since this can encourage private investment and enhance exit conditions for venture capitalists.

29 The simplest way of avoiding economic distortions would be to set a low threshold but to allow registered traders to retain a sliding proportion of the VAT they collect, up to a fixed limit, as a contribution towards their collection costs. Such a system was once used in Germany but had to be withdrawn as incompatible with the European VAT Directive.

30 Many other alternative regimes have been adopted to allow for the problems of specific groups such as retailers and farmers. One of the many aspects of VAT that causes difficulty, is that depending upon the frequency of returns to the authorities, the days of grace allowed after the end of accounting periods, and the time customers take to pay invoices, the trader may have to pay the tax before it is collected from the customer (cash businesses in particular may have the use of the tax monies before they are paid to the authorities). Many countries allow SMEs to operate VAT on a cash basis: that is, they can account for VAT when the customer has paid. In the United Kingdom, firms with a turnover of less than £600,000 can opt for cash accounting or annual accounting. For a full account of schemes for reducing the compliance costs of VAT, see BANNOCK (1990a).

31 BANNOCK (1990a) opined that firms generally paid more tax under forfait than fully accounted systems, but that the opportunity to minimise time costs and avoid the use of an external accountant (as well as excessive scrutiny of their affairs by tax officials) made it worth it for large numbers of firms – about 60 per cent of enterprises in Italy in the mid-1980s opted for forfait systems. These systems do not seem to be as much used as they once were: in France, for example, usage has been discouraged by reducing thresholds in real terms. Why the authorities should wish to discourage the use of forfaits is not clear; it may be because they encourage moonlighting in work not declared to the taxman.

32 ISO 9000, or BS 5750, is a quality assurance standard requiring elaborate systems of control. It was first developed by the public sector for the acquisition of defence and other material where consistency of quality is crucial. In the early 1990s it became fashionable in the United Kingdom to urge, and even require, SMEs to register under the standard. See 'BS-5750: no rush to register', *Small Business Perspective*, January–February 1992.

33 EZs, which have been emulated in other countries with similar unsuccessful results, are an interesting recognition of the unfavourable effects of regulation upon enterprise and the difficulty of making changes to the general business environment. They are to be distinguished from export processing zones (EPZs), or 'freeports', of which there are hundreds around the world.

34 The technicalities of this are considerable, and the rules on state aids somewhat opaque: for example, more aids are allowed in depressed regions than in general. As indicated in BANNOCK & ALBACH (1991), the 1986 Action Programme of the Community specifically included as one of its objectives the adaption of competition law to protect SME agreements on, for example, know-how and certain state aid programmes directed at SMEs, from the normal rules on restrictive practices and distortions of competition.

35 These arguments are very persuasive; although one wonders if the problems of

manufacturing, now a small part of developed economies, are as central to the problems of the day as the authors would have us believe.

36 Increasingly, it seems clear that linkages between national innovation systems and those of other countries may be as important as the content of the systems themselves, possibly more so. See NELSON (1993) for an excellent review of national innovation systems in 14 countries.

37 See NELSON (1993), OAKEY (1994) for references.

38 BANNOCK CONSULTING (1998) cites J. Lerner, 'The government as venture capitalist: the long run impact of the SBIR program', Harvard Business School Working Paper, 1996, which uses the appropriate methodology of matched samples. The United States has several other government programs for funding R&D, including the Department of Commerce NIST Advanced Technology Program and the SBA's Small Business Technology Transfer Program (STTR).

39 The SMART scheme has also had favourable evaluations, though apparently not using rigorous matched-pair methodologies. For example, see MOORE & GARNSEY (1991).

40 Silicon Valley grew from a science park near Stanford University. It has been more successful than the older Boston Route 128 cluster, which BANNOCK CONSULTING (1998) attributes partly to the fact that in Silicon Valley, sources of finance, research and production are much more closely integrated.

41 Jürgen Hauschildt and Ralf H. Steinkühler, 'The role of science and technology parks in NTBF development', in OAKEY (1994), discuss some of the problems with science parks which, where subsidised, give firms located in them unfair advantages over other firms.

42 David Keeble, 'Regional influences and policy in new technology-based firm creation and growth', in OAKEY (1994). Keeble does conclude that science parks can contribute to NTBF growth, as does STOREY (1994), who points out that where adjacent to higher educational and research institutions (as, some would say, by definition they always are) they can help academics to become entrepreneurs. The role of science parks, as distinct from clusters, in the broader sense remains controversial. In the Swedish context, on the other hand, LINDELOF & LOFSTIN (2003) found no significant differences between on-park and off-park firms.

43 The EAS was criticised because failure rates were above average, and for being insufficiently targeted. As STOREY (1994) points out, the scheme cost little since it corrected an anomaly under which unemployed people drawing benefits were penalised by withdrawal of benefit if they earned money from self-employment. Storey concluded that the scheme was cost-effective. He cites research by N. Tremlett, *The Business Start-up Schemes: 18 months Follow-up Survey*, Social and Community Planning Research, 1993. Tremlett found that failure rates under start-up schemes were marginally (but not significantly) higher for participants who went on training courses than those who did not.

A recent evaluation of the UK Princes Trust start-up support scheme reminds us that such schemes assume that there is a market failure in private sector sources of assistance for new business ventures 'although the evidence for such market failure is surprisingly scarce, given the widespread adoption of these measures in western economies' (MEAGER *et al.* 2003). The study points out that it is often asserted that even where these schemes do not create sustainable businesses, the experience received by participants enhances future prospects of employment. The Princes Trust scheme provides loans, grants and mentoring and is substantially funded by government. The study found that there was no evidence that supported entry to self-employment had an impact on subsequent employability. It also found that just over half the participants were not wholly reliant on funding from the programme, and that only 27 per cent stated that they would not have started the business without support. The failure rates for participants calculated do not seem to be very different from the average (although the authors do not make that comparison). What distinguishes this study from many others is the use of large samples and a rigorous methodology using matched samples.

44 Based on research by Experian, the credit information company, and reported upon in an article by Louise Armitstead, 'Government's late payment drive has failed', *Sunday Times*, 3 August 2003.

45 NFIB (2000) cites Professor Dennis De of the University of Reutlingen in Germany as estimating the number of national small business programmes in France at 500, and in Germany at 600 at national and *Länder* level. As noted earlier, the European Commission also has numerous programmes.

46 These reservations applied to the formation of the SBA in the first place, and RILEY (1995) quotes the head of the NFIB as having said that Congress should 'cut government wherever it can, and if that includes the SBA, so be it.'

47 This section draws heavily on BANNOCK (1994a).

8 Training and support

The universal availability of SME support systems

As mentioned in Chapter 7, virtually all developed country governments provide subsidised information services for SMEs, with some form of consultancy or advisory services. Most also subsidise employer and employee training in one form or another, specifically for small firms, to extend public educational and vocational training. These support services are also provided by donors or NGOs in developing countries. The government-sponsored support systems run alongside, and in some cases partly incorporate, semi-public or private not-for-profit services such as those of chambers of commerce and trade associations and, to an extent, compete with purely commercial services run for profit.

Government-sponsored support systems, particularly for information and advice, date mainly from the 1960s and 1970s; though in a few countries (for example, the Netherlands) they date from the inter-war period; and, in Japan at least, the origins go back even further.

Under the umbrella of the Japan Small and Medium Enterprise Corporation (JASMEC) there are 251 Regional Support Centers, 54 Prefectural Support Centers and 8 Venture Business Support Centers. There is also an Institute for Small Business Management and Technology, with nine regional offices.

The United States has SBDCs in some 1,000 locations. These centers are co-operative efforts between State and Federal government, educational institutions and business but were initiated and are supervised by the SBA, which in 1999 provided grants of $72 million. There are also SBA-sponsored Business Information Centers at 45 locations, and assistance is available from the Service Corps of Retired Executives (SCORE) at 700 locations (including SBDCs).

The UK has a support system, Business Link, similar to that in the United States; that is, it involves partnerships with local organisations under the SBS. The 45 business link operators (BLOs), as they are called, have rolling three-year contracts and receive grants in return for the provision of specified services. BLOs have separate contracts with the Learning and

Skills Council for training services (workforce development) and with British Trade International (BTI) for international trading support services. The SBS also provides mentoring through the Business Volunteer Mentoring Association (BVMA). There have been many changes to the UK system since the first national Small Firms Service (SFS) was set up following BOLTON (1971).[1] The Business Link system as such dates from 1992 but has been modified following the establishment of the SBS. Prior to the Bolton report there were already many government support programmes for SMEs. The original SFS was simply a free telephone signposting or referral service and it is interesting that, coming full circle, the SBS is now encouraging BLOs who have been providing direct (charged and uncharged-for) services to move to a 'brokerage model', in which customers are referred to other service providers (HM TREASURY 2002).

The European Commission also provides support services through the European information centres and business information centres (BICs) in all member states. Other European Community initiatives include the *Europartenariat*, which is a network or 'marriage bureau' to assist SMEs that wish to collaborate with firms in other countries, and the European innovation relay centres (IRCs).

Public support for training, as distinct from information and advice, is much less differentiated between small and large firms. However, many if not most countries have continually expressed concerns that SMEs do not participate in training schemes to the same extent as large firms, and there are initiatives directed specifically at small firms – such as Small Firms Training Loans in the United Kingdom.[2] There has also been concern about the training of SME managers, including owner-managers, and most countries have some form of government-sponsored arrangements for this.[3]

As with the general approach to education, the basic rationale for government support for vocational training, information and advice is defined in terms of market imperfections, though there are also broader social considerations. The website of the UK SBS, for example (though similar statements can be found for other countries such as Sweden), states that:

> In a perfect market economy there would be no Government support for business. But the market for business advisory services is imperfect (for example, because many small businesses cannot see the benefits of buying in expertise). The Government addresses this market failure by providing subsidised business advisory services. The Government also supports business in order to promote enterprise and address educational failure, regional disparities and social inclusion.

There are two separate strands of thought here: one is that markets do not supply information and advisory services optimally, but also that small firms do not know what they really need. EUROPEAN COMMISSION (1995) puts the second point more bluntly: 'demand for modern [privately provided] services amongst SMEs still seems to be relatively low, the main reason for this being the low formal competence of many managers and entrepreneurs'. Implicit (and justifying the subsidisation of services) is the (third) argument that SMEs cannot afford the services they need. A fourth, and partly contradictory argument, used to justify government centralised provision, is that there are so many sources of information and advice available from public and private sources that SME owners do not know where to go for assistance, so that some sort of 'signposting service' is needed.

The history of SME support services is not a very satisfactory one anywhere. Once started, they have never been withdrawn, but many problems have been encountered. These problems include: low awareness and take-up, complaints about quality and consistency, lack of evidence of effectiveness in improving business performance, vacillation between targets for support (start-ups and growth firms) and confusion about the extent to which services should be charged for. In this chapter, we cast a sceptical eye upon the need for extensive government support either for SME training, or for information and advice. To clear the ground, however, we now briefly review the economic ideas on information and training which have been used to justify intervention. We then go on to look into the practicalities of this intervention, and the results.

The economics of information and training

Many business services are obviously supplied in a satisfactory way by the market. At one extreme, banking, accounting and legal services, as well as training facilities for IT and other specialised skills such as languages, are widely used by SMEs, and there is again ample supply and demand. At the other extreme, for commercial information, the main focus of public provision, paid services are much less widely used. There are problems identified in economic theory affecting both supply and demand for these services. As we shall show, however, SMEs often receive unpaid advice and support from social networks, including customers and suppliers, as well as through membership of trade and professional associations. There are also semi-public bodies such as, in some countries, public-law chambers of commerce.[4]

Dealing first with the supply side of information, the difficulty here is that information is costly to collect but inexpensive – and increasingly inexpensive with the use of electronic media – to disseminate. Once assembled and disseminated, information may lose its discrete value and can be used by anyone with access to it. In this respect, for example, information is different from single-use physical products: a hamburger can be consumed only once and after consumption cannot be transferred successively to others. Information is different: the knowledge of where to buy a hamburger travels freely and can be used to benefit an infinite number of people. These characteristics of information (as public goods, such as fresh air) make it difficult for firms to make money out of (to capture the benefit of) providing information, even though for the functioning of the economy as a whole the collection and dissemination of information is essential (there are public, as distinct from private, benefits).[5]

On the demand side, SMEs may find it difficult to anticipate what information they need (which is often highly specific and variable), or to know where to obtain it. This may be because the limited managerial resources of the small firm do not allow the owner-manager to gain the necessary perspective, or it may be that the only way to solve unique problems is by search and experience that cannot be bought-in where resources are constrained. There is research evidence that the demand for business services is positively size- and profit-related. This could be either because firms which buy-in information or advisory services tend to be more profitable as a result, or simply because only profitable firms can afford these services. In any case, it could mean that the firms which most need advice are unable to pay for it. For advisory services, the problem is particularly complicated because the unit cost of supply is higher than for pure information and does not fall to the same extent, if at all, as supply increases. Moreover, SMEs may not know what advice they need and may have difficulty in choosing between competing suppliers.

If a business is doing badly this may be the result of a range of factors, not necessarily the obvious ones. It is a very common experience among consultants that they are called in to solve one problem but find that the real problem lies elsewhere. But how to choose a consultant? Since entry costs into the consulting profession are low and there are few economies of scale (except in marketing), there are many competing suppliers. The most appropriate suppliers may not be the large well-known brands, since they are rather distant from SME issues and are in any event likely to charge premium prices. Because information and advice cannot be tested before it is consumed (it is 'experiential'), SMEs will have difficulty in assessing competing suppliers without knowing, in their specific case, what they may be able to offer. This problem is compounded by the tendency for poor-quality suppliers to charge less so that they may prevail over the better-quality suppliers. The resulting communication of bad experience by word of mouth reduces the overall demand for services.[6]

Another factor that may obstruct the optimal functioning of markets for information and advice is that using advisory services can entail, or can be perceived to entail, heavy transaction costs (including the costs of search for the best sources). If the potential user is not convinced that the value of the advice will exceed the transaction costs, then the potential user may not proceed, particularly for users located in rural areas. Transaction costs will certainly be a factor in restraining demand for government-sponsored services, since SMEs will have experience of the high transaction costs of dealing with government in the regulatory context. Against this, an expectation of low transaction costs can explain the existence of private not-for-profit services such as voluntary chambers of commerce (BENNETT 1996).

The foregoing is the crux of the case for the existence of market imperfections in the supply and demand for business information and advice. The case is generally seen to be confirmed by the results of numerous surveys which show that many SME owners admit to a limited knowledge of management – and particularly financial management – techniques (see for example, COSH *et al.* 2001) and therefore need advice and training.

For training, the economic case for imperfections in the market has some similarities to that for information and advice, though it is simpler. It is essentially that the demand for external training courses from SMEs is bound to be lower than for large firms. This is because the proportionate cost and disruption of sending an employee, or the owner-manager, on a training course is obviously higher for a firm with just one owner-manager and a few employees than for a large firm with many employees and several layers of management. It will be cheaper (entail lower transaction costs) for the small firm, at least as far as employees are concerned, to hire someone in the labour market who is already trained. Intervention here is justified by the argument that the social benefits of training exceed the (private) benefits to the small firm, since both individuals and the economy benefit from the training. It is also argued that because they face greater uncertainty, small firms adopt shorter timescales that lead to underinvestment in training compared with large firms. Finally, because every small firm is unique in some sense there will inevitably be a deficiency in the supply of certain types of training suited to their particular needs. The case for specific intervention for small firm training is again buttressed by numerous survey findings. As we shall see, surveys do in fact show that the proportion of firms that send employees or owner-managers on training courses is much lower for small than for large firms.

The case that there are market imperfections in the supply, and particularly in the demand, for information, advice and training for small firms seems a strong one. As pointed out in Chapter 4, however, the existence of market imperfections does not, in itself, justify intervention in any particular instance unless there are grounds for expecting that the benefits of government action will exceed the costs, including the costs of any further market distortions which intervention might introduce. As we shall see, the case for intervention in information and training is based on two unexamined assumptions: first, that the needs of small firms in these respects are significantly undersupplied; and, second, that if they are, it is feasible for government to do something useful about it.

Training of owner-managers and employees

At the outset, it is important to make clear that we are not questioning the general presumption that governments should act to improve the educational or vocational qualifications of the labour force as a whole. In the United Kingdom and in some other countries, including the United States, small and large firms alike agree that the basic skills (the 'three Rs') of school leavers leave much to be desired and that insufficient attention has been paid to the supply of many vocational craft skills such as fitters, joiners and plumbers.[7] Professor S. J. Prais has demonstrated that the UK system provides good university graduates at the top of the educational spectrum but is deficient in the provision of basic schooling and vocational training for the majority. He has shown that relatively low productivity in the United Kingdom compared with other advanced countries can be traced in part to these deficiencies (NIESR 1989). What is being questioned here is the need for specific measures in the case of small firms and the level of understanding of the impact of some general training measures, such as levy systems, upon SMEs.

Evidence on skill shortages and training in small firms

There is no doubt that SMEs do carry out less training, as conventionally defined (i.e. formal training), for employees and managers than large firms. Survey results vary according to sample composition and how questions are phrased, and in particular to how training is defined. Chart 8.1 shows that most small firms have some sort of training provision for new recruits, irrespective of firm size, but in only a minority of owner-managers in the smallest firms, and in only a bare majority in larger firms, do managers have training for themselves. The proportion of employees reporting further training for established staff rose from 56 per cent for the smallest firms to 82.6 per cent for firms with 20–49 people. In the survey on which Chart 8.1 is

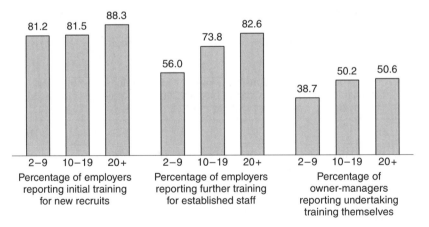

Chart 8.1 Training provision for new recruits, established staff and owner-managers during the past year, by size of enterprise (weighted), United Kingdom

Source: KITCHING & BLACKBURN (2002).

Note: Samples covered over 1,000 respondents in firms employing 2–49 people, including at least one non-owner. Questions on initial training were asked only of firms recruiting during the previous year.

based, care was taken to define training broadly to include on- and off-the-job training.[8] Overall, for the sample as a whole and for established staff, 43.7 per cent of respondents reported on-the-premises, on- and off-the-job training, and 35.3 per cent off-the-premises training, with a further 1.4 per cent reporting distance learning.

Table 8.1 shows that the proportion of small firms providing no formal training falls quite steeply as firm size increases. External training by small firms is not negligible. The table shows that even in the 3–4 employee size band, 29 per cent of the respondents pay for external courses and 23 per cent give time off for staff to attend them. Some of the training is carried out by commercial providers and some by trade associations. Larger firms are much more likely than the smallest ones to pay for external courses or give time off for employees to attend courses. Formal internal training courses, however, are much more widespread amongst larger firms. An earlier SBRT survey found considerable variations in training provision by activity sector: small firms in the retail sector, for example, were much less likely to pay for external training than firms in manufacturing or business services (SBRT 3/98). Other surveys show that the trend for larger firms to do more training extends upwards into the size distribution so that virtually all firms with 500 or more employees carry out formal training.

KITCHING & BLACKBURN (2002) provide an interesting breakdown of the content of training. For established staff, the most common subjects were working methods, IT and product knowledge; for owner-manager training they were working methods, IT and health and safety. Very much fewer reported training on management techniques or finance.

When we come to look at the evidence on firms' experience with skill shortages we find, contrary to the evidence on use of formal training, that the incidence of problems *increases* rather than diminishes with firm size (Chart 8.2).

Table 8.1 'Apart from on-the-job instruction, what training does your business provide for its staff?', by size of business (number of people employed, not including proprietors and partners), United Kingdom, 2000[a]

Employees	0	1–2	3–4	5–9	10–19	20–49	50+	All
No formal training (%)	58.9	59.6	45.1	42.7	27.4	13.1	12.9	42.2
Pay for external training courses (%)	15.5	19.3	28.7	37.8	53.1	67.7	61.3	35.7
Give staff time off to attend courses (%)	6.2	10.2	23.0	19.6	32.7	48.5	48.4	22.5
Organise internal training courses (%)	7.0	9.0	14.8	14.7	32.7	56.6	64.5	21.9
Other (%)	7.0	3.6	9.0	8.4	6.2	4.0	3.2	6.2
Base	129	166	122	143	113	99	31	803

Source: SBRT 12/2000.

Note
a Multiple mentions possible.

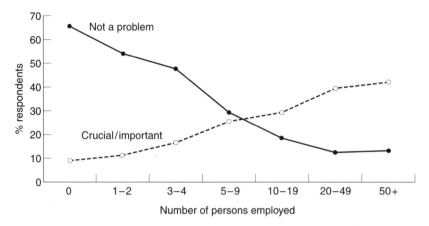

Chart 8.2 'How important are skills shortages as a problem for your business?', by size of business (number of people employed, not including proprietors and partners)

Source: SBRT 12.02.

Obviously the degree of recruitment problems varies cyclically, but these patterns appear to persist throughout the cycle. John Atkinson and Nigel Meager, 'Running to Stand Still', in ATKINSON & STOREY (1994), found a similar pattern, though they also found that in terms of incidence of shortfalls in the number and qualifications of applicants, the seriousness of the problems fell away with size. They interpret this as being the result of greater experience in managing recruitment (large firms inevitably recruit more frequently – and, we would add, as shown in Chapter 2, pay higher wages). However, even if the analysis is restricted to firms that have recruited recently, the strong tendency for larger firms to complain more than small about skills shortages remains.

The myth that SMEs do not train but 'poach' from other firms

The view that small firms significantly undertrain is supported by the beliefs that they lose more employees through dissatisfaction with their job quality and rate of personal progress (have higher employee turnover), and that they tend to solve their skills problems by simply 'poaching' trained and experienced people from other (larger) firms that do carry out training. These beliefs are not justified by the facts. There is no evidence that employees in small firms are any less (or more) satisfied with their jobs than are employees in large firms, either in the United Kingdom or in other countries. Moreover it is improbable that SMEs could 'poach' trained employees from large firms on a massive scale, given that the wages and benefits they offer are on average so much lower.

Any business cannot function for long without competent staff and managers: customer dissatisfaction and competition will lead to its stagnation and eventual closure. Where, then, do SMEs get their trained people? To a large extent the answer must be that SMEs recruit and train on-the-job. As noted, the full extent of training on-the-job by small firms is not reflected in most surveys on training because employers think that 'training' means formal instruction, preferably outside the firm. An increase in the feasibility and importance of on-the-job training as we move down the size distribution is a mirror image of the increase in 'training' provision as firms get larger.

A clue to the extent of on-the-job training is to be found in the characteristics of the staff employed in smaller firms: they tend to be people that need to be trained: younger, unmarried and with fewer higher qualifications (ATKINSON & STOREY 1994). There is more evidence than this, however. SBRT surveys (3/95 and 3/01), apparently uniquely, have attempted to track the origins and destinations of employee recruits and leavers. The results are summarised in Chart 8.3.

The results are striking. Small firms recruit many more students than they lose in employees returning to education and recruit more unemployed people than they make unemployed. They lose some (net) to other small firms, but six times as many to large firms. Small firms also suffer a net loss of employees as people set up in their own businesses. This confirms other research that small firms act as a breeding ground for other small firms. An important consequence of working in a small firm is that some employees are inspired to emulate their employers, having seen 'how it is done'.

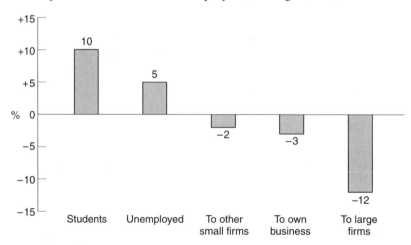

Chart 8.3 Indicator of net change in number of employees between small firms and other groups

Source: SBRT 3/01.

Overall, therefore, and to a significant extent, small firms are recruiting school leavers and the unemployed and losing them, after valuable work experience, to large firms. The survey results implied that the average employee stays with the small firm for seven–eight years. There was also evidence in the survey that employee turnover tended to increase with firm size and not, as is often believed, the opposite.[9]

When asked how they usually addressed skill shortage problems, 44–51 per cent of the smallest firms (1–19 employees) and 67–74 per cent of the larger firms (20 to 50+ employees) said they 'develop internally through training, etc.' while only 1–13 per cent and 13–26 per cent, respectively, would 'attract directly from competitors/other firms'. Larger firms were much more likely than the smallest firms to offer higher pay to attract needed recruits.

The nature of on-the-job training

KITCHING & BLACKBURN (2002) rightly define training broadly as 'any activities at all through which managers and workers improve their work-related skills and knowledge'. This includes formal as well as informal training, though as mentioned they recognise that employers, in responding to surveys, do not always take full account of the latter. Informal on-the-job training is of several kinds: talks and demonstrations, letting trainees try tasks and then commenting on and correcting the results, job rotation and so on. Learning by doing (and by making mistakes) is an essential part of all this, but there is more: a process of *osmosis* in which people learn by just being around in the workplace and observing processes and other people. In fact the very use of the word 'training', which relates to teaching people how to do things, important as it is, vastly understates the complexity of the process by which people learn in business.

In technology there are underlying principles and there are blueprints, other written instructions, and artefacts – tools and machines – but in addition to this *explicit knowledge* there is also *tacit knowledge* which is not, or cannot be, written down. Usually one is insufficient to achieve good results without the other. In the nineteenth century, during the Industrial Revolution in Britain, other countries wishing to emulate industrial success (and in defiance of industrial espionage laws) smuggled out plans, instructions and even machines, but found that they also needed experienced foremen and workers from Britain with the necessary tacit knowledge to apply the technology successfully. Even this was not always enough, for a variety of reasons, including differences in the qualities of available raw materials and supplies (MOKYR 2002).

The point of the distinction between explicit and tacit knowledge is that the possessor of the latter may not know exactly how she acquired it, or even what it is: it emerges only in *application* to a particular situation and cannot be acquired by academic study, only by experience. Understanding of the factors that determine success in business – and in life – have moved on from the IQ or intelligence test which has its origins 100 years ago. IQs seem to measure only the ability to score in tests and thus tend to reflect academic ability: consequently they, and academic records, are not good predictors of success in business. 'Entrepreneurs and those who have built large businesses from scratch are frequently discovered to be high-school or college drop-outs', as mentioned in Chapter 6. More recently has come the concept of 'emotional intelligence' – the ability to empathise with others and control emotions, for example. However, emotional intelligence – more difficult to measure than the IQ – is, it turns out, also a poor predictor of success; social skills, however valuable, are not enough. What really counts is the ability to solve real-life problems – *practical intelligence*, which comes down to having tacit knowledge. Practical intelligence can be measured by examining how people have solved real problems, or how they would expect to solve such problems, the point being that, unlike the IQ test, in real life there may be several right answers, not just one. It seems that 'one of the best ways of improving your practical intelligence is to observe master practitioners at work, and in particular to focus on the skills they have acquired while doing the job'. Observing a master practitioner constitutes much of how an apprentice learns his job in a plumbing business or a machine shop. It is also how junior doctors learn from consultant surgeons, and junior lawyers learn from barristers.[10] This process of observation and learning operates in all businesses of course, small or large, and indeed in all walks of life, especially the arts. However, it is easier and much more effective in a small enterprise where junior recruits are in continual contact with the owner-manager and his senior colleagues (if any) than in a large firm. It is worth emphasising that this learning process is not explicit, like much of the knowledge that is transmitted. Neither the master nor the pupil is necessarily aware of the full nature of the process, although most of us will acknowledge that we learned how to do creative things by having worked with a creator, perhaps in the distant past.[11]

The general failure to understand the distinction between practical (tacit) and technical (explicit) knowledge, and the processes by which they are acquired lies at the root of the errors in public policy towards small business training, though it has much wider implications that go far beyond the subject of this book. The late Michael Oakeshott wrote that 'In a practical art such as cookery, nobody supposes that the knowledge that belongs to the good cook is confined to what is or may be written down in the cookery book' (OAKESHOTT 1962). He went on:

> Practical knowledge can neither be taught nor learned, but only imparted and acquired. It exists only in practice, and the only way to acquire it is by apprenticeship to a master – not because the master can teach it (he cannot), but because it can be acquired only by continuous contact with one who is perpetually practising it. In the arts and in

natural science what normally happens is that the pupil, in being taught and in learning the technique from his master, discovers himself to have acquired also another sort of knowledge than merely technical knowledge, without being able to say precisely what it is.

Conclusions on learning and training

The beliefs that small firms as a group undertrain, and compensate for this by 'poaching' trained and experienced people from other firms, are not merely wrong but the opposite of the truth.[12] It is not that SME owners do not believe in the benefits of training and learning. In the survey by KITCHING & BLACKBURN (2002), 84 per cent of small employers carrying out training (and 71 per cent of non-trainers) felt that training leads to better business performance. It is rather that they realise, perhaps to some extent unconsciously, that the most appropriate (cheapest and most effective) form of training for a small firm is on-the-job. Employers say that they can discern the impact of training in the improved performance of employees. Some of this improvement will result from explicit training on-the-job of the 'this is how you do it' kind, and some from what we have termed the process of osmosis, in which people learn by simply being there and observing what the boss or other seniors do. This process of osmosis operates in various spheres of life, but it is particularly relevant in small firms because much of the knowledge needed in running a business is of the tacit kind. This is why research has found that people whose parents were small business owners are overrepresented among SME owners: it must be not only because they have role models, but also because they have unconsciously absorbed some of the knowledge of *how* to do it.

The relative importance of explicit (what can be written or otherwise articulated) and tacit (which emerges only in action) knowledge perhaps cannot, with present techniques, be measured scientifically. But there are reasons for thinking that uncodified or tacit knowledge is relatively more important for successful management in small firms than in large. This would be expected from the isolation of the owner-manager, the multiplicity of her tasks, the existence of severe time and financial constraints and the greater instability of the business environment faced. As already mentioned in Chapter 6, these characteristics inevitably mean that there is less need, or scope, for written plans and standard procedures. Time pressures are particularly apposite: they mean that the owner-manager cannot possibly do all the things which ought to be done in an ideal situation; selections have to be made intuitively about what must be done and what can be deferred or abandoned. The owner learns from mistakes but if the selection is wrong too often, then the business may fail. For a new start-up by an inexperienced owner, it is no exaggeration to say that the learning process is a race between learning from mistakes and the onset of serious problems. This is no doubt why failure rates for new firms are so high.

All this has implications for owner-manager training. From formal training courses owners can learn about the law, about taxation and other regulatory procedures. They can learn about procedures for the management of cash, debtors and creditors, and even useful hints on raising loans or recruiting staff, for example, all of which are important; but they cannot plausibly acquire the tacit knowledge which is gained only by experience or observation of their peers.[13] Matters are made more difficult by the fact that most of the body of academic knowledge about management is derived from the study of large firms, which is of doubtful relevance in the different circumstances of SMEs.

As far as employee training is concerned, research has failed to find consistent, causal relationships between the amount of training carried out and business performance. KITCHING & BLACKBURN (2002), for example, say:

> Data was inconclusive regarding the links between the provision of training and employment growth (actual and anticipated), sales turnover growth (actual and anticipated) or profit performance. The relationship between each of these factors and each type of training provision is complex: there is no simple positive association between them.

It seems clear from the findings of this chapter that the reason why there is no statistical relationship between employee training and business performance (even though SME owners and researchers alike believe there should be one) is simply that it is not possible to capture fully the training and learning that actually goes on in small firms As we have seen, the extent (and quality) of on-the-job training is just not measurable. This is especially true as far as tacit knowledge is concerned, since even the participants may be largely unaware of learning. The myth that SMEs undertrain can be explained only if formal and mainly external training is counted; and since formal training is clearly only a small part of the learning process in small firms, it is not surprising that statistical relationships with performance cannot be found.

The fact is that SMEs are taking in the young, the unemployed (especially the older unemployed) and training them on-the-job, explicitly or implicitly. The SBRT data quoted above suggests that SMEs not only meet their own training needs, but are also net suppliers of experienced staff to the rest of the economy.[14]

For owner-management training, researchers have also failed to identify any relationship between such training and business performance. STOREY & WESTHEAD (1966) were among the first to draw forceful attention to this uncomfortable fact for management theorists and teachers, but it is increasingly accepted. For example, PATTON *et al.* (2000) say:

Whilst intuitively it is presumed the investment in [management] training will enhance the performance potential of a small firm there is very little empirical evidence to support this proposition.

Patton *et al.* conclude that the heterogeneity of small firms and the difficulties of isolating the appropriate variables and other problems are such that identifying a relationship between manager training and performance is a 'lost quest'. This may well be true because 'management training' can cover a wide field, from partial training in specific techniques to the more ephemeral 'business strategy'. Nonetheless we find it difficult to avoid the conclusion that some management training, at least, is insufficiently tailored to the real needs of small firms. The number of successful entrepreneurs who claim they have never received *any* training after school or college, anecdotally the majority, certainly shows that such training is far from essential.

Attempts to force small firms to do more (formal) training are doomed to failure. SMEs can afford only a limited amount of formal training, though there is ample evidence that when it is economic they do make use of general (not SME-specific) public training services; they also use commercial and trade association services for specific skills such as IT and also for owner-management training. Of course subsidised public training services tailored for them will be welcome, but attempts at forcing are counter-productive. Among governments, a popular approach has been the levy system under which firms pay a payroll levy to a training authority, which is refunded where evidence of approved formal training is provided. There are two problems with this. First, what is officially regarded as 'suitable training' may not in reality be appropriate, with the result that precious resources of SMEs are wasted. Second, SMEs often have difficulty in coping with the paperwork required in obtaining refunds, the result being that the proportion of levy refunded falls with firm size and ends up being a tax on SMEs. Such systems have been tried and withdrawn in the United Kingdom but continue to operate in many countries, including developing countries such as Kenya and South Africa.[15]

Information and advice

Need and uses of sources of information and advice

In the United Kingdom many surveys have been carried out to establish the external sources of information and advice used by small firms (see BENNETT & ROBSON 1999, a review of research on sources of advice). These surveys all show that professional advisers (accountants and solicitors) and trade associations and connections are the most frequently cited sources, followed by the media (where included in the questionnaire), banks and government-funded sources. The order varies, as usual, with sample structure, questionnaire design and also within samples. For example, the smallest firms tend to make greater use of trade connections (customers and suppliers) and the media than of professional advisers which overall, in almost all surveys, come at the top by a large margin. Most firms use several different sources. BENNETT & ROBSON in their survey found an average of 4.5, with a strong clustering between 2 and 7.

In the SBRT 3/02 survey, by far the most common types of information sought were on taxation and government regulations, and technology (including IT),[16] followed by training and staff development, financial management/sources of finance, market information, marketing methods and exporting. It is significant that almost 40 per cent of the respondents needed advice or information on taxation, and all but under a fifth had been successful in finding it (hence the importance of accountants). Of the only slightly smaller number that needed information on regulation, two-fifths had difficulty in finding it. Market information (demand/trends) was the only other area where more than 10 per cent of respondents had experienced difficulty. Regulation therefore seems to be the largest gap by far in the array of needed help. Face-to-face contact and paper pamphlets were the preferred methods of supply, though websites were preferred to telephone help lines.

Use of government support programmes

Official surveys indicate that between 8 and 15 per cent (depending on definition) of the customer base have used SBSs Business Link, which is the main vehicle for government support services in the United Kingdom, and some 15 per cent (unprompted) are aware of the service (HM TREASURY 2002).[17] The Treasury Review stated that:

> Business Links operate against a background of customer apathy. By and large small businesses (particularly very small businesses) are reluctant to recognise the value of external advice and are too occupied with day-to-day matters to search it out. As a result, the SBS has to create demand while at the same time satisfying it through the provision of services.

BENNETT & ROBSON (2000) noted widespread variations in quality for Business Link but that overall, average client satisfaction had increased from 69 per cent in 1997 to 83 per cent in 1999. However, there seems to have been some deterioration since then, with the latest official survey for 2001 indicating satisfaction levels of about 60 per cent. BENNETT & ROBSON (2000) reported higher levels of use of general business information (57 per cent), as might be expected, from Business Link than for personal business advisors (PBAs) (32 per cent), sales and marketing advice (33 per cent) and finance and accounting advice (10 per cent).

Surveys carried out in European countries for the European Commission also show quite low penetrations of, awareness of, and participation in, SME support programmes. UK penetrations were in fact about average, with Austria, Spain and France at the top and Greece, Norway and Iceland at the bottom (Table 8.2). It will be noted that in other European countries, support programmes are less centralised at national level than in the United Kingdom.

Evaluation

Assessing the impact of support services on the business performance of the recipients, as distinct from measuring take-up and satisfaction, is difficult. The problem, as always, is establishing the counterfactual – how would firms have performed in the absence of support? Matters are complicated by the fact that recipients of certain kinds of support are not selected at random. In most cases, officials may select applicants according to prior notions of likely impact, and of course, the users are themselves self-selected. Strictly speaking, account should also be taken of excess burdens including those that result from assisted firms taking business and tax yield away from unassisted firms. (WOOD 1994 argues that benefits of support are offset by losses to unassisted firms unless sales are exported.)

Typically, government-sponsored evaluations do not take account of these complexities. By law, each US SBDC is required to carry out an *economic impact study*: basically, the approach is to compare growth rates in sales and employment of the longer-term clients of SBDCs with corresponding data for the whole state. The results are generally strongly positive.[18] Similar studies have been carried out in other countries, but the results of the use of this crude approach are likely to be very misleading. David Storey, 'Six steps to heaven: evaluating the impact of public policies to support small businesses in developed economies', in SEXTON & LANDSTROM (1999),

Table 8.2 SMEs that are aware of, and participated in, regional, national or European Community support programmes, by enterprise size, Europe-19, 1999[a]

Number of employees	0	1–9	10–49	50–249	Total
Awareness of support programmes (%)	28	33	44	55	31
Participated in programmes (%)	6	11	23	32	9
Financed by:					
– regional government (%)	5	7	14	20	6
– national government (%)	1	3	6	10	2
– European Commission (%)	1	1	6	8	1

Source: European Commission (2000).

Note
a Multiple answers possible.

reviews alternative evaluation methods and concludes, rightly in our view, that only methods which compare performance of randomly matched pairs of assisted and unassisted firms with similar characteristics, and which take account of selection bias, are appropriate. In STOREY & WESTHEAD (1996), an evaluation of the impact of management training support (referred to above), it was found that the more sophisticated the evaluation procedure, the weaker the link between support and performance. ROBSON & BENNETT (2000) concluded in their review that: 'There is little evidence of statistically significant relationships between government-backed providers of business advice, such as Business Link, and firm performance.'[19]

In summary, we can say that there is no real evidence of a need for official sources of advice and support on commercial matters because alternative channels are available. Public subsidised services are more likely to inhibit private provision. Of course, all support network operators can claim instances where their help has been productive, and free or subsidised help is bound to have some takers. However, services of this kind could never cover the whole of the SME population except at prohibitive costs anyway. On top of this there are a number of practical pitfalls in the way of public support services. These practical difficulties have all been encountered in Britain, where the idea of universal support has probably been pursued with greater vigour than in any other country except Japan, though they are to be found everywhere.[20]

Problems in providing support for information and advice

Underlying the lack of demand for, and apparent ineffectiveness of, government-backed information and advice services, there are numerous problems on the supply side. Decisions have to be taken to balance a desire to achieve higher penetration of the business population and to contain the use of inevitably limited resources. To achieve this balance, and to secure various policy objectives, most government support service networks make some charges, at least for higher-intensity services such as on-the-premises use of personal business advisers. There may also be a focus on particular sectors of the business population, such as start-ups or firms with growth potential. All these choices face difficulties: for example, should start-ups that might fail be encouraged? How to select firms with growth potential? Charges never seem to reflect full accounted costs, although in some countries unrealistic objectives of breaking even at some time in the future have been set (though never met).[21] A moment's consideration shows that if costs could be fully recovered, then the service could feasibly be provided by the private sector and government sponsorship would be unnecessary. There is a school of thought which believes that if users pay something for the service they will value it more and take advice more seriously though in the case of the UK, BENNETT & ROBSON (2000) found that fees had little systematic relation to user satisfaction.[22]

There are also problems in the design and content of business support services: are government officials with little or no business experience suited to design these services (even with the help of consultants)? Can suitably experienced PBAs be recruited with small, as opposed to large, business experience? As shown above, how can services be evaluated and reasonably consistent standards of quality achieved? Then there are problems with the content of services that have received insufficient attention. It is assumed that government-sponsored networks have access to knowledge about best practice in small business management, but do they? Does anyone know the best way of handling the vast range of business difficulties encountered by a very heterogeneous range of SMEs, when successful firms often break all the generally accepted rules? Business support services were probably initially inspired by the success of extension services in agriculture. The parallels are weak, however: in agriculture, there is a sound scientific (empirically tested) basis for advice on seeds, fertilisers, irrigation and crop rotation (as indeed there is for aspects of technology such as drill rotation speeds and lubrication or heat treatment), but such knowledge does not exist for general management practices. Moreover, agricultural extension services predominantly delivered advice on the farm, which would be prohibitively costly for general business support services.

Another issue is that academics have established that business people make use of extensive networks of contacts for information and advice, and that these networks can be segmented into local, national, family, social, customers, suppliers and so on (CURRAN & BLACKBURN 1994). This had led to the notion that networks in areas where they appear to be deficient – such as contacts with business angels – can be supplemented and extended by public initiatives. GIBB (2000) has criticised the view that 'networking' can be meaningfully regarded in terms of accessing separate channels or in other ways as a distinctive activity. He rightly says that: 'Networking and the "know-who" that goes along with it is the very essence of entrepreneurial activity and small business management . . . It is critical to the firm's transaction costs, the development of trust and its "community".'

Artificially created networks do not seem to work because they abstract from prior human contact, community feeling and trust. At one time, there was a view that the gap between the extent of informal risk finance (business angels, see Chapter 6) in the United States and Britain could be narrowed by supporting network services. These services have struggled to achieve much outside services run by trade associations.[23] Similarly, a group discussion among SME owners in Hamburg found little support for the so-called 'marriage bureaux' of the European Commission. It was felt that such activities 'should be left to the relevant SME interest groups run by entrepreneurs' (BANNOCK & ALBACH 1991).

Despite these inherent difficulties, the provision of business support services has spread (or rather has been spread by governments and donor agencies) around the world to the transition and developing countries.

BATEMAN (2000), an OECD official writing in a personal capacity of business support centres (BSCs), says:

> The practical inspiration for the majority of BSC networks in Central and Eastern Europe was quite clearly the UK's experience with LEAs and TECs . . .
>
> The new liberal approach has led to the establishment of BSC networks which can be typified as weak, poorly functioning, excessively commercial, determinedly short-termist, and financially unstable.[24]

Similarly, in the Third World, the spread of support service networks funded by bilateral, multilateral agencies and non-governmental organisations (NGOs) has also led to problems and dissatisfaction. The World Bank, in a review (IBRD 2001), concluded that fresh thinking was needed for BDS:

> Motivating the search for a 'new paradigm' for BDS was the shared recognition that traditional interventions have failed to provide quality, affordable BDS to a large proportion of the target population of small enterprises. There was a general feeling that publicly-provided and publicly-funded services have not achieved their objectives: enterprise productivity and competitiveness, job creation, poverty alleviation, and social mobility. Moreover, good performance measurement was lacking to be able to evaluate and compare programs.

Conclusion on support services

The IBRD's conclusion was that support services, including services provided by trade associations, should be re-focused to encourage market provision and to avoid crowding out the private sector.[25] This logic applies equally to developed countries. The IBRD (2001) report says that BDS are already being provided for profit in developing countries in ways that are not readily visible to donors and other outsiders. Commercial business support services, on the other hand, are highly visible in developed countries. OECD (1999) estimates that the market supply of business services (R&D and technical, marketing, management consultancy and human resource development(HRD)) had been growing at 10 per cent per annum in developed countries. KEEBLE *et al.* (1991) showed that numbers of enterprises in computer services in the United Kingdom grew by 89 per cent between 1985 and 1989, in management consultancy by 83 per cent, in professional and scientific services by 45 per cent and in other business services by 43 per cent. Most of the new and existing enterprises in these fields were of course SMEs, and their customer base numerically must also have been largely among SMEs. This shows that there is a growing use of commercially provided external information and advice services. To crowd out any of this activity by the provision of subsidised public services is to damage the very growth of the SME sector to which these services are dedicated. Public services of this type also undermine the efforts of the large array of trade associations, chambers of commerce and other private sector organisations.

As with SME-specific training initiatives, government support networks are based on misapprehension about need and are fighting a losing battle to supply something for which there is little effective demand or necessity. If there *are* market failures in the supply of information, they are probably heavily concentrated in the supply of information about regulatory requirements – information the government has a duty to supply, with its natural monopoly of in-depth knowledge. That is what public services should focus upon, as well as on referral or signposting services for the enormous range of information sources that are available within government and the private sector.

Notes

1 See BENNETT *et al.* (1994) for an insightful account of the history of Training and Enterprise Councils (TECs).
2 In some countries – for example, Germany – the concern about lack of training by SMEs does not really arise because after completing full-time schooling pupils not continuing in full-time education are required to attend vocational schools. Moreover, in a wide range of activities, not merely in crafts such as woodworking but including hairdressing and interior decorating, an individual may not set up a business unless qualified as a master craftsman (*Meister*) which requires training under a person so specified. Ironically the Germany craft-guild system (for a description see DORAN 1984), much admired around the world, is now heavily criticised at home on the grounds that it prevents experienced workers from entering self-employment, restricts competition and keeps up prices.

    Other countries have used levy systems to force training on firms, as described below. The United Kingdom has used a levy system in the past. In 2001, TECs, which had superseded the Manpower Services Commission (MSC) arrangements in 1988, ceased to operate, their training activities being taken over by the National Learning and Skills Council and their information and advisory services by BLOs under the SBS. (The MSC had been set up in 1973; there were different arrangements in Scotland.)
3 'Undertraining' in SMEs is a preoccupation in many developed countries (though not all: not, as mentioned, in Germany, where the system largely precludes it). In France, according to a report in *Le Monde* (20 September 2003), new legislation was to be introduced to fulfil a government commitment to lifelong vocational learning. The report stated that in the year 2000, only 10 per cent of workers in SMEs with fewer than 20 employees had access to vocational training, compared with 65 per cent in firms with over 2,000 employees. The comparable figures for engineers and managers were 16 per cent and 67 per cent, respectively, for small and large firms. Everywhere, employees (and unions) naturally want to feel that training will enhance their career prospects. There is a belief, justified or not, that on-the-job experience does not count for as much as paper qualifications. A useful idea in the French legislation will be a

Passeport formation which, notably, will include a record not only of formal training but also of job experience.

4 'Public law', in this context, means that all enterprises are members of bodies recognised by government, as in France, Germany, the Netherlands, Spain and Italy, for example. The United States, Canada and the United Kingdom have voluntary or private law bodies (BENNETT 1996).

5 The benefits to society as a whole of these kinds are referred to as 'externalities' or 'spillovers'; there are also 'disbenefits', or 'negative externalities', from private activity, such as environmental pollution. These negative externalities provide a classic case for intervention for which there is no need where externalities are positive.

6 As everywhere in this book, we avoid the use of economic jargon wherever possible. Where sellers know more than buyers (or the reverse, as in the case of banking; see Chapter 4) this is known in economics as 'information asymmetry'. Where poor-quality providers prevail over the better ones, this is known as 'adverse selection'. Adverse selection arises in the second-hand car market where some cars are 'lemons' but the ordinary buyer cannot identify them, the result being that prices do not fully reflect quality.

7 Of the smaller firms surveyed in SBRT 12/2000, 13.2 per cent thought that the main cause of skills shortages in their business was 'inappropriate skills developed at school/college'; this proportion did not vary systematically by firm size.

8 SME owners tend to interpret 'training' narrowly to exclude much on-the-job training. This probably means that all surveys understate informal training in SMEs. KITCHING & BLACKBURN found in their face-to-face interviews (the main survey was by telephone) that 'some employers implicitly assume that "proper training" needs to be provided in a formal, off-the-job setting, away from the workplace, by an external provider, possibly involving qualifications or accreditation of some kind'. We argue below that in fact people in small firms are being trained all the time, whether they or their employers are aware of it or not.

9 Some qualifications need to be made to these results. The first is that although the survey covered over 800 SMEs employing 9,000 people, of the 14 per cent who had left, employers were able to identify their destination for only half (two-thirds for recruits). Since larger firms were less able than small to identify origins and destinations, however, this would imply understatement of the shifts of employees from small to large firms. However, it also means that sample sizes were small for some components of the analysis. It is worth noting that confidence in the data is supported by the fact that the survey has been repeated three times with non-identical samples (1989, 1995, 2001) and with very similar results.

10 Quotations from Dr Raj Persaud, 'Practical intelligence lends a hand', *Financial Times*, 14 August 2001. Dr Persaud's article refers to the work of Professor Robert Sternberg, a psychologist at Yale University, and in particular to the latter's article 'Analytical, creative and practical intelligence as predictors of adaptive functioning', *Intelligence*, 29, 2001.

11 It is significant that when asked, 'Who is directly responsible for skills development in your business?', SBRT survey respondents said that for firms with 1–9 employees, the proprietor/MD/Chairman was responsible for training in 69–81 per cent of cases.

12 In the foreword to SBC (2003), the Chairman of the Small Business Council, William Sargent, writes: 'For years policy makers have laboured under the impression that small businesses don't train. This attitude has been frustrating for myself and other members of the Council because it is simply not true.' (The SBC's paper draws on KITCHING & BLACKBURN 2002, whose report was commissioned by the SBC.)

13 This is not to imply that entrepreneurial training is without value. The importance of technique should not be underestimated and there are some talented teachers that have an empathy for business, even where they have not run businesses themselves, which allows them to communicate some tacit knowledge. It is doubtful if even these teachers, however, can 'make' entrepreneurs unless the innate ability is there.

14 We have found no similar data for other countries although in Germany, according to the Institut für Mittelstandsforschung (IfM), small firms are also net suppliers of trained labour to the rest of the economy.

15 There have been other experiments, such as training credits where SMEs are rewarded with grants for approved training, but these suffer from similar deficiencies. A better solution would be freely provided and widely exchangeable training vouchers. Why small firms regard training levies as just another tax is exemplified in research by the Small Business Project, Johannesburg. The South African skills levy amounts to 1 per cent on payrolls over R250,000 (about £25,000). Firms can claim back up to 65 per cent of the levy, often conducting approved training and skills planning. Out of 49 small companies interviewed, only four had claimed back a portion of the levy. One said 'We train all the time – but it's not the sort of training recognised by the authorities.'

16 In SBRT 9/01 survey, 88 per cent of SMEs used computers – up from 36 per cent in 1985. Non-users were very small firms, mainly in catering, retail, agriculture and construction. Of firms with 50 or more employees, 100 per cent had computers and 90 per cent of firms with 20 or more employees used e-mail.

17 The awareness figures are surprisingly low given that Business Link has been heavily promoted. The SBRT 3/96 survey found that 45 per cent of its respondents claimed to know the name and location of their local Business Link; though this survey underrepresented new start-ups, who were less likely than larger firms to be aware of support organisations.

18 CHUSMAN & McMULLAN (1996) found that benefits (after allowing for incremental tax revenues from incremental sales and adjustment for levels of client satisfaction) exceeded costs by about 60 per cent.

19 Among SMEs the most popular support provided in the United Kingdom was subsidised access to private commercial market research and consultancy services under the Enterprise Initiative. This was so popular that access to the scheme was rationed. It has since been discontinued. WREN & STOREY (2002) found that assistance for advice on marketing provided under the Enterprise Initiative had no impact on survival of smaller SMEs; however, it was most effective for mid-range firms, where it raised survival rates by 4 per cent over the longer run, and growth rates in surviving firms by up to 10 per cent per annum.

20 Comparisons are difficult and data sparse but, as shown in Chapter 7, in 1988/9 Britain spent more on information and consultancy than Germany, though much less on support for SMEs overall (BANNOCK & ALBACH 1991).

21 The necessity to achieve targets and budgets has often created tensions as support networks have tried to press charged services onto SMEs.

22 In 1999, 37 per cent of service use for Business Link incurred a fee.

23 There was not, and is not, any evidence that formal support networks in the United States can explain the difference in the extent of use of informal finance. More likely explanations have to do with taxation, levels of wealth and cultural factors.

24 Local enterprise agencies (LEAs) are local voluntary organisations in the United Kingdom mounted by local authorities and business organisations, including banks. Prior to the development of Business Links, these bodies received some funding from central government; some were absorbed by BLOs,

while others continued to operate independently. At their peak there were approaching 300 LEAs in the United Kingdom. A specific objective of government policy was to reduce the number of conflicting support organisations, as these were seen to create confusion amongst SMEs; the virtues of competition were forsaken in this instance. Bateman's thrust is not actually against business support as such; he believes funding should have been directed to local authorities. His main critique is of neo-liberalism, the tenets of which favoured free-market policies as the sole solution to the development of the transition countries.

25 The report suggests, for example, that business development services (BDS) facilitators can help commercial suppliers to develop new products and promote good practice. They can also educate SMEs on the potential benefits of services, or provide incentives to try them.

9   Small firms in developing countries

Introduction

So far, this book has been about small firms in developed countries but the main findings (with a few important exceptions) are more urgently applicable to the poorer countries of the developing world and to countries in transition.[1] It is hardly necessary to emphasise that the fact that 23 per cent of the world's population live in extreme poverty (living on less than $1 a day) (IBRD 2001c) is a human tragedy as well as a threat to global peace and security. Some progress has recently been made (the proportion of the world population living in extreme poverty fell from 29 to 23 per cent between 1990 and 1998), but some parts of the world (notably sub-Saharan Africa) have also slipped backwards and continue to have very much higher infant mortality and lower life expectancy than middle- or higher-income countries.[2] The outlook would be very bleak if some parts of the world (notably East Asia and the Pacific from the 1960s and, more recently, China) had not shown that rapid emergence from underdevelopment is possible. However, it does not seem that overall there is much evidence of convergence in the sense that poorer countries are catching up with the leaders, at least since the 1970s.[3]

In this chapter, we start with a brief review of theories of development and aid policy, then look at the role of SMEs, particularly in the contrasted experiences of East Asia and Africa. We go on to examine the institutional constraints on SMEs in LDCs and countries in transition. Finally we enquire into the roles of national governments and donors in attempting to promote SMEs and their role in development.

Thinking on economic development

Theories of growth

There is a massive economic literature on growth and development. One stream of this literature is specific to the issue of how countries can break out of underdevelopment, and is mainly post-Second World War in its origins. Another stream of literature is older, and deals with the factors that determine economic advance in all countries at a more theoretical aggregative level. Both of these streams of thought started with simplified, if not mono-causal, interpretation, but are flowing into a broader, more complex view, which increasingly emphasises the role of intangible and institutional factors. These generalisations are, of course, simplifications and the two streams have at times spilled over into one another.[4]

At the more general level, abstract economic growth theory has moved through a number of phases. The classical economists after Adam Smith saw increased prosperity coming about through the division of labour, but Malthus and Ricardo identified limits to economic growth arising from diminishing returns as expansion led to the use of marginal and inferior land and population pressed against the means of subsistence.[5] Neo-classical economists identified the role of capital accumulation which allowed increasing return to scale – which in turn permitted growth rates to exceed the rate of growth of both population and capital. More recently, Schumpeter elevated innovation and technological progress to the driving position in economic growth. Early modern theories of growth, which were initially concerned with modelling steady-state growth on the assumption that technological progress was random and could not be embodied in the models (was exogenous), are now giving way to more complex (but not mathematically explicit, or even empirically verifiable) theories in which investment in education and research influence innovation and thus economic growth (endogenous growth theory).

What has happened in the evolution of growth theory is a growing appreciation that economic growth is not determined solely by the amounts of inputs of labour (even embodying skills and knowledge) or capital (even embodying new technologies),[6] but a more complex process in which *institutions and even cultures* are important constraints or facilitators of growth. The importance of institutions has been much stressed in economic literature, particularly recently.[7] However, the term 'institutions' is rarely defined by those that use it, nor is its relation to 'culture' at all clear.[8] What is clear is that the customs and rules that operate in economic life, such as property rights, are enormously important, as we shall argue. That the quality and relevance of institutions are difficult, if not impossible to incorporate in mathematical models only goes to show how inadequate these models can be to interpret economic reality.

Aid and development policy

The evolution of thinking of theoretical economists – and, significantly, by economic historians such as NORTH (1981) – towards an appreciation of the fundamental importance of institutions has been reflected in the changing policies of bilateral and multilateral aid agencies in the post-Second World War period. Large amounts of development assistance funding have been provided to LDC and transition countries – upwards of

$50 billion annually since the mid-1990s – though this aid has fallen both absolutely (by 15 per cent between 1995 and 2001) and as a percentage of the national incomes of the donor countries.[9]

In the early post-war years there was a heavy emphasis on the importance of *planning*, on the part of both donors and recipient governments.[10] This was inspired by wartime experience and by the apparent success of the planned economies. The common view of the theoreticians of development was that poor countries lacked the savings and investment necessary for growth, which resulted in a vicious circle of underdevelopment. This situation provided a justification for foreign aid, much of which was devoted to physical capital formation for infrastructure – roads and dams, for example – and industrial and agricultural investment.

As long ago as the 1950s the late Peter Bauer, virtually a lone voice against development orthodoxy, then and until quite recently, argued that there could be no vicious circle of underdevelopment in the sense of lack of savings. Since all countries were once poor, but some developed and some did not, inability to save could hardly be the explanation.[11] Towards the end of his life (he died in 2002), Bauer wrote: 'Poverty or riches and personal and social satisfaction depend on man, on his culture, and on his political arrangements. Understand *that*, and you understand the most important cause of wealth or deprivation' (BAUER 2000, emphasis in the original).[12] In other words, it is *institutions and culture*, not resources, that we need to look at when seeking the causes of underdevelopment. In fact the very poor do save, as Bauer earlier asserted. De SOTO (2000) has calculated that the value of savings in LDCs is 'forty times all the foreign aid received throughout the world since 1945'. This saving is embodied in property which, through lack of legal title (an institutional issue), cannot be used as collateral for borrowing and productive use: it is, in de Soto's words, 'sterilised'.

To return to the evolution of development policies, we find that, since attempts to alleviate the savings and investment gap did not lead to sustainable development in the 1960s and 1970s, more attention in aid programmes was focused on improvements in health and education. This shift was inspired by the findings mentioned earlier: that even in the advanced countries, growth could not be fully explained by capital and labour inputs alone but that *intangibles*, in the form of technological development and human capital, played an important part.

In the 1980s the focus of attention in development policy turned to the role of *macroeconomic management* and allowing markets to work. The view was that the economic systems of LDCs could not channel resources into growth where interest rates, capital movements and prices were subject to selective controls, large parts of the economy were directly controlled by the state, and (partly as a result) there was inflation and economic instability. The World Bank and the International Monetary Fund (IMF) drew up and supported economic structural adjustment programmes (ESAPs) to reduce budget deficits and inflationary pressures, to free interest rates, remove price controls and privatise state assets. While these policies, where fully implemented, did bring some improvement in terms of growth and inflation, they caused social unrest and were not sufficient to transform the situation (WORLD BANK 1994). A similar pattern, and some initial chaos, was also reproduced in Central and Eastern Europe, where similar policies were pursued in the early 1980s. It became clear that macroeconomic liberalisation alone was not sufficient to trigger sustainable growth until the *institutional framework and incentive structures* could be improved.

In the late 1990s and into the Millennium, development policies have again shifted towards more broadly based strategies that focus both on the short-term alleviation of poverty and the promotion of private sector development through the removal of regulatory and other institutional barriers.

Stages of growth

There are various approaches to looking at the way economies change as they develop. Historically, the now developed countries all went through stages in which at first agriculture accounted for the major part of economic activity, with a steady movement from mainly subsistence to traded output and higher productivity. The development of markets permitted industrialisation as more of the population moved off the land and into towns, with an intermediate stage of 'proto-industrialisation' in which craft activities in rural areas developed into small-scale manufacturing.[13] It should be noted that trade, and other services such as retailing, in fact lead to industrialisation. This is important, because governments in capitalist and communist countries alike have tended to regard trading as an unproductive activity not to be encouraged, whereas in reality the trading sector, including international trade, acts as a driver of growth, creating markets for manufacturers and permitting the accumulation of capital for investment. With industrialisation, the growth of incomes quickens and urbanisation proceeds. At first, industry accounts for an increasing share of employment and the national product but then, like agriculture, reaches a stage of decline as the service sector and urbanisation continue to grow at high levels of income, while international trade becomes relatively less important with the growth of the service sector. Most rapid growth in income *per capita* occurs at the industrialisation stage.

These generalised phases of urbanisation and successive sectoral change come out more or less well from a cross-section analysis[14] of countries at various levels of income today (Table 9.1). We should not expect a close correspondence, of course, because the figures in the table cover all countries, some of which are stuck at a particular stage of development or underdevelopment. Meanwhile the averages obviously conceal varied experiences.

Table 9.1 Sectoral distribution of GDP, *per capita* growth rates, urbanisation and international trade by income group, 148 countries, 1965–99

Income groups ($US)	% of urban popu- lation	% of GDP, 1999		% of foreign trade of GDP		% of annual real-GDP growth (1965–99)
		Agri- culture	Industry services	(1970)	(1999)	
Low-income: < $755	31	26	30	20	50	1.8
Middle-income: $756–9,265	50	10	36	26	55	2.4
High-income: >$9,266	77	2ᵃ	27ᵃ	29	43	2.4

Source: World Bank, *World Development Indicators 2001*.

Note
a European Monetary Union (EMU) countries only. The averages conceal wide variations in growth: for example, among low- and middle-income groups combined, GDP *per capita* growth was 5.6 per cent for East Asia and Pacific, 2.4 per cent for South Asia and –0.2 per cent for sub-Saharan Africa.

The role of SMEs and constraints in the business environment

The informal sector

The economies of LDCs and countries in transition are characterised by three sectors: state enterprises, a formal sector and an informal sector. The division of private sector activity into formal and large informal sectors is a characteristic of underdevelopment. Formal enterprises are registered and pay direct and indirect taxes (with varying degrees of compliance). Informal enterprises are generally not registered, nor do they pay direct taxes, although they may be unable to escape indirect taxes on inputs from large registered enterprises. There are no comprehensive official statistics on the informal sector, and their output and incomes are generally not, or not wholly, included in the national accounts.

Developed economies, of course, also have informal sectors but they are relatively small and cover largely illegal economic activity. What distinguishes the informal sector in LDCs, though not in most transition countries, is that it is officially tolerated and is very large. From estimates by ENSTE & SCHNEIDER (1998) covering developed and developing countries from all continents except Australia, it can be seen that as a percentage of recorded GDP the size of the 'shadow economy', as they term it, falls progressively with development measured by GDP *per capita*. What these estimates show is that among developed countries, the informal sector generally accounts for 10–20 per cent of GDP. In Eastern Europe this ratio rises to 20–30 per cent but in LDCs it rises to 40–75 per cent or more.[15]

The toleration of informality in LDCs is a recognition of the fact that the mass of micro- and small enterprises (MSEs) could not survive if they had to bear the full compliance costs of regulation. There are two widespread misconceptions about this. One is that regulation does not affect the informal sector because they do not observe tax, employment and other laws. However, there are other costs of being informal, and limits to the toleration exercised: harassment by police, who (for example) may not allow street traders to operate in urban areas; and corruption, in which poorly paid officials require bribes from small entrepreneurs in the informal as well as the formal sectors to turn a blind eye to non-compliance or alleged non-compliance. In addition, informals cannot obtain titles to land – and in consequence, bank credit – in the absence of collateral. Tax systems act as a barrier to escape from informality, since informals have the choice of remaining informal and not paying taxes, or registering their business and being faced with steep taxes.

A second misconception is that *formal* businesses in LDCs are only lightly regulated anyway.[16] On the contrary: regulation of business actually tends to be more severe in poor countries than in richer countries, not only in terms of compliance costs as a percentage of GDP *per capita*, but absolutely in terms of the complexity, uncertainty and delay involved in compliance.

Cross-section studies and institutional differences

The World Bank has carried out or sponsored a number of cross-section studies which have measured the relationship between various aspects of regulation and other institutional factors, such as the cost and effectiveness of judicial systems for the enforcement of business contracts.[17] These studies show that across large numbers of countries, heavier regulation is associated with more informality, more corruption, less productivity and more unemployment (World Bank 2003). Table 9.2 shows, for example, measures of the weight of regulation by country income group, indicating that the complexity of regulatory procedures tends to be inversely related to income levels.

The picture comes into sharper focus still when we relate the average costs of starting a business to GDP *per capita* for areas of the world at different stages of development (Chart 9.1). It can be seen that, in relation to incomes, costs are much higher in Africa than in the transition countries of central Europe, which in turn are higher than in those countries in South Asia which have succeeded in industrialising.

The measure of regulatory costs in the cross-section studies reviewed above are fairly crude and simplified, but the results are consistent with the findings of the (very few) surveys of compliance costs carried out in developing countries (see EVANS *et al.* 2001). These studies also confirm the same steeply regressive character of compliance costs found in the advanced countries which mean that regulatory costs bear particularly heavily on SMEs.

Table 9.2 Measures of regulation by country income groups

Group	Number of procedures to start a business	Number of procedures to enforce a contract	Index of employment laws
Low-income	11	30	53
Lower-middle-income	12	27	55
Upper-middle-income	10	27	55
High-income	7	18	43

Source: World Bank (2003).

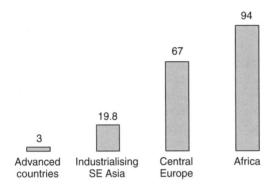

Chart 9.1 Business entry costs as a percentage of GDP *per capita* for country groups

Source: BANNOCK *et al.* (2002), based on DJANKOV *et al.* (2001).

The role of SMEs

We saw in Chapter 1 that the number of SMEs and their share in employment tends to fall with economic development. This reflects the contraction of the informal economy with increased *per capita* incomes, as observed above, and a shift to the right in the firm-size distribution: LDCs have much less employment in medium and large-scale firms than in advanced countries, where average firm sizes are larger. These shifts – from cottage and household industry to medium and large-scale industry – have been observed in the past path of development of the now developed countries, and also apparently in the more recent development of East Asia. Miyokei Shinohara, 'A survey of the Japanese literature on small industry', in HOSELITZ (1968), systematically documented this pattern, and it has been recently confirmed for Indonesia by TAMBUNAN (2000).[18] Bannock and Binks, in BANNOCK & DALY (1994), were able to identify some statistical relationships to explain a 'dynamic transition process from informal household industry to modern self-employment and smaller firms leading to larger firms in a sophisticated market economy'. This process starts with the service sector – not, as often supposed with manufacturing – and the nature of self-employment itself changes with development. In the modern economy, the self-employed are not engaged primarily in petty trading, artisanal work or subsistence activity as they are in developing countries, but in personal and business services.

We have discussed the decline but persistence of SMEs in economic activity and mentioned their various roles in training, capital accumulation, innovation, subcontracting, use of marginal resources[19] and as complements to large firms in modern economies. In LDCs and in the more distant past of the now advanced countries, the balance of importance of these various roles in economic advance seems to be different. Technical innovation and complementarity to large firms may well be less important roles for SMEs in LDCs, if only because some technology in a globalising world is transferred from the lead economies, and because there are so few medium and large-scale firms in LDCs. Capital accumulation, in which agriculture and petty trading allow investment in more capital-intensive activities (services and simple household manufacturing) is a more important role for SMEs in LDCs than in developed economies, if only because of the low stage of develop-ment of the financial infrastructure.[20] This is why Peter Bauer could argue that lack of savings was not a cause. There are no statistics of capital forma-tion by small firms in LDCs (nor, in a comprehensive sense, in advanced countries either). Much of this capital accumulation is unrecorded anyway and does not require, as Bauer pointed out, monetary savings or investment, for example in 'the planting of cocoa or rubber trees on smallholdings where the output is collected and distributed by traders. These categories of capital formation are indispensable for the advance from subsistence production' (BAUER 2000). And, of course, the advance from subsistence to production is the essential condition for the creation of an exchange economy, which in turn allows for the division of labour and economic advance.

Equally important, and even more important in LDCs than in advanced countries, is the role of SMEs in the development of the skills of the workforce and the commercial culture necessary for development. Bannock and Binks, in BANNOCK & DALY (1994) quote E.T. Schumacher, author of *Small is Beautiful*, a passage which is strikingly similar to that of Peter Bauer cited earlier in this chapter:

> Among the causes of poverty, I am sure, the material factors are entirely secondary – such things as lack of natural wealth, or lack of capital, or an insufficiency of infrastructure. The primary causes of extreme poverty are immaterial; they lie in certain deficiencies, in education, organisation and discipline.
>
> (SCHUMACHER 1973)

Schumacher went on to argue that the development of small-scale activity helps to promote these immaterial qualities. By mounting small firms, employers and employees alike learn by doing, gain experience of the technical and organisational issues in economic activity and help to spread the commercial culture which has to replace traditional attitudes as development proceeds. This process of learning is slow and involves trial – and, equally instructive, error. It is so important and so often unappreciated that much of Chapter 8, dealing with advanced countries, is devoted to on-the-job training. This form of learning is even more important in developing countries as well as in transition countries, where commercial attitudes were suppressed in long years of communist rule.

Statistical evidence on the role of SMEs

The qualifications made on the reliability and difficulties of interpreting small firm statistics in the advanced countries apply with much greater force to those for the developing and transitional world.[21] For LDCs, as noted, MSEs in the informal sector are nowhere fully covered in official statistics. The only reasonably reliable and comprehensive data available are those of the GEMINI surveys (see Appendix), but even these are single-year survey estimates based on regional clusters, and relate mainly to sub-Saharan Africa (LIEDHOLM & MEAD 1999). The GEMINI data show very high 'birth' rates (19–25 per cent), belying the view that entrepreneurship is lacking in Africa. The authors suggest that in the African countries, about 40 per cent of the increase in the labour force found work in MSEs in the 1980s and 1990s. As in developed countries (see Chapter 2), about three-quarters of these jobs in the long term came from new firms and the rest from expansion of existing enterprises. In the vast majority of cases, new jobs resulted from 'small additions to micro-enterprises with fewer than five employees after expanding, but the process of graduation to more than 10 employees also made a significant contribution to job creation', 1 per cent of firms grow substantially and 'more than half of today's medium-sized firms began with fewer than five employees' (MEAD 1994).[22] Table 9.3 shows the average distribution of the MSE population by employment size in six African countries studied by LIEDHOLM & MEAD (1999). These distributions seem to be fairly typical of poorer LDCs. It can be seen that almost 97 per cent of enterprises in Africa employ fewer than five employees. As in the UK figures given for comparison in Table 9.3, over two-thirds of enterprises have no employees apart from the owner(s).

The essential difference is that in the African countries there are relatively very many fewer firms with 11–50 employees. A distribution by employment share (which is not given in the source) would show an even more pronounced difference, because larger firms by definition have more employees per firm.

When we look at the fast-growing economies of East Asia that have succeeded in industrialising, we find that SMEs have been very prominent, and in most cases appear to have been the driving element.[23] In Taiwan,

Table 9.3 Total number of enterprises, by employment size band, average for six
African countries compared with the United Kingdom

Employment band	Africa (%)	United Kingdom	%
0	66.3	0	69.3
1–5	30.4	1–4	20.0
6–10	2.3	5–9	5.3
11–19	0.6	10–19	3.0
20–50	0.4	20–49	1.5
50+	n.a.	50+	0.9

Sources: Africa: derived from LIEDHOLM & MEAD (1993); United Kingdom: SBS data.

Notes
Africa: unweighted averages for Botswana, Kenya, Lesotho, Malawi, Swaziland and
Zimbabwe *c.* 1991, United Kingdom 2001. The surveys in Africa cover only MSEs with fewer
than 50 employees, including proprietors, predominantly agricultural enterprises are excluded.
n.a. = not available.

SMEs (>100 employees) accounted for 27 per cent of industrial production
in 1971 and 38 per cent in 1991. In the service sector, the corresponding share
was about 48 per cent in both periods. The SME share of exports of manu-
factures fell from 66 per cent to 57 per cent over the same period (HU 1999).

The growth and industrialisation of the East Asian economies generally
seems to have been associated with a large and increasing presence of SMEs,
though as might be expected from our earlier account of development
dynamics, the role of very small firms (fewer than 10 employees) has tended
to decline (IQBAL & URATA 2002). Korea is often cited as an exception
because of the perceived dominant role of large conglomerates (Chaebol),
in contrast (for example) to Taiwan, Hong Kong and, earlier, Japan. The
Korean case is particularly interesting because there have been apparent
reversals in the trend of SME shares in employment and value added, which
declined throughout the 1960s and early 1970s but rose strongly after that.24
By 1997, SMEs (5–300 employees) accounted for over 69 per cent of
manufacturing employment and 47 per cent of value added in Korea, and
about 40 per cent of exports (NUGENT & YHEE 2002).

There is general agreement that SMEs have not only benefited from the
liberalisation of the Chinese economy but have been largely responsible for
its rapid growth since the 1980s (GIBB & LI 2003). The early 1960s reversal
of the disastrous Chinese policy of concentrating 130 million family farms in
1957 into 26,000 'people's communes' in 1958 was only the first dramatic
sign of what was to come (MADDISON 1998). The number of small enterprises in industry (fewer than 200 workers) rose from 344,000 in 1978 to
8 million in 1996, while their share in output increased from 57 per cent to
66 per cent over the period 1980–96. About three-quarters of industrial
employment is accounted for by SMEs (WANG & YAO 2002), considerably more than most advanced countries (though not Japan).

What can statistics tell us about the role of SMEs in development?

A cross-section study by BECK *et al.* (2003) concludes that 'fast growing economies tend to have large SME sectors'. However, it 'does not support the view that SMEs exert a causal impact on growth and poverty'. Some readers might think that if SMEs are quantitatively related to *per capita* income growth rates, then their role must have something to do with making growth possible. However, this does not follow, because a large role for SMEs could be a product rather than a cause of growth. The difficulty with this type of quantitative cross-section analysis is that it cannot capture the *qualitative changes* that take place in the role of SMEs as development proceeds, and which may be subject to long lags. Statistical analysis may also show that inputs of labour and capital (adjusted for human capital) can explain much of economic growth, but growth accounting of this sort does not tell us *how* societies organise changes in the accumulation of capital and the inputs of labour to achieve the explained growth. TFP calculations may tell us that the efficiency with which inputs are utilised is increasing, or not.[25] This can be important because unless TFP does improve, growth will run into diminishing returns – but again, TFP calculations do not tell us by what mechanisms that efficiency is attained (or not).

An early attempt by IBRD (1993), and subsequently others, to explain Asian growth, derived an explanation from factors, which included macro-economic policies, education, high rates of investment, open economies and export promotion, but these made no mention of the striking commonality of the large role of SMEs. Nor did IBRD (1993) emphasise the role of institutional factors, which the World Bank is now rightly persuaded are of central importance in development.

NELSON & PACK (1997) divide the theories of East Asian development into two groups. The first group, which they call 'accumulation' theory, stresses the role of investments in physical and human capital. The second, 'assimilation' theory, stresses 'the entrepreneurship, innovation and learning that these economies had to go through before they could master the new technologies they were adopting from the more advanced industrial nations; it sees investment in human and physical capital as a necessary, but far from sufficient, part of the assimilation process.'[26] It is the assimilationist point of view for which we argue here, and for the role of SMEs in that process.

To say that SMEs everywhere play an important role in development (an active, not merely a passive role) is not a prescription for some predetermined proportion of the number of SMEs, or for their share in employment. We seen that in these terms there appear to be significant differences between countries, even at similar stages of development. We have also seen that the 'quantity' of SMEs tends to decline with development, with reversals as external economic circumstances change, but that the 'quality' of SMEs also changes, as with the evolution from household industry to modern industry and self-employment. It may be that the quantity of SMEs is particularly important at the early stages of development, as it seems to have been in most East Asian countries and recently in China and was, historically, in the West, including Britain and the United States (Chapter 3): but quality is also important. As noted above, BECK *et al.* (2003) did find a relationship between the quantity of SMEs and economic growth rates, but did not find that this reflected a causal relationship. GUILLÉN (2001) concluded from his case studies of Spain, Argentina and Korea that:

> The mere numerical presence of SMEs relative to larger firms, business groups, or foreign multinationals is not very relevant to the global economy. What matters is to what extent the SME sector succeeds in exports, foreign investment and technological development.

It is this ability to modernise which seems to characterise SMEs in the countries of East Asia. HU (1999), for example, demonstrated this for Taiwan.

The opposite of all this appears also to be true: countries which have static SME populations outside the informal sector, in which little progress is being made in restructuring, exporting, innovation and efficiency, will be stuck at a backward stage. This seems to be the case in much of Africa. Unfortunately, few LDCs have SME statistics which are sufficiently reliable or which cover a long enough time period for adequate time series analysis. Venezuela is an exception, and a fascinating study by MULHERN & STEWART (2003) charts the decline of that country's *per capita* GDP growth rate from 1.7 per cent per annum in 1960–78 to –1.9 per cent in 1979–92. They show that the share of SMEs in manufacturing employment, number of firms and value added declined throughout. Their finding was that lack of innovation and efficiency improvements explained the long-term decline in SMEs.

Constraints on SMEs in LDCs

When the institutional environment for business in LDCs is examined, it becomes clear why development is so sluggish. Indeed, the wonder is that so many people do start and grow businesses at all. It is often asserted that people in poor countries lack entrepreneurial drive and skills. Anyone travelling across Africa, however, can see signs everywhere that vast numbers of people *are* struggling to engage in business activity. Particularly for those without access to land, people have no choice but to engage in business if they are to survive. There are few big companies; many of them are state or foreign-owned, and mostly shielded by perimeter fencing. Town streets throng with itinerant traders and, where permitted, stalls and kiosks. On the edges of towns, in homes and on industrial estates, on back lots and rural roadsides, are many thousands of small enterprises making and repairing things. Supplies of materials are hard to get and afford, but use is made of recycled materials – sandals are made out of car tyres, teapots and kettles out of petrol cans. Some enterprises are using more advanced tools and equipment – furniture being made on foot-treadle or electrically-powered routers, replacement parts for vehicles on lathes; casting door and window-fittings, even a mini re-rolling mill.[27] De SOTO (1989) paints a similar picture for Peru, with a special emphasis on the role of (illegal) SME transport undertakings.

Farther out from a typical African town are farmers and subsistence enterprises and everywhere fruit stalls, small bars, cafes, hairdressers and other activities housed in little buildings made from corrugated iron or packing cases. There are markets, not only for food and handicrafts but also more specialised activities such as trading in used clothing, some of which may be imported. Apart from climatic differences and obvious twentieth-century intrusions such as vehicles and telecommunications services run by owners of mobile telephones, the small business scene must be very similar to what it was in parts of Europe in the eighteenth and early nineteenth century.

It is easy, looking at small enterprise in LDCs, to draw the superficial conclusion that all the business-owners need is access to funds to buy materials and equipment, and more knowledge. This conclusion might be right; but behind these obvious constraints lies a mass of institutional factors that prevent a transition to formalisation. The little workshops and retail outlets do represent savings but are often built on communal land which, although it may be conferred to the owners in reasonable permanence, is without legal title – or, worse, simply occupied in shanty towns in defiance of laws. This means that property cannot be used as collateral for bank borrowing. Informal sources of finance are underdeveloped and usually constrained by harsh laws that drive moneylenders underground and force up already exorbitant interest rates.[28] People do not want to borrow much from banks anyway, because even formal sector interest rates net of inflation are typically very high (10 per cent or more) and even when they do, monopolistic banking systems with few branches outside large towns make it very difficult. Nor do people want to make money savings when funds can be invested in trading activities (or animals, which are reproducible assets) giving a better return. The finance constraints on SMEs in LDCs are different in character from those in developed countries; though in themselves they are not, as is often asserted, the main obstacle for development.

A small-business-owner in the informal sector contemplating formalis-ation, even where that is a realistic possibility thanks to rapid expansion of business and its prospects, has other problems to face: the inevitability of high tax rates and greatly increased regulatory compliance costs. Registration and licensing, for example, are slow and costly, and getting public permissions through in reasonable time will probably involve the payment of bribes to underpaid officials. The legal enforcement of contracts is also likely to be prohibitively expensive because commercial justice is largely based upon European systems brought in in colonial times. All these things also deter inward investment and foreign trade.

Box 9.1 summarises some of the economic and institutional constraints that typically obstruct development in a sub-Saharan African country.

The list is not, of course, complete: for example, women, who actually play the driving role in SMEs in many African countries, face discrimination and even legal obstacles to building a business.[29] It is also important to note that many of these institutional constraints are *inter-related* and *self-reinforcing*. For example, complex and inefficiently administered regulation creates opportunities and incentives for corruption, and the influence of lack of title to land on the financing problem would not necessarily be removed if legal

Box 9.1 Constraints on enterprise development in sub-Saharan countries

Poor macro-economic environment	Instability, inflation and high real interest rates, restrictions on movements of exchange/dividends/capital
Large state sector	High cost of inputs for SMEs, restricts market opportunities, contributes to fiscal deficits
Taxation systems	High compliance burdens, e.g. delayed VAT refunds
Corruption	Payments necessary to avoid harassment and to obtain public services such as permits
Rule of law	Costly and cumbersome legal systems and prevent enforcement of contracts
Land ownership	Much land is owned by the state but vested in communal tenure and controlled by local leaders; there is no effective market in most land
Business registration and licensing	High compliance costs: slow procedures and inefficiency in inconveniently located government offices
Employment law	High compliance costs and labour inflexibility in the formal sector
Impediments to foreign trade and inward investment	Customs clearances and trade paperwork slow and costly; various restrictions on investment, including severe limitations on use of expatriate staff

title to land were more easily obtained. Although taking collateral and realising it are proper legal procedures in most African countries, in practice the courts are very reluctant to permit lenders to dispossess property owners in default, which naturally makes them reluctant to lend even against security. Moreover, there may be other obstacles to the provision of finance. In Kenya, the central bank does not allow unsecured lending to SMEs, for example, and any pledging of agricultural land requires the prior permission of the land control boards. To change one law often simply reveals that other problems remain. For example, in this case, unless there are public registers of mortgaged assets (as generally there are not in Africa) banks legitimately fear that the same asset could be pledged to more than one lender, leaving them with no security.

Most of the institutional issues in Box 9.1 are, to a diminishing extent, common to the transition countries in Europe, although Europe had considerable advantages over the African countries. The extent of communist control was such that after independence these countries had to make a fresh start and re-write their laws and regulations. Property rights were quickly restored, the democratic rule of law re-established and much of state industry privatised. Extreme poverty was less of a problem, and educational standards and infrastructure were superior. Nevertheless, authoritarian state traditions of bureaucracy proved hard to change.[30] The tax system and very high social security contribution rates in some countries (particularly, for example, Russia), still reflect elements of communist values such as discrimination against wage flexibility and trading activities. The banking system and capital markets remain very backward compared with EU standards (HAINZ 2003). The informal sector often tends to take the form of underreporting of sales for tax purposes rather than outright avoidance, though in the most backward countries in particular that remains a major problem, as does corruption.[31] There are also considerable differences between the countries of transitional Europe – with some, like Hungary and Poland, rapidly approaching advanced country standards and others, such as Belarus and Uzbekistan, with a long way to go.

Removing constraints

Government policy

If the view that institutional factors are impeding development is right, and we believe that these factors are at least a large part of the story, then the direction of policy should be fairly clear. All of the constraints on business in African countries in Box 9.1 appear to be within the power of national governments to change. In fact, most of these constraints are now on the agenda in African countries and elsewhere.

Macroeconomic policies have improved, as they have in the West. This is partly pure economics, but mainly a question of fiscal discipline by government and the granting of a measure of independence to central banks to pursue appropriate monetary policies. Privatisation of state enterprises helps to curb government deficits (in LDCs, state industries often operate at a loss or need bailing out from time to time). Provided there is some re-regulation to ensure competition, then privatisation can help to reduce input costs of SMEs (in transport, energy and telecommunications, for example). It is also observable, in the West and LDCs alike, that privatisation, in increasing pressures for efficiency, results in a much greater degree of subcontracting, which also creates opportunities for SMEs. Privatisation is difficult to carry out: there was little choice in the former command economies, but in Africa vested interests have slowed change. It is important to point out that selling off or giving away state enterprises is not a first step. Carried out too early, it can lead to the creation of elites and compound lack of competition unless prior steps are taken to ensure the workings of markets in a general sense.

The removal or easement of the other constraints present all kinds of difficulty. Not least is the fact that LDC governments lack the skilled manpower and technical capacity to engage in thoroughgoing reform. Everything seems to be in need of change, and controversial reforms have to be studied, laws changed and implemented properly: ill-considered change can make things worse. It is not enough to change laws; the public admin-istrative machine has to be reformed and motivated, right down to the local authority and street enforcement level. Corruption cannot be eliminated until regulation has become simpler and more transparent. The ideal is that bribes should be converted into taxation, leaving firms better off – or, at least, no worse off – but it takes time. In Africa, in particular, neither direct nor indirect taxes can easily be introduced in the informal sector, even in a graduated way. So few businesses keep any sort of accounts: instead, recourse has to be made to lump-sum taxes that are costly to administer and require a registration system; some reduction in bribe-taking, and some reform in civil service pay scales is necessary.[32] Unfortunately, most sub-Saharan African countries introduced VAT in their formal sectors in the 1990s.[33] It seems that IMF economists, enamoured of the theoretical neutrality and enforcement qualities of such taxes, advocated VAT as a plank for much-needed fiscal reform. However, VAT, in its European form particularly, is not a suitable tax for LDCs, or even transition countries. As explained in Chapter 5, the heavy compliance costs of VAT require scarce book-keeping skills, bear heavily on SMEs and in practice encourage outright evasion.

Re-establishing the rule of law and making commercial law more easily accessible in the enforcement of contracts takes time and requires some prior legal reforms. Alternative dispute resolution systems, effectively arbitration, can help, but are difficult if not impossible to make viable on a paying basis (there is a role for donors here). The reform of employment legislation to reduce compliance costs, if not its adverse effects on labour flexibility, is a political minefield. In Africa, even though employment law effectively protects only a small minority of the labour force, attempts at reform have so far been defeated in most countries. In Africa and in most European transition countries, employment law is generally even more onerous to employers than in the European Union, where it is also on the agenda for reform.

Progress is being made in some countries in improving the efficiency of customs offices, business registration and licensing systems, and other public services. What is being learned is that not only can compliance costs for business be lowered by reform, but government collection costs can also be reduced and revenue enhanced. Mozambique, with donor assistance, adopted a radical approach to customs systems reform: it hired Crown Agents, a privatised UK agency, to operate the system, with an immediate 40 per cent increase in revenue and greatly reduced delays. Other examples of the impact of donor assistance in reforming institutions are given below.

Land use and ownership is at the very root of society, and reform here is the most contentious and difficult of all. In much of sub-Saharan Africa, as already mentioned, land is basically owned by the state but vested in communal tenure with control by traditional local leaders. Individual land use is not centrally registered and legal title cannot therefore be established. Only in South Africa is the principle of ownership protected by the constitution, although even there, land tenure in the former Bantustans is still under the control of local leaders. Land ownership issues are very complex. In Malawi, much land is not registered and foreigners are not allowed to own land at all. In Zambia, the state does grant 99–year leases but until recently land was deemed to have no value in law (BANNOCK *et al.* 2002). In much of Latin America the situation seems to be broadly similar (DE SOTO 1989). The European countries in transition were in a similar position under communist rule, where by law there was no private ownership except, in some cases, for residential purposes. There have been many problems with this, as in East Germany where previously dispossessed persons emerged to reclaim ownership. In the countries of Central Europe, pre-war civil codes and land registries could be, and were, re-introduced. Land ownership in these countries is no longer regarded as a constraint on development; the concern rather is that richer foreigners will come in and acquire what is, for them, cheap property.

In his two important and influential books, Hernando de Soto (1989, 2000) recounts how the now advanced countries had to reform their legal systems and regulations as a precondition for development. This meant breaking down authoritarian 'mercantilist' institutions such as craft guilds, which gradually retreated into towns before an influx of informals from the countryside and abroad, as well as the establishment of modern property rights.[34] He argues that people in the informal sector in LDCs are not culturally predisposed to work outside the law, as is shown by their own extra-legal systems and their successful efforts to produce and consume in an honest way. These informals are forced to operate outside the legal system because that system is not adjusted to reality. It is not that inhabitants of LDCs are incapable of saving, investment, exchange, specialisation and technical progress – it is because bad laws prevent them from doing so (DE SOTO 1989).[35]

In the absence of any better evidence, we take the level of regulatory compliance costs to be at least a partial indicator of the extent of institutional barriers to development. These costs are very high in relation to income levels in Africa and seem to be lower in countries that have made more economic progress, as shown above in Chart 9.1. World Bank cross-section studies also bear out these relationships. Certainly, rapid progress in China (MADDISON 1998), Central and Eastern Europe, and also now in India, reflect the liberalisation of economic controls.

One study, carried out for the UK Department for International Development (DFID), compared progress in institutional reform in seven sub-Saharan African countries and three Central European countries over the period 1995–9 (BANNOCK *et al.* 2002).[36] It may seem strange to compare Africa and Central Europe, but despite the obvious differences there are similarities in the need for, and progress towards, institutional reform in the two areas . Major political and economic change took place in Africa from the 1960s as these countries achieved independence, but it was not until the early to mid-1990s that post-independence, unrepresentative and interventionist governments evolved into multi-party democratic systems. Central Europe achieved independence from communist regimes (around 1990) but, as in Africa, the transition proved painful. It was not until the mid-1990s that both areas were in a position to lay the foundations for real democratic market development. The Central European countries had many advantages, notably the ability to restore and modernise pre-war institutions, and they also moved more quickly and decisively than their African counterparts. Across the sample of 10 countries there was a fairly clear relationship between the pace and degree of institutional reforms undertaken and the pace of *per capita* income growth. The three Central European countries, which had carried out most reforms, came out best, followed by Uganda and Ghana, where there were more reforms than elsewhere in Africa, and well ahead of Zambia and Kenya, where the number of reforms was least.[37]

The role of governments and donors

Bernie Cornfeld used to market his mutual funds under the rubric: 'Do you *sincerely* want to be rich?' This message is equally relevant to the governments of LDCs and the advanced countries who want to help them: it is not enough to will the ends, you also have to will the means. The recipe for sustainable development, we now know, is not planning or massive investment, or even education, though all these things can be helpful – it is simply to set people free to better their own condition. Of course, most governments in LDCs are now trying to do this and donors are trying to help them, but it is difficult and many vested interests lie in the way. There is a widespread misconception that the problems of development are technical in nature, whereas in fact they are political. The now advanced countries somehow (always painfully, and over a long period) achieved the necessary reforms to allow people to focus their energies on creating new wealth rather than in rent-seeking – getting a share of the wealth that is already available. LDCs have to do the same, and this means de-politicising economic activity through strong, stable government that furthers the institutions that will promote private effort: essentially dealing with the issues illustrated (though it is not a complete list) in Box 9.1.

If the institutional setting is right, then SMEs – an important part of the process of development, though not the whole – will thrive.[38] LDCs have similar, if simpler, SME policy instruments to those of the advanced countries described in Chapters 7 and 8, which are subject to the same irrelevancies and weaknesses. The assumption is that because the advanced countries use these instruments they have contributed to the success of those countries and thus must be transferred to LDCs. Because access to finance *is* a problem for SMEs in LDCs (whereas on the whole we assert that it is not, in the developed countries), there has been a particular focus on the creation of state-owned credit and venture capital institutions and upon credit guarantees and other devices. More attention has been paid to these things than to the root causes of SME finance problems, which include lack of competition in banking systems, problems with collateral, overregulation (and often underregulation) of micro-finance institutions, lack of mortgage registers[39] and the sheer inability of firms in the informal sector to generate sufficient earnings for reinvestment. Instruments that are merely minor supplements to a sophisticated financial infrastructure in developed countries are expected in LDCs to bear the whole weight of the deficiency in the business environment – and predictably fail to do so.[40]

Fortunately, the international aid community, as noted in Chapter 8, is now beginning to turn its back on the transference to LDCs of SME policy approaches from the West and instead focus upon the real underlying institutional problems. Although there may be one or two minor exceptions, the massive amounts of aid applied to LDCs since the Second World War have had no measurable impact on development.[41] Despite increasing aid to Africa, for example, the problems there remain intractable. While earlier there was a lot of aid for East Asia (often for political reasons), there is little evidence that it was in any way responsible for the 'East Asian Miracle', though it probably helped in the cases of Korea and Taiwan. Similarly, quickening progress in China and India apparently owes nothing to foreign aid. Basically, countries have to help themselves. Peter Bauer argued that aid is counter-productive because 'Official transfers enhance the hold of governments over their subjects, and promote the politicisation of life'; in other words, it encourages rent-seeking as well as biasing development policy towards unsuitable external models (BAUER 1984).

Donors can help in providing technical assistance for institutional reform, however. As already mentioned, the limited capacity of LDC governments to analyse and reform domestic legislation of the kind covered in Box 9.1 is a major constraint, particularly since a knowledge of what works and does not work in other countries is so valuable. DFID has, for example, provided help to Kenya and Uganda in such matters, and this has had a measurable effect. Both relate to the reform of business registration and licensing systems. In Africa, and indeed in much of transitional Europe, business registration systems are slow, costly and cumbersome. Before she can register a business, the entrepreneur may have to produce documents proving that past taxes have been paid, premises have been approved, separate special permits have been obtained where necessary for a whole range of traders and so on. Typically, the entrepreneur will have to visit several government office, sometimes at a considerable distance and with a long wait in each, and possibly also receive prior inspections from one or more officials. Streamlining of these systems, including a separation of inspection and licensing, has made possible major reductions in compliance costs as well as improved compliance (more businesses register when it is made easier for them to do so). These advances are not only important for the direct savings in time they make for business people, but also for the reduction in opportunities for corruption which result from simpler systems. They also have a valuable 'demonstration effect' in that they can help convince authorities that deregulation does not result in chaos and that there are benefits to the government administration as well as to business.

Assistance for regulatory reform can be productive only if the political will is there to implement change. This will is often not there or is heavily qualified by fears that deregulation will harm the poor (as macroeconomic deregulation, in removing price controls, frequently has in the short term) or that powerful interests will resist – or alternatively unduly benefit from – the change (as in privatisation). For these reasons it is not enough to provide purely technical help – for example, to review legislation – but to assist in advocacy for change: explaining the potential benefits, devising means to ensure that losers get some compensating benefits, for example. It is best to start the process of reform by offering help with less contentious matters (such as business registration) where quick results are possible, rather than the more difficult issues such as land reform or employment law.[42] Help with advocacy, as well as giving necessary support for the business groups who have the ultimate responsibility for advocacy, can come close to interfering with the domestic affairs of the host country, but as long as donors make clear that they are merely there to help in what must be domestic decisions, this need not be a problem. In theory, the ultimate objective must be to assist and encourage LDCs to carry out all this work themselves, but this, too, is difficult to achieve, for a variety of reasons.

However difficult the process of reform, there is no real alternative. The LDCs can never develop until the energies of the majority of the population trapped in the informal sector can be released for development. This will not happen without thoroughgoing reform. Although the advanced countries, for the time being, at any rate, can afford high regulatory costs, the poor cannot. In fact one of the problems is that the LDCs are trying to develop with a burden of regulation vastly higher than that which the now advanced countries supported when they industrialised. As mentioned in Chapter 5, in Britain it was not until 1809 that the Factory Acts excluded children under the age of nine from working specifically only in cotton mills, and not until the 1844 Act that working hours for children aged 9–13 were limited to six-and-a-half hours a day (these laws did not apply to SMEs). By 1820, in terms of GDP *per capita*, Britain and the Netherlands had become the richest countries in the world, more than four times African levels at the time (Britain is now 12 times higher). By 1913, the United States had overtaken Britain to become the most powerful economy in the world, but there was no child labour legislation covering the whole country until the 1930s, nor were minimum wage laws introduced until 1938.[43] While the regulation of juvenile labour, which does occur extensively in LDCs (though in micro-enterprises often in a familial context) is hardly a felicitous example, extreme poverty can be worse and there are dangers in using this and other issues such as adult labour and environmental standards as an excuse for shutting out imports from LDCs. These things should be matters for the people in developing countries to decide for themselves.[44]

Notes

1 'Developing countries' is a euphemism for 'poor countries', which effectively are market economies that have not yet reached the stage of growth of industrial-isation. There are several variants of the term – less developed countries, or least developed countries (LDCs); Third World; non-OECD countries, etc. – but precise definitions are elusive and, for our purposes, unnecessary. The World Bank estimates that of a world population of 6 billion (1999), 40 per cent have incomes (GNP per head) of under $755 per annum and only 15 per cent have incomes of more than $9,266 per annum. 'Countries in transition', as in Eastern and Central Europe and China, are countries moving from planned (commu-nist) to market economies; while 'Newly Industrialised Countries' (NICs) are countries which are industrialising but have not yet reached advanced country status (though some of them now have *per capita* incomes similar to OECD countries) (IBRD 2001c).
2 Between 1965 and 1999, GDP *per capita* in sub-Saharan Africa fell by 0.2 per cent per annum. In 1999 the infant mortality rate was 92 per 1,000 live births, compared with 5 per 1,000 in the European Union (IBRD 2001c).
3 Whether or not convergence has been taking place is controversial and depends upon the countries included, the time period taken and how convergence is defined. According to Angus Maddison, 'Explaining the economic performance of nations', in BAUMOL *et al.* (1994), the capitalist core countries (European Union, United States, Canada and Australia) among a total sample of 43 have

had the highest incomes and fastest long-term growth between 1820 and 1989, and inter-group convergence increased over the period. Performance in Asia was very heterogeneous, with high-income spreads in recent times, but Asia overtook Latin America over the period, while Africa had the lowest incomes and growth and also high income spreads (though much lower than Asia).

4 See Guillén (2001) for a lucid and up-to-date survey of theories of development and globalisation, which also covers the work of such writers as Rostow, Prebisch and Gerschenkron, which we do not discuss here.

5 In the early 1970s, the Club of Rome Report brought back notions of limits to growth in the form of resource constraints. More recently still, environmental constraints are believed by some to place new limits on growth. Others believe that the price mechanism and technological development can remove these constraints as they have, at least so far, abated the threat of oil shortages which first loomed in the early 1970s. We have given a very truncated account of the evolution of theories of economic growth. For further references see textbooks on economics, for example SAMUELSON & NORDHOUSE (2001).

6 In the 1960s, DENISON (1967) and others were able to disaggregate the elements of growth so that after allowing for changes in inputs of labour and capital it could be seen that there was a large residual. This residual could be explained only by advances in knowledge and other sources of growth in total factor productivity (TFP).

7 The classical economists were well aware of the value of property rights and the rule of law for economic advance. Adam Smith, for example, wrote: 'The acquisition of valuable and extensive property, therefore, necessarily requires the establishment of civil government' (SMITH 1776).

8 *The Shorter Oxford English Dictionary* (1968 edition) gives no less than seven definitions of 'Institution', of which the most relevant for our purpose is 'An established law, custom, usage, practice, organisation or other element in the political or social life of a people'. 'Culture' has five definitions, of which 'The training of mind, tastes and manners . . . the intellectual side of civilisation' seems most appropriate. In the economic context, NORTH (1981) has the following definition: 'Institutions are a set of rules, compliance procedures and moral and ethical behavioral norms designed to constrain the behaviour of individuals in the interests of maximising the wealth or utility of principals.' The rules governing the relationship between lords and serfs in the medieval manor system, and contemporary regulation of business, are both aspects of institutions.

As JONES (2003) points out, consideration of the effect of cultures on economic development now risks offending political correctness; earlier (JONES 1995) wrote that most economists think that culture has little or no significance because it adjusts to economic imperatives. Jones maintains that the persistence of French culture in Quebec and the 'messy relations between Islam and Christendom' show the importance of culture. Jones draws a distinction between institutions and culture, in that the former 'can be created or abolished by a conscious act of will; they are essentially creations of politics and power. The term 'culture' is best applied to values and patterns of customary behaviour, which at least in the short term are harder to invent, induce or abolish' (JONES 2003). MARSHALL (1890/1961), to whom Jones refers, was well aware of the importance of culture, which he referred to as 'custom'. Writing before the age of political correctness, he was able to make forthright comparisons between cultures. He pointed out that one of the characteristics of modern economic advance was a greater sympathy and correctness in dealing with strangers as distinct from neighbours or family. He wrote of this as 'a growing source of a kind of deliberate unselfishness, that never existed before the modern age'. Referring to Britain, he wrote: 'That country, which is the birthplace of competition, devotes a larger part of its income than any other to charitable uses, and spent twenty millions on purchasing the freedom of the slaves in the West Indies' (MARSHALL 1890/1961).

9 World Bank, *Global Development Finance*, 1, 2003. The numbers include net official flows in the form of 'soft' loans, grants and technical assistance from bilateral agencies (i.e. national governments) and multilateral agencies such as the World Bank and the Regional Development Banks (RDBs). Japan and the United States are the largest contributors, followed by France, Germany and the United Kingdom. However, only Denmark, the Netherlands, Norway and Sweden have met the (not universally agreed) target of 0.7 per cent of their national income.

10 The evolution of international development efforts can be traced in successive editions of the World Bank's *World Development Reports*.

11 See BAUER (1984, 1991, 2000) for convenient and very readable collections of his articles.

12 Quoted by Razeen Sally, 'Editorial: essays in the spirit of Peter Bauer', *Economic Affairs*, December 2003.

13 'Proto-industrialisation' is a term used to characterise market-oriented cottage industries in eighteenth-century Britain and other places (as distinct from craft enterprises meeting only local needs). Proto-industries developed under the 'putting-out system' in which merchants contracted with people in rural areas to make goods such as textiles at home, providing them with a market and often (as in the case of textiles) with the necessary materials. Whether this form of SME activity in some way triggered the growth of the factory system is a matter of controversy (see MATHIAS & DAVIS 1989).

14 Cross-section studies analyse the characteristics of a 'population' (in this case of countries) at a single point in time, as distinct from time-series analysis, which compares changes between successive points in time.

15 THOMAS (1992) takes a broad view of informality, which helps to get this phenomenon into perspective. His definition of 'informality' is that it covers economic activity not recorded in national accounts. He distinguishes between: (i) the *household sector*, such as the unpaid work of housewives; (ii) the *informal sector*, with which we are principally concerned here; (iii) the *irregular sector*, which covers legal activity that is not declared to tax authorities (such as cash payments for house decoration); and (iv) the *criminal sector*. All but (i) involve market transactions, while (iii) and (iv) involve illegality.

16 Much of this regulation, for example employment law, is copied from developed countries and its severity enhanced in many cases. For example Ethiopia, one of the poorest countries in the world, has the most generous paid-vacation allowance of any country, at 39 working days a year (World Bank 2004). Of course, employment laws are usually only enforced in the formal sector and benefit only better-paid workers; those in the informal sector get little or no protection. In former colonies, and particularly in former British, French and Portuguese territories in Africa, much business regulation is based on laws established by the mother countries many years ago, including laws intended to exclude indigenous people from certain business activities. It is interesting that some of these laws have not been modified following independence, the most likely explanation for this being that they are as useful to new indigenous vested interests as they were to the colonialists.

17 These studies are being extended in ingenious ways to cover more and more measurable institutional elements. DJANKOV *et al.* (2003) see institutional issues as a trade-off between dictatorship and disorder, and emphasise that what counts is the effectiveness of institutions: 'economic and social change in each country should be considered in the light of its own institutional possibilities'.

Thus the 'big bang' theory of allowing markets to work in transition countries did not work as well in Russia, where it resulted in disorder, as it did in some Eastern European countries that had been under dictatorship for a shorter period and had in many respects more effective institutions.

18 Tambunan recognised that the persistence of industrial clusters of SMEs and flexible specialisation muddies the clarity of these conclusions. See PIORE & SABEL (1984) and our discussion in Chapters 7 and 10.

19 By 'use of marginal resources', we refer to the way SMEs make use of redundant buildings, untrained labour and the ways in which they recycle machinery and other physical assets where, as is so often the case, they cannot afford the best.

20 Even in advanced countries, about 70 per cent of the sources of funds of industrial and commercial companies come from internal sources (even more for SMEs). This is sometimes taken as a criticism of the efficiency of capital markets in allocating resources; but in fact, out of prudence, firms cannot become overdependent on outside finance even where it is available. Nicholas KALDOR (1996), for example, asserted: 'contrary to the conventional view of economists (though significantly, *not* that of businessmen), internal and external sources of finance are *complementary* to each other, and not substitutes; to be in a "safe" position, the entrepreneurs' own capital and reserves must grow at the same rate as the scale of operation of the business' (emphasis in the original).

21 In the European transition countries, firm-size structures are rapidly moving towards EU patterns. For example in Poland, 67 per cent of private sector employment is in enterprises with fewer than 250 employees (in the United Kingdom, 65 per cent) (*Report on the Condition of Small and Medium-sized Enterprise Sector in Poland in the years 2000–2001*, Polish Agency for Enterprise Development (PAED), 2002). Statistics for some Central and Eastern European (CEE) countries are very detailed, but these countries have problems with the accuracy of their registers (which do not adequately remove closed enterprises) and are suspect. The Polish Agency, for example, estimates that 15 per cent of all employees (almost 750,000) worked in the 'grey economy'.

22 The GEMINI data in LIEDHOLM & MEAD (1993) indicate that on average, only 20 per cent of the MSE labour force are hired workers compared with 71 per cent for the United Kingdom (we calculate from SBS data).

23 In World Bank terminology, which we follow here, East Asia and Pacific includes China (with Hong Kong but apparently not Taiwan, the Republic of China, which is not recognised as having a separate existence), Thailand, Malaysia, Indonesia, Vietnam, Korea (North and South) and quite a few other countries. Singapore is included in 'other high income'. Between 1965 and 1999, GDP *per capita* grew at 5.6 per cent per annum in East Asia (6.4 per cent in China and 6.3 per cent in Singapore), compared with 2.4 per cent for OECD countries, 1.4 per cent in Latin America and –0.2 per cent in sub-Saharan Africa.

24 The Korean data relate to establishments, not enterprises, and cover firms of 5–300 employees (5–200 before 1973). There were changes in government policies towards small firms over the period (SMEs were 'neglected' in the 1960s) but the study by Nugent and Yhee does not give the impression that government policy made a great deal of difference. GUILLEN (2001) takes a similar view.

25 TFP is the residual in a calculation of the difference between changes in inputs of labour and capital (including human capital), and output. Where growth cannot be fully explained in this way by changes in inputs, the residual is a measure of the efficiency with which the inputs have been employed. This residual will be the result of improvements in technology and organisation. Since there is no common denominator by which labour and capital can be combined in a TFP calculation, it is assumed that the ratios of the two do not change over

the period of the analysis (that is, production functions are fixed). This is a weakness of TFP calculations because changes in organisation and technology can and do lead to changes in factor proportions. The calculations therefore assume away some of the very things which play such an important role in economic development. An article by KRUGMAN (1994), based on work by Lawrence Lau and Alwyn Young of Stanford and Boston universities, respectively, challenged the widespread belief that the growth of East Asian economies was a 'miracle'. Krugman argued that since TFP was not increasing, the growth of the East Asian economies was simply the result of the mobilisation of inputs, not improved efficiency, and would eventually cease, as in the earlier case of the Soviet Union (KRUGMAN 1999). (In fact, growth did cease with the financial crisis of 1997, but has subsequently resumed.) Krugman's findings are controversial. Bart van Ark and Marcel P. Timmer, 'Realising growth potential: South Korea and Taiwan, 1960 to 1998', in MADDISON *et al.* (2002), did find significant TFP growth in Taiwan and Korea and concluded that Krugman's conclusion that growth in these countries would be subject to diminishing returns (referred to below) was 'highly doubtful'. We doubt that it is a coincidence that TFP growth was much greater in Taiwan, where SMEs played a larger role, than in Korea, where they played a smaller one.

26 As Nelson & Pack say, technology transfer is not just a simple matter of getting access to blueprints. Much of the necessary knowledge to implement the technologies is not codified; it has to be learned by trial and error and adapted to local circumstances, and this is done in firms (including SMEs). Also, given the financial constraints on SMEs, they have to find ways of investing out of retained earnings from profits, a double trick to master. See CARREE (2002) for an empirical study on Taiwan.

27 For an illustrated account of the Jua Kali informal industry in Kenya, see KING (1996). 'Jua Kali' means 'hot sun' and brings out the fact that many of these workers lack premises.

28 In South Africa in 1992, raising the exemption for micro-lenders under the 1968 Usury Act to a higher (but still very low) level led to an enormous increase in the number of operators, indicating a large pent-up demand for and potential supply of finance. The so-called 'Grameen Bank' system of peer-group saving and lending in Indonesia and Pakistan has shown that poor people can reliably save and borrow.

29 In Lesotho, married women may not enter into contracts, including borrowing money, without the permission of their spouse. (The government has stated that this will be subject to legislative change.)

30 In its *Transition Report 2002*, the European Bank for Reconstruction and Development (EBRD) gives figures for the 'bribe tax' of dealing with officials and regulation as 5.9 per cent of available working time for Central and Eastern Europe and the Baltic (CEB) for a small new private company, and 8.7 per cent in south-eastern Europe (SEE).

31 EBRD's figures for the 'bribe tax' as a percentage of sales for a small company were 1.2 per cent for CEB and 2.2 per cent for SEE in 2002, both sharply down compared with 2001. The percentage of sales reported for tax purposes was 85.5 and 71.3 per cent, respectively.

32 Poorly paid as they are, it is said that most civil servants in many African countries have up to 20 dependants. 'Tax farming', in which local authorities are allowed to retain a proportion of central government tax revenue, is being experimented with in some countries – an interesting throwback to the private tax farming system of early modern Europe.

33 Perforce, the European transition countries, particularly those preparing for EU entry, have done likewise.

34 'Mercantilist' is the word de Soto uses. It refers to an economic philosophy of the sixteenth and seventeenth centuries in Europe, which emphasised the importance of state power over individuals and the maximisation of export surpluses. Rightly criticised by Adam SMITH (1776) as an impediment to economic progress, mercantilism nevertheless did, by strengthening state power in national economies, lay the foundations for the liberal policies that later swept away authoritarian restrictions.

35 De Soto's thinking has much in common with that of Peter Bauer, who preceded him, though they do not agree about everything – the role of culture, for example. Neither has yet been fully assimilated into development orthodoxy. Both were deeply influenced by detailed empirical work they carried out on the ground. Bauer's early studies included the rubber industry in south-east Asia and trade in West Africa, and de Soto studied the informal sector in his native Peru.

36 The 10 countries were: Ghana, Kenya, Malawi, South Africa, Tanzania, Uganda, Zambia; Hungary, Latvia and Poland. Initiatives to establish machinery and measures to tackle most of the issues in Box 9.1 were recorded, with dates, and compared with the rates of change in income *per capita* over the period.

37 Given the small number of years in the analysis, and the fact that many factors, including regional effects and commodity prices, affect economic growth, the statistical relationship between policy reforms and income *per capita* was remarkably robust (an R^2 of 0.71 significant at the 1 per cent level with a P-value of 0.004). South Africa did worse than its policy and institutional mix would predict, probably because of the disruption following the end of Apartheid in 1994. South Africa is, in any event, very different in many respects from the other sub-Saharan countries included in the analysis: it is, for example, very much less dependent upon agriculture and has a large manufacturing sector.

38 It is worth emphasising that we are not suggesting that SMEs are the whole solution to the development problem, but this book is about SMEs. Many other factors are important, one of which is access to export markets. All the industrialised countries protected their industries at various stages of their development (for example, the United Kingdom, the United States and Japan) and continue to discriminate against imports from LDCs, especially of agricultural products. LDCs are enjoined to open up their markets, but given the historical role of exports in development it would be better to give LDCs more access for their exports than to grant them aid ('Trade not Aid'). FDI in LDCs, which is about three times the value of aid, can also be helpful; some LDCs, seeing it as a form of neo-colonialism, are ambiguous in their attitudes towards FDI, though this is changing – most LDCs now welcome FDI and have set up organisations to attract it.

39 LOVE & MYLENKO (2003) found that the existence of private credit registers was associated with lower financing constraints and a higher share of bank financing.

40 Financial instruments in LDCs are generally poorly designed and administered: lossmaking state banks with inadequate credit assessment or control procedures, or credit guarantee schemes which guarantee too large a proportion of the loans they cover so that the lending banks have insufficient incentives to avoid moral hazard, are typical examples. Most of these institutions, and other SME policy instruments, are funded by well-meaning donors and NGOs.

41 ERIXON (2003) cites academic studies which have shown that aid has not had any significant effect on investment in physical capital (governments seem to lower their own investment in favour of consumption).

42 Regretfully, in general the more difficult and contentious the reform, the more likely it is to make a difference. What is easy to do may not help a great deal but

it can give confidence in the process of reform. Change is not made 'once and for all', it needs to be a continual battle – witness the problems the developed countries have had in their own reforms (Chapter 5).

43 The income comparisons in this paragraph are based on MADDISON (2001).

44 According to a letter from Professor Ira Sohn to the *Financial Times* (10 February 2004), the EU trade commissioner is studying proposals that would 'ban imports from countries that did not share [government's] national values and standards'.

10 The big picture

Major themes

Members of the public who patronise small firms when they call their insurance broker, collect dry cleaning or seek the help of a computer consultant and buy a manufactured product through the mail, rarely pause to think about the abstractions examined in this book. Small firms are just there as part of life – as, indeed, are the big firms that assemble aircraft, supply soft drinks or manage multiple retailers. Small businesses are visible on the high street and at the roadside, but they are not all exposed to contact with the public at large: many supply only other firms, and even more are home-based.

Does it really matter how many small or big firms there are, how many they employ and what their relative roles are in our standards of living and the prospects for economic advance? Yes, it does matter, because everyone is interested in standards of living and their prospects for the future, as well as in other things upon which small firms have a bearing, including the dispersal of economic power, opportunities for individual employment and self-expression and variety in life.

Many of the findings of this book are at variance with what GALBRAITH (1967), in his memorable phrase, called 'the conventional wisdom'. In particular, our findings contradict the still pervasive notion that SMEs everywhere form a backward sector in a modern economy upon which they are a drag and from which they need help to catch up. The interesting thing is that most of our findings are well supported by academic research. One of the objectives of this book is to bring together the results of the latest research in the hope that the conventional wisdom can be altered. Of course, not all scholars will agree with everything that is said here; some aspects of the SME scene remain controversial.

In this final chapter, we begin by summarising the major themes of the book. We then go on to discuss what more might be done to deal with the issue of regulation, and conclude with some remarks about the future of small firms.

In Chapter 1, we defined 'small business' as including owner-managed firms in all sectors of the economy with, for statistical purposes, between

0 and 250 employees. We acknowledged that the cut-off point was arbitrary, but explained that this did not matter much: in the United Kingdom, 99.1 per cent employ fewer than 50 people and 99.8 per cent employ fewer than 250. When measured by share of employment, the cut-off does make a difference: those that employ less than 50 people account for only 35.9 per cent of private sector employment, and those with less than 250 for 55.4 per cent. These kinds of numbers are fairly typical of the advanced countries, but SME statistics always have to be treated with caution: many countries omit small firms in agriculture; figures for the United States and Japan leave out the self-employed without employees; and there are other possible complications.

Chapter 2 emphasised the wide variety of SMEs but found that the prime motivation for most of them is not making money but independence and self-expression. On average, the returns SME owners earn are similar to those in large firms, despite the greater risks these owners bear. Employees in SMEs, on average, do earn less than those in large firms. This is not because they are being exploited; owner-managers do not seem to make more than they could earn in a large firm and, when they do, their employees share in their good fortune. This 'dual economy' aspect of small-large firm comparisons can probably be explained by the greater capital intensity of large firms, and perhaps by their greater market power; there is no evidence that large firms are more efficient in their overall use of resources.

Chapter 3 argued that SMEs complement large firms and perform an indispensable role in the economy and in economic development. The tendency for the numerical predominance of SMEs (and their share in employment) to decline somewhat as countries get richer does not alter this. It used to be thought that lack of access to economies of scale would lead to the eventual eclipse of SMEs. Their persistence in modern economies, however, shows that the reality is more complex. SMEs persist because they perform different roles from large firms, and often do not compete directly with them. Even today, SMEs remain very prominent in innovation, in exporting in the globalised economy and in making use of physical and human resources which are unsuitable for use by large enterprises. A few growth-SMEs regularly emerge to challenge larger incumbents, and in doing so contribute additionally to the flexibility and dynamism of economies. The *role of SMEs in development* is the first of the five major themes of the book.

Chapters 4 and 5 introduce the second major theme, which is that the main constraints on SMEs and their role in economies are not lack of production economies of scale, management skills or even access to finance, as is generally believed, but the *continued rise of the regulatory State*. Increasingly, governments are imposing regulatory requirements on business which bear more heavily on small than on large firms. Dealing with these requirements is subject to economies of scale to which SMEs do not have access, and as a result their role in the economy is being distorted away from the market optimum.

Chapter 6 probes more deeply into the very different nature of *management* in small firms, which are not simply scaled-down large firms – a third major theme. This helps to explain why the systems imposed by regulation are so intrusive and damaging to the way small enterprises function. This chapter does nevertheless raise the possibility that there are constraints in the provision of finance for innovative small enterprises; constraints which are more severe in Europe than in the United States.

All governments recognise the importance of SMEs and wish to promote them. Chapters 7 and 8 review the remarkably similar SME policies pursued by governments, and find these wanting. Most *instruments used by governments to promote SMEs* fail to achieve their objectives, or have only a very minor impact: our fourth major theme. Policies are mostly at variance with the analysis of the nature of SME constraints made earlier in the book, and with the expressed preferences of owner-managers. While the regulatory problem is now being recognised by governments, the measures taken to deal with it have also proved ineffective.

Chapter 9 deals with the urgent issue of economic development in the Third World and transition countries. This chapter confronts the increasingly recognised importance of the issues of *governance and institutions* that are holding back development, our fifth major theme. What is holding up private sector wealth creation in these countries is not lack of money, or entrepreneurial talent, or infrastructure, but simply that the mass of the populations have so little scope to better themselves by their own efforts. Perhaps surprisingly, private enterprise in the developing countries suffers even more from overregulation (in relative terms) than the West, without having the well-defined property rights, other institutions and stable governments which in the past have made development possible in the now advanced countries. Breaking out of underdevelopment is possible, as has been shown in South East Asia and is beginning in China (anomalously perhaps), India and elsewhere. In all these cases SMEs have played a major part, as they did earlier in Japan and earlier still in Europe and the United States.

Controlling regulatory compliance costs

As concluded in Chapter 7, governments need to accept the existence of limits on the extent to which selective micro-policy instruments can favourably affect the small business sector. Instead, they should focus on macro-measures that affect all businesses and which will then inevitably benefit small firms most. Of these measures, a reduction in the burden of regulation and the discriminating effects of taxation should be the prime targets. This is, of course, easier said than done because attempts to deal with either regulation or taxation unleash powerful opposition.

There are no grounds for thinking that pressures for more regulation will abate. The only solution we can see is that a price has to be put on it. The present system, under which existing regulations are rarely modified and new ones introduced piecemeal (with the costs initially borne by business and then wholly or mainly passed on to consumers in a diffused, unseen and unappreciated way) is a recipe for an unending increase in business costs which will bear down particularly on small firms. If legislatures were to agree on compliance cost budgets in advance and these budgets were allocated to ministerial departments like other forms of government expenditure, then for the first time there would be some real countervailing pressure against the growth of regulatory compliance costs. The principle would be that new compliance costs could be imposed only if they were within the budgeted limits. At first, for practical reasons, the system might be applied only to new regulatory compliance costs, but ultimately it should be extended to existing costs so that Ministers would have an incentive to find ways of reducing existing compliance costs so as to make room for new ones. The system would need to be watertight so as to cover all government agencies, not merely central government departments.

The first steps towards such a system have already been taken with the introduction of regulatory impact assessments (RIAs) in many countries. The extension of the system to existing legislation would require systematic measurement, and the techniques have already been developed in the field of taxation, as shown in Chapter 4. The United States has already tried some elements of regulatory budgeting and the problems are not insuperable.[1] It all sounds very bureaucratic, but how can you administer the government machine without bureaucratic mechanisms?

Two important questions arise. First, is such a system politically feasible? And, second, how would such a system to give greater transparency to regulatory costs impact on small firms? On political feasibility there are some grounds for optimism, though since such a system would mean curbing government freedom of action it would not be embraced without reluctance. The problem of the inflation of compliance costs resembles in a way that of price inflation, which also can allow governments to pre-empt real resources without raising taxes. In recent years many governments have ceded independent control of monetary policy to central banks, including, in Europe, the United Kingdom via the Bank of England and in the Eurozone via the European Central Bank (ECB). In the United States the Federal Reserve System is, of course, independent of political control.[2] In a way, dealing with traffic congestion is another parallel. This is a problem similar to regulatory compliance that has been growing inexorably over a long period, and in many places, congestion has now reached a point where putting a price on road use by tolls or other charges in congested areas is increasingly seen as an acceptable solution.[3]

What is politically possible varies with the scale and urgency of the problem and, as Keynes said, may be influenced by the scribblings of economists. The time when there is acceptance of a need for firmer measures to control the rise of regulatory compliance costs, or at least to make these costs more transparent, may not yet have come; but it surely will.

The second question, how budgetary control of regulatory compliance costs would benefit SMEs and their role in the economy, is easier to answer. Assuming that the system were successful, then a reduction in the rate of growth of compliance costs would disproportionately benefit SMEs since, as shown in Chapter 4, they typically account for two-thirds of these costs, vastly more than their share in private sector GDP. If it proved possible actually to reduce compliance costs, then if output prices and taxation remained unchanged, the result would be a re-injection of real resources into the small business sector. Some of the savings might 'leak' into increased leisure or consumption, but there would also be increased investment and output to the benefit of economic advance.

There would also be some reduction in government administrative costs, since a small proportion of regulatory costs is also borne by government. It should be emphasised that we are writing here only of compliance or administrative costs and not taking into account the excess burdens or efficiency costs, which also accompany regulation, as recounted in Chapter 4. It should also be emphasised that there are potential gains from making regulation more fit for their purpose – that is, making regulation more efficient, as distinct from controlling its ambitions and volume. The proposed compliance costs budgeting system would increase pressures and incentives for more efficient regulation, since under such a system savings would allow governments to respond to calls for more regulation without increasing overall burdens. This is what pricing does: it encourages the more efficient use of resources.[4]

Although reducing the growth of overall compliance costs will disproportionately benefit SMEs, it will still leave them in a relatively worse position than larger firms. This discrimination cannot be justified on either economic grounds or, arguably, in terms of social equity. The principle of progressive taxation, in theory if not always in practice, is generally accepted; should this principle not also be extended to cover the impact of compliance costs – which, like taxation, are a levy on private resources to contribute to general welfare? To introduce a progressive element into the burden of regulatory compliance costs would, in part at least, translate into direct state expenditures (negative taxes) to compensate SMEs for the relatively higher costs they bear, scaled to firm size. In principle, this could be done using information derived from the survey measurement system advocated under the proposed compliance cost budgeting arrangements. Unfortunately, the incidence of compliance costs is not a simple function of firm size (which in turn is susceptible to measurement in several different ways), but varies with activity sector and other specific characteristics of individual firms. If it were to be done it would be important to resist the temptation to come up with an accurate and fair system and settle for rough and ready allowances, segmented for a few successive stages of firm size and set well below the average measured level of compliance costs for each segment.[5] We leave it to the reader to judge whether or not the introduction of a system for compliance cost compensation is politically feasible or likely. We should guess not, at least until thinking has advanced to the point where comprehensive compliance cost budgeting has been established. It can be argued that the progressive element in many countries in corporation taxes allows some compensation for the regressivity of compliance costs, and that the extension of this principle to direct taxes might be a simpler, if politically more sensitive, way of achieving the objective.

Another question is: what can be done in developing countries about the regulatory and other institutional issues identified in Chapter 9? As argued there, these matters are not only to do with getting compliance costs down but also, and to a greater extent than in the advanced countries, with development. The essence of the problem is the same as in the West, but its resolution is more urgent and the means available to deal with it fewer. Elaborate systems for compliance cost budgeting are not feasible in most poor countries because of the paucity of administrative resources in their governments. With donor assistance, a start can be made by introducing RIAs and reviewing some of the worst instances of regulatory obstacles and costs. Useful beginnings have been made in the provision of assistance of this sort by several donors and by research on regulatory and administrative obstacles to inward investment by the World Bank, as mentioned in Chapter 9. Progress has been slow – as, indeed, it has been for similar efforts in the advanced countries – but it should gain momentum as it is seen that regulatory reform can benefit the most disadvantaged elements in society and that the worst fears of unfavourable consequences do not materialise. For that reason, it is best to begin with 'easier' problems such as licensing and business registration, where there are weaker vested interests in the way of change, rather than with more important but intractable issues such as land tenure where the problems are deeply embedded in the social fabric. Dealing with these deeper issues – indeed, the resolution of all the issues in development – requires political will. In the absence of this will, donors can do very little to help other than to exercise persuasion to convince host governments that releasing the energies of their own people for productive purposes is the only path to take. The moral authority of donors to give such advice would be enhanced if there were evidence that the problem was being tackled more firmly in the advanced countries.

Realistic time horizons for regulatory reform in developing countries are very long, but the potential rewards are enormous and very much greater than in the advanced countries. These rewards will also be massively cumulative once started: for example, regulatory reform can reduce opportunities for corruption, help to transform the attractiveness of inward investment as well as releasing the better-off from rent-seeking and freeing the energies of the poor towards productive self-help. Increased wealth creation and reduction in corruption can expand the scope for raising tax revenues so as to allow governments to invest in public services and improve the institutional environment for the functioning of markets. Fundamentally, these were the elements of the process by which present-day advanced countries embarked upon the path to development. It took a very long time – research by economic historians keeps extending progress along that path backwards in time (to way before the eighteenth century) – but for many reasons contemporary progress can be faster now, as witness the relative speed of recent development in South and East Asia.

Reducing tax discrimination against SMEs

In the developed world, the promotion of SMEs requires some abatement of the discriminatory elements in taxation identified in Chapter 5. Ideally, this would result from thoroughgoing reforms to shift the base of taxation from direct taxes on income to the taxation of *expenditure* (indirect taxation). Indirect taxation has less distorting effects upon capital accumulation and investment by SME owners, as well as upon the economy at large. Radical reforms of this kind would also lead to a massive reduction in the compliance costs of taxation, which is (or was) the major source of compliance burdens on businesses. The political feasibility of such a shift – as with attempts to control compliance costs – is, of course, an issue. There are some general trends in evidence towards the simplification of the number of tax bands (though not the simplification of systems as such) and even in the reduction of direct taxes, particularly in Europe. There has also, since the 1970s, been a shift from direct to consumption taxes which, compliance cost issues aside, will have benefited SMEs. Radical reforms are, however, notoriously difficult to achieve because such reforms inevitably result in losers as well as winners; this is why the long-term pressures for more and more complexity are so strong. In the meantime, some measures can be taken to improve existing tax systems, not least by allowing businesses to shelter profits from tax while they are retained in the business for a period before they are used for business development, and by simplification within existing systems.

In developing countries the problems are different in some ways, and the challenge is to widen the tax base. In practice, two things are needed. First, burdens on SMEs have to be shifted from paying bribes to paying taxes. Second, which is part of the same process, the 'tax cliff' between the informal and formal sectors has to be converted into a climbable gradient. Improvements and simplification in the regulatory environment, by limiting the scope for corruption, can contribute to the first objective. For the second objective, tax rates need to be more progressive. This is not easily achieved, since in the informal sector basic book-keeping information is rarely available upon which to base more elaborate taxation. A partial answer here (and one which is beginning to be adopted) is to adopt forfait systems, long used in Europe, in which lump-sum taxes, varying according to business activity, are levied as part of a business licensing system.

Better regulation, not support

If action were taken on compliance costs and taxation – that is, to improve regulation – there are only a few other things that governments need to, and usefully can, do to promote SMEs. We have advanced suggestions at several points in the book. It emerged in Chapter 7 that many countries, particularly in the developing world, might usefully adopt Small Business Acts to give legal force to small business policy and improve the machinery available for small business advocacy, policy formulation and implementation. We also concluded that public purchasing is, unintentionally, yet another source of discrimination against SMEs, and one which needs attention in many countries. In Chapter 8, we argued that extensive support systems for information and advice should everywhere be curtailed and re-focused upon regulation information and referral, to avoid crowding out private sector initiatives. Attempts to force approved training activities on small firms should be abandoned. In some countries, more attention needs to be given to innovation finance and to competition policy; the latter should focus more upon removing barriers to new entrants than upon forcing large companies to change their behaviour, which can be counter-productive.

The future of small business

It is an error to assume that the structure of market economies and the technologies and modes of organisation adopted are evolving, or should evolve, towards some pre-determined state. Things are more complicated than that. The technologies and organisational forms which are most appropriate or most efficient at one stage in history seem to depend upon the state of knowledge, consumer tastes, social values and no doubt much else. They also seem to be determined for quite long periods, and in part at least, by what has gone before (*path dependence*). Technology itself, for example, is not an independent variable. It is reasonable to suppose that because large firms and government account for most of capital expenditure and R&D, that effort will concentrate upon technologies suited to large-scale organisations (Graham Bannock, 'Technology and the quality of life', in ALEXANDER 1975). Even then, however, developments by smaller enterprises can kick things in another direction. The emergence of the transistor and microchips, and later the Internet, were initiated by large organisations; but mini- and personal computers and universal software systems, and their applications to e-commerce, were pioneered by small enterprises and then taken up by large firms.[6] This is an illustration of the complementarity of small and large firms in the economic system that was emphasised in Chapter 3.

We have been careful in this book not to assert that there is any knowable optimal level of the numbers of small enterprises and their share in employment and activity. All we can say is that distortions of capital markets through the differential effects of taxation and the growth of regulatory compliance costs can be expected to move production structures away from what would obtain in an 'ideal' free-market system and depress the role of SMEs below the optimum. Although we cannot know how damaging this distortion is for efficiency and output, we can conclude, as we have, that a wise objective of policy is to attempt to minimise these distortions and keep economic systems as open as possible in respect of organisational structure.

How uncertain the future is, and yet how in some respects it can be gripped by path dependence, is a paradox of increasing interest to economists and economic historians. The fascinating work of PIORE & SABEL (1984) and their colleagues has traced the history of flexible small-scale production and mass-production as alternatives at various times and places to the present day. Recent experience, as we showed in Chapter 3, exhibits SMEs co-existing with large firms, industrial districts composed of SMEs competing with large firms operating on a quite different basis and small firms collaborating with large in the design and manufacture of specialised products and components. Motor manufacturers have experimented with the abandonment of the assembly-line, apparently flying in the face of some aspects of the Second Industrial Revolution that seemed to presage a future characterised by mass-production of standardised products. What SABEL & ZEITLIN (1997) argue is that this 'fragility and mutability' of methods of production is not new but has been the experience in many places and activities in the history of industrial capitalism. Their work deals with manufacturing, but their conclusions are equally applicable to the service sector, now the dominant part of the economy and where most SMEs are to be found.

Fifty years ago a large manufacturing company might well have bought in a lot of parts and components from smaller firms but it probably did all of its specific research (including market research), managed its own cleaning and catering facilities, maintained its own buildings and even dealt with the disposal of some its waste products. Today most of these activities, as well as newer ones such as IT, call centres or even manufacturing itself, may have been subcontracted out, much of it to SMEs and some of it to lower-labour cost countries abroad. SMEs, too, increasingly find it economic to farm out specialised administrative and other functions. Some of these functions include regulatory-intensive activities such as payroll management, a sure sign that regulatory cost pressures are acute. As another example, the intensification of financial service regulatory burdens in the United Kingdom after the 1990s has led to the emergence of 'umbrella' or 'network' organisations of small independent financial advisers that take responsibility for some of the regulatory compliance burden, as well as negotiating terms with product providers. There has also been an expansion in the number of SMEs offering advice and assistance on other aspects of regulation – for example, employment legislation and health and safety – and of course trade associations are kept busy in similar respects. Before the

Second World War, most SMEs could manage their business tax affairs themselves; today, the majority use professional accountants, the complexity of taxation having increased to the point where not to do so would result in unnecessary tax burdens or even penalties. Evidence that the market is moving to spread and reduce the costs of regulatory compliance through specialisation in these ways should help to convince sceptics that complaints about regulatory burdens reflect the incidence of real costs and not, as is sometimes suggested, merely anti-regulation – that is, 'anti-social' – sentiments.[7]

As frequently emphasised in this book, regulation is necessary for many reasons: to facilitate the workings of markets, to protect consumers and employees and to maintain health, safety and environmental standards, for example. In practice, some regulation is not enforced and there is just too much of it. Unfortunately, also, much regulation is badly designed and administered and is unnecessarily costly in compliance terms, or even counter-productive. A minor but crystal-clear example is the regulation of the taxi trade, which in many cities frustrates its own objectives of protecting consumers as well as unnecessarily burdening operators and restricting the opportunities for small firms (see Box 10.1 for the United Kingdom).

Enormous obstacles are ranged against those who wish to reduce or reform regulation. First, there is bureaucratic inertia and incomprehension. Administrators do not like to deregulate, and believe from their narrow standpoint that objections against excessive compliance costs by businesses are exaggerated. The problem here, of course, is that many individual regulations *are* tolerable; it is the cumulative total that is not. Second, vested interests, as well as consumer lobbies which politicians may be reluctant to alienate, will resist change. There is always some interest that benefits from regulation. For example, the progressive raising of the threshold for the compulsory audit of company accounts which has taken place in the United Kingdom since the 1970s was at first resisted by banks, credit rating agencies and the Inland Revenue, on the grounds that it would lead to fraud, losses to creditors and the restriction of credit. However, little happened except that the costs for many owner-managed companies were reduced.[8] Powerful trade unions resist any changes to employment legislation. Certainly, workers do need some protection from stupid or unscrupulous employers, but this legislation is invariably unnecessarily complex and costly to administer, and often discriminates in its effects upon certain groups, particularly women.

Producers are often the most powerful supporters of regulations that raise barriers to entry for new competition. The farming lobby and manufacturing interests in the United States, for example, have since the 1970s supported the regulatory subsidisation of ethanol (a substitute for petrol made from corn) on the apparently bogus grounds that it would reduce dependence on imported oil and bring environmental benefits (Ronald N. Johnson and Gary D. Libecap, 'Information distortion by politicians and constituent

Box 10.1 Why taxis are often hard to find

The Office of Fair Trading (OFT) carried out an investigation of the regulation of taxis (OFT 2003). It proposed removing restrictions on the number of licensed taxis, which would reduce waiting times and improve public safety. Long waiting times create a gap in the market, the report said, 'which is partly filled by illegal cabs – 1.8 million people used an illegal taxi in 2002'. The limited supply of taxis can also add to difficulties faced by police in dealing with public disorder in town centres at night. The OFT also recommended that local authorities should continue to set maximum fare levels but allow freedom to set lower fares. Quality and safety controls should continue; 'however, the way that they are applied can impose unnecessary costs and hinder new entrants to the market'. This was a reference to requirements for vehicle design, which (outside London) may prevent the use of standard and less costly vehicles. Case studies of local authorities that have removed quantity restrictions showed that the supply of taxis increased by an average of about 50 per cent. Unsurprisingly, the OFT proposals were not welcomed by taxi-driver unions. According to *The Times* (12 November 2003) a spokesman for the Transport and General Workers' Union said: 'What will be better for consumers is more robust regulation to outlaw the cowboy cabs.'

Another aspect of taxi regulation illustrates how alternative approaches to regulatory objectives might be considered. The authorities have required all 22,000 London taxis to be modified to allow entry and exit by persons in wheelchairs, at a cost of about £2,000 per vehicle. Some 3,000 cabs, mainly run by part-time operators, were withdrawn from the fleet following the imposition of this regulation. Research by the author established that the use of taxis by people in wheelchairs is relatively rare (perhaps once per year per cab) and mainly restricted to National Health Service customers, and therefore Radio cabs only. Alternative arrangements to meet these needs without the necessity for modification of the whole fleet could have been considered.

groups in promoting regulatory transfers: the case of ethanol', in MAGNUSSON & OTTOSSON 2001).

The significant reduction of regulatory burdens requires political will, rigorous analysis and advocacy, and measures to mollify or compensate losers. Political will is obviously necessary to overcome resistance from vested interests.[9] Analysis and advocacy are necessary to demonstrate the benefits of regulatory reform, which are often indirect and usually delayed in their incidence. It needs to be shown that competition, for example, can be the most powerful means for benefiting consumers – as in airline deregulation or telecommunications – and that excessive employment protection legislation can have the opposite of its intended effect by deterring employment. Ironically, it is not the generally accepted primacy of health, safety and the environment that is threatened by sensible regulatory reform, but less dramatic things: we showed in Chapter 5 that tax paperwork accounts for approaching half of the compliance burdens on small firms, for example.[10]

An important issue for consideration is that the advanced countries have now developed a deep-seated culture in which regulation is seen as the only way of solving problems – and, worse, that if regulation fails, as it generally does, the only solution is more regulation. All problems cannot be put down to 'unrestrained market forces', nor can regulation compensate for the breakdown in the traditional values that disciplined societies in the past. There is some irony here in view of recent Chinese history, but Confucius said that 'the right method of governing is not by creating legislation or by law enforcement but through the moral education of the people' (WARNER 2003).

Conclusion

Given the complexity of the factors affecting the organisation of economic activities, it would be hazardous to make detailed predictions about the future of SMEs. Much will depend upon the response to the downward pressures exerted by the state in terms of regulatory costs and tax discrimination. There are certainly some favourable forces at work: on balance, technological development has moved in favour of SMEs.[11] Rising wealth and, contrary to common opinion, globalisation, are also in their favour. When the challenges of economic development in the Third world are met, as they eventually must be, there will be a massive increase in the role of SMEs in the poorer parts of the world. Small firms are, in fact, needed more than ever and while market economies endure, there will always be a large place for them.

Notes

1 As mentioned in Chapter 5, US attempts to control paperwork burdens have not been entirely successful, but they do seem to have resulted in a slower growth in regulatory burdens than elsewhere. One of the problems has been the difficulty of extending the process to include all arms of government.

2 It would not be reasonable to give central banks too much of the credit for the international decline in inflationary pressures in the 1990s and into the Millennium. This decline is also attributable to other causes, but improved discipline must have helped. The real challenge for central banks will come if and when widespread deflation emerges, as it has in Japan.

3 There are other parallels. Writing in the *Financial Times* (27 February 2002), John Kay argued 'the case for bringing to fiscal policy the detachment that has worked well for monetary policy'. He pointed out that the 'Golden Rule',

introduced by the New Labour government in the United Kingdom, under which fiscal policy should be neutral over the whole economic cycle; the European Growth and Stability Pact (GSP), designed to limit public deficits as a percentage of GDP for members of the Eurozone; and the persistent desire of the US Congress to achieve balanced budgets, all show that politicians can see the merit in limiting their discretion over fiscal policy. Kay advocates the establishment of a fiscal policy commission with a role analogous to that of the central bank.

4 The importance of the RIAs and other existing machinery for monitoring regulation, which so far has only had limited results, would be greatly enhanced under the proposed system.

5 Such a system would have the advantage of increasing pressures for the control of compliance costs, since the higher these were, the higher allowances and direct public expenditure would be.

6 We showed in Chapter 6 that utilities and other large firms have increasingly been devoting resources to corporate venture capital (CVC) to open windows on new technologies from emerging small firms which might destroy their markets or create new opportunities.

7 Discussions about small firms are often influenced by the ideological persuasions of the proponents. Those on the Left are basically unfavourable to SMEs as vestiges of proprietorial (and inequitable) capitalism that are difficult to control in the public interest. The Right see SMEs as standard-bearers for the benign market system which, left to itself, will achieve socially optimal structures and scale. Both the Left and the Right welcome employment creation by small firms (though the former regret the inferior pay and conditions in SMEs), but neither face up to the role of the indispensable complementarity of small firms and large, and the tensions that creates for social policy. There are, of course, many shades of view on both sides, from those who would prefer to see small firms regulated out of existence in favour of unionised Big Business, to the near-anarchic (Poujadist) Right, who would like the activities of the modern state to shrink to maintaining law and order and an active competition policy. A good example of the view of the Left is in HARRISON (1994). His concern is that the Right, in the 'questionable statistics of Birch and the *laissez-faire* ideological tracts of Gilder' (George Gilder wrote a best-seller, *The Spirit of Enterprise* (1984); for Birch, see Chapter 3), have a vested interest in the survival and resurgence of small firms. The vogue for SMEs, he believes, 'could distract us from the need to continually monitor and find new ways to socially regulate the behaviour of the multinational enterprises and their alliances'. Harrison argues that there has been no shift to SMEs, which simply provide a new route for big companies to exploit their workers, while large firms remain the drivers of economic progress.

8 The threshold is expected to be further raised from a turnover of £2.8 to £5.6 million, the legal definition of a small firm, from 2004.

9 Regretfully, political will is frequently directed at meeting the demands of lobbyists. *The Times* (7 January 2004) reported that the government was 'proposing that every new and converted house in Britain be required to install temperature-controlling safety devices on its hot water taps by 2006. The move has been applauded by the Royal Society for the Prevention of Accidents, the Child Accident Prevention Trust and perhaps unsurprisingly by the Thermostatic Mixing Valve (TMV) Manufacturers Association.'

10 The growth of regulatory burdens in the area of employment and other issues in Europe may be reducing the predominance of taxation in the total burden. I am indebted to Francis Chittenden for drawing this to my attention.

11 The importance of contemporary technological developments is not only that they can liberate SMEs from some of the constraints of economies of scale – for example, lowering capital costs and by making flexible production in small plants, or in making small service activities more viable – but also that they can help in the diffusion of information. In his continuously stimulating account of the rise of the knowledge economy and its links with economic advance, Joel Mokyr mentions that 'In the seventeenth and eighteenth centuries technical and scientific writings in Europe switched from Latin to the various vernacular languages'; this improved access to knowledge was an important factor in the developments that led to the Industrial Revolution (MOKYR 2002). The Internet is doing the same thing today, helping to give SMEs a more equal access to the knowledge needed for their specialised roles – and also, of course, an economic means for marketing themselves, if necessary, on a global basis.

Appendix

Coverage, sources and comparisons of small business statistics

Statistical coverage

Commonly (although the United Kingdom is an exception), statistics on small business exclude agriculture and also forestry and fishing. Thus data published by the European Commission relate to 'non-primary private enterprises' and the US data to 'non-farm businesses'. The Official Small and Medium Enterprise Agency (part of MITI) also does not cover the primary sector in Japan. The reason for the exclusion of agriculture is probably that historically powerful Ministries of Agriculture collected their own statistics and had their own policies for farmers. Nonetheless, most farms are small businesses and increasingly share the characteristics of other SMEs. In many developing countries, most statistics may exclude subsistence farmers participating in the market economy to only a limited extent.

There are a number of other particularly important features of small business statistics which are a frequent source of error and confusion. The first point is that the terms 'business', 'company' or 'firm' are too imprecise to be of use in counting SMEs. A 'company' is generally an incorporated business, and it may also be referred to as a 'business' or a 'firm', although that can apply also to a sole proprietorship (an unincorporated business owned by one person) or even a partnership which has five or more joint owners. A company or business may not be independent (as shown above, a key characteristic of an SME) but owned or controlled by another company or even a sole proprietorship or partnership. More precise are the terms 'establishment', which is typically the smallest reporting unit capable of responding to a statistical inquiry (such as a branch or factory) and 'enterprise', which is an ultimate unit of control that may own several establishments (or companies).

'Enterprise' and 'establishment' are British terminology, and these and the other terms in the previous paragraph have similar meanings in Japan and the United States.[1] In other countries such as Germany for example SME statistics may relate to quite different levels of aggregation (BANNOCK 1976). The European Commission, in its SME statistics, adjusts national data for member states so as to achieve rough comparability and its figures on SMEs relate to enterprises; it does not publish data at establishment level.

A second point about SME statistics has to do with the treatment of the self-employed without employees, the '0' employee size class. These should be included: a plumber working alone on his own account is an independent business even though he has no employees. He is treated as such in both European Commission and UK official statistics on SMEs, but US data do not include '0' employee firms within their SME numbers. The treatment of 0' employee firms is a common source of error. For example, a publication of the Observatory of European SMEs concludes that 'in Europe 19',[2] SMEs account for approximately two-thirds of total employment, this figure amounts to almost 46 per cent for the USA and 33 per cent in Japan' (EUROPEAN COMMISSION 2002c). However, these differences are apparently mainly related to differences in the coverage of the US and Japanese figures (US data, for example, exclude '0' employee firms). Probably most countries (Germany is another example) do not generally include the self-employed without employees in their SME statistics. Equally, data on self-employment may or may not classify owner-managers of incorporated businesses as self-employed (about half of OECD countries do not, OECD 2000)).

A third pitfall in SME statistics also relates to the coverage of the employment numbers. In some cases, part-time as well as full-time employees are included. For total employment figures, the convention is that two part-time equals one full-time employee, but this convention is not always observed. Another difficulty is the treatment of unpaid family workers. The convention is to exclude them, but it is necessary to understand the coverage of the figures because exclusion of unpaid workers and the mixing up of part- and full-time employees can make a nonsense of productivity calculations, for example.

These issues of coverage are particularly important for countries in transition and developing countries where the grey economy or the informal sector may be very large (see Chapter 9).[3] It might be assumed that by definition there are no reliable statistics on small businesses in the informal sector, and this is no doubt true: however, in CEE transition countries, in particular, it is believed that figures on numbers of businesses are more reliable than data on their output and sales because of underreporting. Data on the profitability of SMEs is everywhere suspect, not only for this reason but because owner-managers have a perfectly legitimate choice between drawing a high or low salary which is, of course, a cost before determining profit.

The foregoing is by no means an exhaustive account of the pitfalls in SME statistics: others will emerge as we look at the sources of these figures, and indeed have emerged throughout the book.

Sources of statistics

The ideal situation for SME statistics would be one in which all live businesses, irrespective of legal form and whether or not they had employees, were registered on a comprehensive national database and allocated a unique enterprise identifying code to prevent duplication. In practice, no country has realised this idea, though France seems to have approached it. Since 1997, the SIRENE database in France has been fed with data from a large range of organisations, including the tax and social insurance authorities, postcode files, chambers of agriculture, trade, commerce and industry and education and health authorities. Compliance by firms is assisted by the obligation to use the SIRENE number in any dealings with the public administration.

At the other extreme, in the United Kingdom most new unincorporated businesses are not obliged to register anywhere except with the tax authorities, and even then only where they expect to incur a business income tax liability or need to register for VAT – and, in the latter case, only where anticipated turnover exceeds £56,000 (2003/4). In any case in the United Kingdom, as in the United States, privacy (disclosure) laws limit the transfer of information between, say, the tax authorities and statistical offices, or even the publication of statistical data which might result in the disclosure of information about individual businesses.

In countries with public law chambers and/or local business registration systems, such as Germany and much of Central and Eastern Europe, there is a further source of statistics. In Germany, the lower tier local authorities (*Gewerbeamt*) collect business registration and deregistration information and send copies to the provincial (*Länder*) statistical office. Totals are transmitted to the Federal Statistical Office and used by the *Institut für Mittelstandsforschung (IfM)* to estimate the number of start-ups and liquidations, though these data are not thought to be very reliable and chamber data even less so, largely because of underreporting of closures.[4] In Hungary, Bulgaria and other CEE countries, quite elaborate SME statistics based on registrations, though valuable, are subject to the same limitations.

Very few countries carry out full enterprise censuses in an attempt to compile comprehensive statistics on the business population. Germany and the United States are among the exceptions but coverage is not complete and these censuses are carried out at long intervals (10 years in the case of Germany). In the United States the Quinquennial Enterprise Census, carried out in years ending with a 2 and a 7, does not provide data on the smallest firms, and the results appear with a delay of three years or more.

All developed countries do carry out censuses and sample surveys in particular activity sectors such as manufacturing and agriculture, and these are a useful source of information. However, all surveys normally depend upon the use of registers or sampling frames which, as we have seen, are difficult to compile as far as comprehensive coverage of small firms is concerned. The UK Census of Production, for example, does not require returns from firms employing fewer than 20 people. The United Kingdom does have an Interdepartmental Business Register, using the Company Register, VAT, published and other sources, which has comprehensive cover for larger firms but is incomplete for SMEs, particularly the self-employed.

A survey estimation technique which eliminates the need for sampling frames is the micro-enterprise, baseline or saturation survey. In this approach enumerators, as far as possible, identify on the ground and interview all businesses in selected clusters (say, in areas 1 km^2) in strata (such as rural areas, commercial districts and residential areas in cities). These results are then grossed up to national totals. Saturation surveys have been carried out in many developing countries under the GEMINI project funded by USAID (LIEDHOLM & MEAD 1999), in Zambia funded by DFID and on a pilot basis in Bulgaria. In the advanced countries, given the availability of other data, statisticians have been loath to use this technique, but it has been successfully tried on a pilot basis in the United Kingdom (LEYSHON 1987) and has been used in the United States for local commercial market research purposes.

There are various other official sources of data on SMEs, but all have their limitations. Employment censuses are usually on a pay-point (close to establishment) basis but omit the self-employed without employees. Often numbers of self-employed can be derived only by labour-force surveys benchmarked against population censuses, as in the United Kingdom. VAT registers are extensively used as a source of data in the United Kingdom, though strangely not in other European countries in some of which the registration threshold is much lower than in the United Kingdom and therefore coverage greater. The United Kingdom uses a unique conflation of VAT, the Labour Force Survey (LFS) and other data to produce estimates of numbers of enterprises, which are probably quite reliable and even superior in some respects to the official numbers for the United States and other countries (BANNOCK & DALY 1994). These countries, as we have seen, do not have integrated zero employee and employer SME numbers. Business income tax returns are another potential source of data, but the main deficiency with these is that these returns do not necessarily include employment numbers and are not made on an enterprise basis so there is double counting. Statistics Canada benefited in the 1970s from a change in the law to allow the use of tax returns for statistical purposes, but there were many problems.

So far, we have been describing official national sources, but there are also many private sources of statistics on SMEs. None of these private sources has the range of coverage of official data, but by providing depth and richness they add greatly to our knowledge of the subject. There are general business opinion surveys, often broken down by firm size, *ad hoc* surveys by academics and others, and also some regular or occasional enterprise surveys, a few specifically targeted at SMEs. Examples for the United Kingdom are the NatWest/Small Business Research Trust (SBRT) *Quarterly Survey of Small Firms in Britain*, the surveys of the Cambridge Small Business Research Centre (CSBRC), and the Confederation of British Industries (CBI) *Industrial Trends* survey. Two of these surveys provide very long runs of data: the CBI since 1972 and the SBRT since 1984. In the United States, the National Federation of Independent Business (NFIB) carries out regular surveys of its large membership. The difficulty for most private surveys is the lack of a suitable enterprise sampling frame. Many make use of Dun & Bradstreet (D&B), which has credit assessment data on a large number of enterprises in many countries. Surveys based on D&B sources, and indeed all the surveys mentioned, underrepresent the smallest firms.

There are also a number of multinational enterprise surveys. For example, the European Commission sponsors business outlook surveys throughout the European Union, and the World Bank carries out surveys in many countries, including LDCs and (with the EBRD in Central and Eastern Europe. Grant Thornton and Business Strategies carry out a European Business Survey. Of interest, too, is the Global Entrepreneurship Monitor (GEM), which since 1999 has carried out surveys of new venture creation and self-employment identified by random telephone surveys of adult populations now in some 37 countries, as well as a survey of experts involved in entrepreneurial activity. The GEM is carried out by independent researchers at business schools and universities.

What the figures show: overall SME data

Table A1.1 shows why, as far as numbers of enterprises are concerned, the exact placing of the threshold between 'large' and 'small' forms matters little. Of the 3.7 million business enterprises in the United Kingdom, according to the official estimates, 99.1 per cent employ fewer than 50 people; raising the threshold to the EU-wide level of fewer than 250 employees pushes up the percentage to 99.8 per cent. There are in fact only 3,245 enterprises with 250–499 employees and a further 3,540 with 500 or more. Most, though not all, of these are quoted companies and public corporations owned by the state.

When we look at the share of small enterprises in employment, as distinct from numbers of firms, the predominance of small firms is greatly reduced. The 99.1 per cent of enterprises that employ less than 50 people account for only 43.4 per cent of total private sector employment, although enterprises with less than 250 employees (99.8 per cent of all enterprises) account for more than half of total employment. The 6,800 or so large firms (only 0.2 per cent of all enterprises) account for almost 45 per cent of total employment;

the 3,500 or so largest, with 500 or more employees, account for 39.6 per cent of all employment.

Table A1.2 gives a similar picture for Western Europe (Europe-19): 99.8 per cent of the 20 million enterprises are SMEs and account for two-thirds of employment, there being only 40,000 firms with 250 or more employees. Comparison with Table A1.1 (which includes the primary sector, unlike Table A1.2) shows that the United Kingdom has relatively more micro-enterprises but fewer SMEs than the European average. SMEs as a whole account for a smaller proportion of total employment in the United Kingdom (55.4 per cent) than in Europe-19 (66.4 per cent). The explanation of these differences is partly structural: for example, the United Kingdom has a more developed service sector and has very large numbers of sole proprietors without employees in the construction sector.

Table A1.3 shows the role of SMEs according to activity sector. In terms of number of enterprises SMEs predominate in all sectors – indeed, only in mining, quarrying, water and energy is the proportion of SMEs less than 99 per cent, and then, at 98.4 per cent, only just. In terms of employment, however, there are big variations. SMEs predominate in agriculture and construction (100.0 per cent), real estate and business services (70.2 per cent), education (84.5 per cent) and other social and personal services (73.1 per cent). In other sectors their contribution to employment varies from less than 13 per cent in mining, etc. to 53.8 per cent in hotels and restaurants. The sectors are not, of course, of equal importance in absolute terms: although accounting for about half of employment in manufacturing and distribution and repairs, SMEs account for over 2 million and 2.3 million jobs, respectively, in these sectors.

Table A1.1 Enterprises and their employment as percentage of total by employment size class, number, United Kingdom, 2001

Class size	Enterprises (%)	Cum. (%)	Employment (%)	Cum. (%)
0	69.3	69.3	12.8	12.8
1–4	20.0	89.3	9.9	22.7
5–9	5.3	94.6	6.3	29.0
10–19	3.0	97.6	6.9	35.9
20–49	1.5	99.1	7.5	43.4
50–99	0.5	99.6	5.5	48.9
100–199	0.2	99.8	4.9	53.8
200–249	0.0	99.8	1.6	55.4
250–499	0.1	99.9	5.0	60.4
500 or more	0.1	100.0	39.6	100.0
Total	100.0		100.0	
Base (000)	3,746.4		18,434.0	

Source: SBS; includes public corporations and the primary sector.

Table A1.2 Non-primary private enterprise: enterprises and their employment by employment size class, number and percentage, Europe-19, 2000

Item	Micro	Small	Medium	Total	Large	Grand total
Employment size	0–9	10–49	50–249	0–249	>250	
Number of enterprises (000)	19,040	1,200	170	20,415	40	20,455
(%)	93.1	5.9	0.8	99.8	0.2	100.0
Employment (000)	41,750	23,080	15,960	80,790	40,960	121,750
(%)	34.3	19.0	13.1	66.4	33.6	

Source: 'SMEs in Europe, including a first glance at EU candidate countries', *Observatory of European SMEs*, 2002/2, European Commission.

Table A1.3 Enterprises, total number, total employment and share of SMEs, United Kingdom, 2001

Activity	Total enterprises (000)	% SMEs <250	Employ- ment (000)	% in SMEs
Agriculture, forestry, fishing	181	100.0	452	>97.1
Mining, quarrying, energy, water	6	98.4	221	>13.0
Manufacturing	293	99.2	4,103	50.7
Construction	692	100.0	1,666	84.5
Wholesale, retail, repairs	542	99.8	4,652	50.0
Hotels and restaurants	123	99.8	1,560	53.8
Transport, storage, communication	236	99.8	1,657	39.1
Financial intermediaries	64	99.5	1,076	21.4
Real estate, business services	867	99.0	3,491	70.2
Education	117	99.9	289	84.5
Health and social work	233	99.8	3,253	41.9
Other social/personal services	392	99.9	1,200	73.1
All industries	3,746	99.8	22,622	55.4

Source: SBS.

European variations in the density of SMEs

Table A1.4 shows large variations in the average employment size of enterprises – from 2 employees in Greece to 6 in the United Kingdom and 10 in the Netherlands and Ireland. Another form of comparison is to calculate the number of enterprises per 10,000 of the population.[5] These two measures are related – countries with small average enterprise size tend to have relatively large numbers of enterprises in relation to their populations and vice versa, and again there are quite large variations.

The southern European countries (Greece, Italy, Spain and Portugal) have about 680–750 enterprises per 10,000 of the population, with average enterprise sizes of 2–5 employees. In the United Kingdom, Germany,

Table A1.4 Non-primary private enterprise: number of enterprises, average enterprise size, population and number of enterprises per 10,000 of population, by country, Europe-19, 2000

Country	Enterprises (000) (1)	Average enterprise size no./ employees (2)	GDP per capita (US$) (3)	Popu-lation (4)	No. of ents./ 10,000 of population (5)
Austria	225	10	27,001	8,106	278
Belgium	545	6	26,619	10,251	531
Denmark	180	9	29,495	5,337	337
Finland	210	6	25,260	5,181	405
France	2,490	7	24,215	58,892	423
Germany	3,550	8	25,893	82,143	432
Greece	800	2	16,817	10,543	759
Ireland	95	10	29,174	3,787	251
Italy	4,125	3	25,161	57,189	721
Luxembourg	20	10	46,743	439	456
Netherlands	555	10	27,836	15,926	348
Portugal	685	5	18,021	10,008	684
Spain	2,700	5	20,124	39,466	684
Sweden	270	8	24,843	8,872	304
United Kingdom	3,490	6	24,938	59,766	584
European Union[a]	19,930	6		375,905	530
Norway	175	6	30,166	4,491	257
Switzerland	320	8	30,138	7,185	224

Sources: Columns (1) and (2): EUROPEAN COMMISSION (2002b); column 3: *National Accounts of OECD Countries, Main Aggregates, 1, 1989–2000*, OECD, 2002; data are in purchasing power parities (PPPs) at current prices; column (4): *Historical Statistics, 1970–2000*, OECD, 2001.

Note:
a Europe-19 includes Iceland, Liechtenstein, Norway and Switzerland and has a total of 20,455,000 enterprises.

France and Belgium, the number of enterprises per 10,000 of the population falls in the wide range of 400–600, with the Netherlands and Switzerland and the Scandinavian countries having notably fewer (250–350). These group-ings suggest an *income effect*, with the higher the income *per capita*, the larger the average enterprise size and the fewer the number of enterprises in relation to the population. Within Europe, however, such a relationship is not in fact well supported by the data and there seem to be 'cultural differ-ences' at work.[6] When we extend the picture to include a larger range of countries, including developing countries, perforce for reasons of data availability, using a different measure (the proportion of the workforce that is self-employed as a proxy for SME density) the hypothesised relationship becomes clearer (Chart A1.1). Bannock and Binks, in BANNOCK & DALY (1994), found that levels of GDP *per capita* explained some 70 per cent of the variations in the self-employed as a proportion of the workforce, for 30 countries at various stages of development.

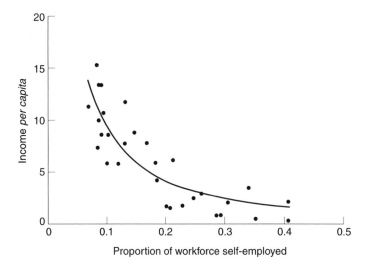

Chart A1.1   Per capita income and the proportion of own-account workers in the active labour force, *c.* 1985 (actual and fitted values)

Source: Bannock and Binks, in BANNOCK & DALY (1991).

Comparisons with the United States, Japan and elsewhere

Thanks to the efforts of EUROSTAT in making adjustments wherever necessary, the data on numbers of SMEs and their employment in Europe should be reasonably comparable, though they can be no better than the national data (as adjusted) on which they are based. Despite EUROSTAT's efforts, there is room for doubt about the validity of the large differences in SME density in Europe shown in Table A1.4. Can we really believe, for example, that the number of enterprises per 10,000 of the population in Switzerland is less than half that in Denmark, a country with similar levels of income, and not much more than half of those in France and Germany, countries with which Switzerland has close cultural affiliations? We just do not know.

Outside Europe, comparisons of SME statistics are even more problematical. According to the US SBA there were an estimated 5.80 million non-farm firms with employees in 1999 (SBA 2001). The same source gives a figure of 10.09 million self-employed, a total of 15.89 million enterprises.[7] With a population of 275.4 million, this gives 577 enterprises per 10,000 of the population, very similar to the United Kingdom at 584. Japan seems to have a lower SME density. Japan has 4.851 million enterprises (1999) according to official statistics, but these figures do not include the self-employed without employees. If we use the establishment total of 6.184 million, which is probably closer to the reality, then with a population of

126.9 million, Japan has 512 non-primary enterprises per 10,000 of the population. This is about 12 per cent less than the figures for the United States and United Kingdom. (Japan's enterprise population has been shrinking since the mid-1980s under the impact of deflation.)[8]

Sometimes concern is expressed that a country has 'too many' micro- and small enterprises and 'too few' medium-sized enterprises (we discussed similar concerns about self-employment and 'birth' and 'death' rates in Chapter 2). In Table A1.5 we compare the absolute number of manufacturing enterprises for four countries in three employment size bands, having adjusted for differences in population. It can be seen that the United Kingdom in the late 1980s had considerably fewer enterprises in the 20–99 employee sizeband than Germany or Japan, but only a little fewer than the United States. For the 5–19 employee size band the United Kingdom had many more enterprises than the United States, but very many fewer than Germany or Japan. For firms in the 100+ sizeband the United Kingdom had more than the other countries and particularly in comparison with Japan and the United States. This exercise in comparative statistics illustrates the difficulties: the lower size band for the United Kingdom is not the same as for the others (resulting in understatement), while the Japanese data also has a different threshold for the lower band (resulting in overstatement). It was also necessary to adjust the Japanese data from an establishment to an enterprise basis, otherwise this, too, would have led to an overstatement.

EIM Business and Policy Research have produced estimates for the European Commission of business populations in the EU candidate countries (EUROPEAN COMMISSION 2002c). The 13 candidate countries are mostly countries in transition to market economies, such as Romania, Poland and Hungary, but also include Turkey, Malta and Cyprus. It is not surprising, therefore, that the enterprise density, which we calculate at 337, is within the range for Europe shown in Table A1.4, but well below the EU-15 average of 530. EIM state that their numbers are subject to uncertainty.

Table A1.5 Enterprises in manufacturing, by employment size band, adjusted for population, UK = 100

Employment size	United Kingdom 1986	Germany 1987	Japan 1987	United States 1990
5–19	100.0[a]	268.2	148.3[b]	61.7
20–99	100.0	228.1	223.2	108.9
>100	100.0	94.7	54.1	47.4

Sources: United Kingdom and Germany: BANNOCK & ALBACH (1991); Japan: MITI (1995), data have been crudely adjusted from establishment to enterprise basis; population: MADDISON (1991).

Notes
a 6–19.
b 4–19.

Enterprise statistics for developing countries are never comprehensive, or at least always suspect, for reasons explained in Chapter 9. The only sources that can be used with some confidence are those from the baseline or saturation surveys mentioned above. In respect of SME density, Zambia is probably fairly typical of sub-Saharan countries in Africa. We calculate that there are 368 non-farm enterprises per 10,000 of the human population in Zambia from the data in PARKER (1996). For the saturation surveys carried out in five other sub-Saharan countries in the early 1990s and reviewed in MEAD (1994), we calculate an average enterprise density of 397.[9]

In both the candidate and the sub-Saharan countries, the SME density appears to be somewhat lower than the EU-15 or Europe-19 averages and there are also differences in the size distribution of enterprises. In the candidate countries, micro-enterprises (0–9 employees) account for 95.4 per cent of all enterprises compared with the Europe-19 average of 93.1 per cent. For Africa, the size breakdowns are not quite the same as in the European data, but in seven sub-Saharan countries in LIEDHOLM & MEAD (1993), enterprises with 10 or fewer employees accounted for an average of 99.0 per cent of all enterprises. So it seems that enterprise populations are more skewed towards micro-enterprises in Africa and in the candidate countries than in Europe.

What would be more significant from an economic point of view would be comparative data on SME contributions to *value added* as well as to employment. However, it is just not available. There are figures for sales turnover for some countries, but such data can be misleading. Turnover double counts aggregate economic activity, since the sales of one company may be inputs to others – for example, manufacturing and retailing. For 2001, the SBS estimates the share of enterprises with fewer than 250 employees in total private sector turnover in the United Kingdom at 51.4 per cent, compared with their share in employment of 55.4 per cent. Value added, which measures the contribution to GDP, is a better measure but there are no official estimates. BANNOCK & ALBACH (1991), after fairly elaborate calculations, put the SME contribution to non-primary private sector GDP at 32.2 per cent for the United Kingdom in 1986, and 46.0 per cent for Germany. For the United States (under 500 employees, 1982) one estimate by the SBA of the share of SMEs in non-primary private sector GDP was 50 per cent, and another estimate for Japan for the same year was 60 per cent (STANWORTH & GRAY 1991). All these estimates are subject to qualifications, and do not necessarily reflect the present-day position.

Notes

1 However, this does not mean that US and British SME statistics are necessarily comparable, as we show below. To confuse matters, the UK statistical authority, now the Office of National Statistics (ONS), no longer publishes a size analysis

for its *Manufacturing Census* from 1987 in terms of enterprises and establishments but for 'enterprises' or 'businesses', which correspond roughly to 'establishments' in the old terminology. The old term 'enterprise' has been supplanted by 'enterprise groups'.

2 'Europe-19' refers to the 15 EU member states plus Iceland, Lichtenstein, Norway and Switzerland.

3 The World Bank classifies the world into low-, middle- and high-income countries. *Developing countries* (LDCs) fall mainly into the bottom category. The term 'LDC' means 'poor' countries which have yet to industrialise to any great extent. *Countries in transition* have economies which are moving, or have recently moved, from a planned to a market economy, e.g. Russia and CEE countries, and are all in the middle-income group. The high-income or *advanced countries* are mostly members of the OECD. The *informal sector* is not an easily defined term but consists of that part of the population of LDCs engaged in subsistence agriculture and labour-intensive low-value added activities. *Informals* are often not registered, and do not pay business income taxes. The term is often used as an alternative to the '*grey*' or '*shadow*' *economy* for countries in transition but is narrower, since the latter includes underreported income in the formal sector.

4 I am indebted to Dr Gunter Kayser, Director of the *IfM*, for this information.

5 We refer to this as a 'measure of SME density'. 'Population' is total population, though it could be argued that the labour force would be more appropriate.

6 Economists often ascribe things to 'cultural differences' in the absence of information, and that is the case here. An unknown part of these differences can probably be explained by differences in statistical coverage; other reasons are discussed in Chapter 3.

7 Since some of the firms with employees will be presumably unincorporated with self-employed sole proprietors or partners, we should anticipate a degree of overlap between the employer-firm and self-employment data that would lead to an overestimation of the US enterprise total. However, if the ratio of firms with employees to the total enterprise population in the United States were the same as in the United Kingdom, then the US enterprise population would not be lower than the SBA total of 15.89 million but very much higher, at 18.9 million. The SBA also provides a figure of 24.91 million for the number of non-farm business tax returns filed for 1999, but multiple business ownerships mean that this figure greatly exaggerates the number of independent enterprises.

8 I am indebted to Dr Hiroshi Teraoka of Chukyo University for assistance in interpreting Japanese statistics.

9 The saturation surveys cover only enterprises with fewer than 50 employees (100 in Zambia), but this has little effect on the comparisons made here since the number of larger firms is tiny.

Bibliography

ABERNATHY *et al.* (1983)   William J. Abernathy, Kim B. Clark and Alan M. Kantrow, *Industrial Renaissance*, Basic Books.

ACS & AUDRETSCH (1990)   Z.J. Acs and D.B. Audretsch, *Innovation and Small Firms*, MIT Press.

AGF (1988)   *New Technology-Based Firms in Britain and Germany*, Anglo-German Foundation.

ALEXANDER (1975)   K. J. W. Alexander, *The Political Economy of Change*, Basil Blackwell.

AOYAMA (1999)   Yuko Aoyama, 'Policy interventions for industrial network formation: contrasting historical underpinnings of the small business policy in Japan and the United States', *Small Business Economics*, May.

ATKINSON & STOREY (1994)   John Atkinson and David Storey (eds), *Employment, the Small Firm and the Labour Market*, Routledge.

ATTACK (1986)   Jeremy Attack, 'Firm size and industrial structure in the United States during the 19th century', *Journal of Economic History*, June.

AUDRETSCH (2001)   D. B. Audretsch, 'Research issues relating to structure, competition and performance of small technology based firms', *Small Business Economics*, February.

BAIN (1959)   Joe S. Bain, *Industrial Organisation*, John Wiley.

BANNOCK (1976)   Graham Bannock, *The Smaller Business in Britain and Germany*, Wilton House.

BANNOCK (1977a)   Graham Bannock & Partners Ltd, *Making Markets Work: Support Services for Equity Markets for Growth Companies in Europe*, European Commission Directorate-General Telecommunications, Information Market and Exploitation of Research.

BANNOCK (1977b)   Graham Bannock & Partners Ltd, *Credit Guarantee Schemes for Small Business Lending: A Global Perspective*, report for ODA (DFID).

BANNOCK (1990a)	Graham Bannock, *Taxation in the European Community: The Small Business Perspective*, Paul Chapman.
BANNOCK (1990b)	Graham Bannock, *VAT and Small Business Revisited*, NFIB Foundation.
BANNOCK (1994a)	Graham Bannock, *The Promotion of Small and Medium Enterprises in Europe*, Council of Europe.
BANNOCK (1994b)	Graham Bannock & Partners Ltd, *European Second-Tier Markets for NTBFs*, European Commission DG XIII-D4: SPRINT/EIMI.
BANNOCK (1999)	Graham Bannock, *Corporate Venturing in Europe: A Study for the European Commission DG-XXIII*, EIMS, 98/176.
BANNOCK (2001a)	Graham Bannock, 'Reforming value added tax', *Economic Affairs*, 21(2), 2001.
BANNOCK (2001b)	Graham Bannock, 'Controlling regulation', *Economic Affairs*, 21(2), 2001.
BANNOCK & ALBACH (1991)	Graham Bannock and Horst Albach, *Small Business Policy in Europe*, Anglo-German Foundation.
BANNOCK & DALY (1994)	Graham Bannock and Michael Daly (eds), *Small Business Statistics*, Paul Chapman.
BANNOCK & DORAN (1991)	Graham Bannock and Alan Doran, *Venture Capital and the Equity Gap*, National Westminster Bank.
BANNOCK & PARTNERS (1994)	*Globalisation and SMEs in the UK*, for DTI/OECD, mimeo.
BANNOCK & PARTNERS (1997)	*Credit Guarantee Schemes for Small Business Lending, A Global Perspective*, Volume 1, for ODA.
BANNOCK & PEACOCK (1989)	Graham Bannock and Alan Peacock, *Governments and Small Business*, Paul Chapman.
BANNOCK CONSULTING (1998)	*Innovation Finance in Europe: A Pilot Project in Benchmarking for the European Commission Services*, mimeo.
BANNOCK CONSULTING (2001a)	*An Estimate of the One-Off Transition Costs to the UK of Joining the Euro*, mimeo.
BANNOCK CONSULTING (2001b)	*Company Flotation in Europe: A Basic Guide for Smaller Companies*, European Commission, mimeo.
BANNOCK CONSULTING (2001c)	*Capital Gains Tax and Enterprise, Part 1: The US Experience*, Study for the BVCA by Bannock Consulting, mimeo.
BANNOCK CONSULTING (2001d)	*Innovative Instruments for Raising Equity for SMEs in Europe*, mimeo.

BANNOCK *et al.* (2002)   Graham Bannock, Matthew Gamser, Mariell
                             Juhlin and Andrew McCann, *Indigenous Private
                             Sector Development and Regulation in Africa and
                             Central Europe*, a 10-country study for DFID,
                             mimeo.

BATEMAN (2000)   Milford Bateman, 'Neo-liberalism, SME
                             development and the role of business support
                             centres in the transition economies of Central
                             and Eastern Europe', *Small Business Economics*,
                             June.

BAUER (1984)   Peter Bauer, *Reality and Rhetoric: Studies in
                             Economics of Development*, Weidenfeld &
                             Nicolson.

BAUER (1991)   Peter Bauer, *The Development Frontier*,
                             Harvester Wheatsheaf.

BAUER (2000)   Peter Bauer, *From Subsistence to Exchange and
                             Other Essays*, Princeton University Press.

BAUMOL (2002)   William J. Baumol, *The Free-Market Innovation
                             Machine*, Princeton University Press.

BAUMOL *et al.* (1994)   William J. Baumol, Richard R. Nelson and
                             Edward N. Wolff (eds), *Convergence of
                             Productivity*, Oxford University Press.

BECK *et al.* (2003)   Thorsten Beck, Asli Demirgüç-Kunt and Ross
                             Levine, *SMEs, Growth and Poverty: Cross-
                             Country Evidence*, World Bank, mimeo.

BENNETT (1996)   Robert J. Bennett, 'Can transaction cost
                             economics explain voluntary chambers of
                             commerce?', *Journal of Institutional and
                             Theoretical Economics*, 152(4).

BENNETT & ROBSON   Robert J. Bennett and Paul J.A. Robson, 'The
(1999)   use of external business advice by SMEs in
                             Britain', *Entrepreneurship and Regional
                             Development*, 11.

BENNETT & ROBSON   Robert Bennett and Paul Robson, 'The Small
(2000)   Business Service: business support, use, fees and
                             satisfaction', *Policy Studies*, 21(3).

BENNETT *et al.* (1994)   Robert J. Bennett, Peter Wicks and Andrew
                             McCoshan, *Local Empowerment and Business
                             Services: Britain's Experiment with Training and
                             Enterprise*, UCL Press.

BERG (1993)   M. Berg, 'Small producer capitalism in
                             eighteenth century England', *Business History*,
                             January.

BERGER & UDELL (2002)   Allen N. Berger and Gregory F. Udell, 'Small
                             business credit availability and relationship
                             lending: the importance of bank organisational
                             structure', *The Economic Journal*, February.

BERLE & MEANS (1932)	A. A. Berle and G. C. Means, *The Modern Corporation and Private Property*, 1968 revised edition, Harcourt Brace & World.
BINKS *et al.* (1993)	M. Binks, C. Ennow and G. Reed, *Small Businesses and their Banks*, Forum of Private Business.
BIRCH (1979)	David L. Birch, *The Job Generation Process*, MIT, mimeo.
BLACKFORD (2003)	M. G. Blackford, *A History of Small Business in America*, 2nd edition, University of North Carolina Press.
BOLTHO *et al.* (2001)	Andrea Boltho, Alessandro Vercelli and Hiroshi Yoshikawa (eds), *Comparing Economic Systems: Italy and Japan*, Palgrave.
BOLTON (1971)	J. E. Bolton, Chairman, *Small Firms: Report of the Committee of Inquiry on Small Firms*, Cmnd. 4811, HMSO.
BRAUDEL (1990)	F. Braudel, 'The identity of France', *People and Production,* II, Collins (French original 1986).
BROCKHAUS (1987)	R. H. Brockhaus Snr, 'Entrepreneurial research: are we playing the correct game?', *American Journal of Small Business*, Winter.
BROWN (2000)	D. Brown, 'The importance of pedlars in industrialisation', *Textile History*, 1.
BRTF (2003)	Better Regulation Task Force, *Annual Report 2001/02.*
BRUCHEY (1980)	Stuart W. Bruchey (ed.), *Small Business in American Life*, Columbia University Press.
BUCKLAND *et al.* (2003)	William Buckland, Andrew Hatcher and Julian Birkinshaw, *Inventuring: Why Big Companies Must Think Small*, McGraw-Hill Professional.
BUNZEL (1962)	John H. Bunzel, *The American Small Businessman*, Alfred A. Knopf.
BYGRAVE & TIMMONS (1992)	William D. Bygrave and Jeffry A. Timmons, *Venture Capital at the Crossroads*, Harvard Business School Press.
CARREE (2002)	M. A. Carree, 'Industrial restructuring and economic growth', *Small Business Economics*, June.
CARTER & RAM (2003)	Sara Carter and Monder Ram, 'Reassessing portfolio enterpreneurship', *Small Business Economics*, December.
CBI/NATWEST (1999)	*Study into Corporate Ventures and Alliances*, Confederation of British Industry and NatWest Bank.
CHAMBERLIN (1933)	E. H. Chamberlin, *Theory of Monopolistic Competition*, Cambridge.
CHANDLER (1962)	Alfred Chandler, *Strategy and Structure,* MIT.

CHANDLER (1977)   Alfred Chandler, *The Visible Hand*, Harvard
                         University Press.
CHANDLER (1990)   Alfred Chandler, *Scale and Scope*, Harvard
                         University Press.
CHELL (1985)   Elizabeth Chell, 'The entrepreneurial
                         personality: a few ghosts laid to rest',
                         International Small Business Journal (3).
CHITTENDEN *et al.* (2003)   Francis Chittenden, Tim Ambler and Monika
                         Sharmutkova, *Government Policy for SMEs: Do
                         Regulators 'Think Small First'?,* Manchester
                         Business School Working Paper, 451.
CHURCH (1993)   R. Church, 'The family firm in industrial
                         capitalism: international perspectives on
                         hypotheses and history', *Business History*, 35.
CHURCHILL & LEWIS   N. Churchill and V. Lewis, 'The five stages of
(1983)   small business growth', *Harvard Business
                         Review*, May–June.
CHUSMAN & McMULLAN   James J. Chusman and W. Ed McMullan, 'Static
(1996)   economic theory, empirical evidence and the
                         evaluation of small business assistance
                         programs', *Journal of Small Business
                         Management*, April.
CLAPHAM (1950)   J. H. Clapham, *An Economic History of Modern
                         Britain: The Early Railway Age 1820–1850*,
                         Cambridge University Press.
CLAPHAM (1952)   J. H. Clapham, *An Economic History of Modern
                         Britain: Free Trade and Steel 1850–1886*,
                         Cambridge University Press.
COMPETITION   *The Supply of Banking Services by Clearing
COMMISSION (2002)   Banks to Small and Medium-Sized Enterprises*,
                         Commission Report.
COOPER *et al.* (1990)   Arnold C. Cooper, William C. Dunkelberg,
                         Carolyn Y. Woo and William J. Dennis Jr,
                         *New Business in America: The Firms and their
                         Owners*, NFIB Education Foundation.
COSH *et al.* (2001)   Andy Cosh, Mark Cox and Alan Hughes,
                         *Evaluation of the Golden Key Package
                         Component of the Small Business Initiative*,
                         British Bankers' Association.
COUNCIL OF EUROPE   Graham Bannock, *The Promotion of Small and
(1994)   Medium-Sized Enterprises in Europe*.
CRESSY (2002)   Robert Cressy, 'Funding gaps: a symposium',
                         The Economic Journal, February.
CURRAN (2000)   James Curran, 'What is small business policy in
                         the UK for? Evaluation and assessing small
                         business support policies', *International Small
                         Business Journal*, April–June.

CURRAN & BLACKBURN (1994) — James Curran and Robert Blackburn, *Small Firms and Local Economy Networks: The Death of the Local Economy?*, Paul Chapman.

CURRAN & BURROWS (1988) — J. Curran and R. Burrows, *Enterprise in Britain: A National Picture of Small Business Owners and the Self-Employed*, Small Business Research Trust.

DE MEZA (2002) — David de Meza, 'Overlending', *The Economic Journal*, February.

DE MEZA & WEBB (1987) — D. de Meza and D. Webb, 'Too much investment: a problem of asymmetric information', *Quarterly Journal of Economics*, 102.

DE SOTO (1989) — Hernando de Soto, *The Other Path: The Invisible Revolution in the Third World*, I.B. Tauris.

DE SOTO (2000) — Hernando de Soto, *The Mystery of Capital: Why Capitalism Triumphs in the West and Fails Everywhere Else*, Bantam Press.

DEAKINS & FREEL (2003) — David Deakins and Mark Freel, *Entrepreneurship and Small Firms*, 3rd edition, McGraw-Hill Education.

DEEKS (1976) — John Deeks, *The Small Firm Owner-Manager: Entrepreneurial Behaviour and Management Practice*, Praeger.

DEFOE (1724) — Daniel Defoe, *A Tour Through the Whole Island of Great Britain*.

DENISON (1967) — E. F. Denison, *Why Growth Rates Differ*, Brookings Institute.

DENISON (1974) — E. F. Denison, *Accounting for United States Economic Growth 1929–1969*, Brookings Institute.

DENNIS (2000) — William J. Dennis Jr, 'Wages, health insurance and pension plans: the relationship between employee compensation and small business owner income', *Small Business Economics*, December.

DEVEREUX & SCHIANTARELLI (1989) — M. Devereux and F. Schiantarelli, *Investment, Financial Factors and Cash Flow: Evidence from UK Panel Data*, Institute for Fiscal Studies, Working Paper, 89/10.

DJANKOV *et al.* (2001) — Simeon Djankov, Rafael La Porta, Florencio Lopez-de-Silanes and Andrei Schleifer, *Courts: The Lex Mundi Project*, World Bank, mimeo, subsequently in the *Quarterly Journal of Economics*, February.

DJANKOV *et al.* (2003) — Simeon Djankov, Edward Glaeser, Rafael La Porta, Florencio Lopez-de-Silanes and Andrei Schleifer, *The New Comparative Economics*, World Bank Policy Research Working Paper, mimeo.

DODD (1993)	Donald B. Dodd, *Historical Statistics of the United States*, Greenwood Press.
DOI & COWLING (1998)	N. Doi and M. Cowling, 'The evolution of firm size and employment share distribution in Japanese and UK manufacturing', *Small Business Economics*, May.
DONCKELS & MIETTINEN (1997)	Rik Donckels and Asko Miettenen (eds), *Entrepreneurship and SME Research: On its Way to the Next Millennium*, Ashgate.
DORAN (1984)	Alan Doran, *Craft Enterprises in Britain and Germany*, Anglo-German Foundation.
EDWARDS (2003)	Paul Edwards, *The Impact of Employment Legislation on Small Firms*, European Industrial Relations Observatory.
EDWARDS & FISCHER (1994)	Jeremy Edwards and Klaus Fischer, *Banks, Finance and Investment in Germany*, Cambridge University Press.
ENSTE & SCHNEIDER (1998)	Dominik Enste and Friedrich Schneider, *Increasing Shadow Economies All Over the World – Fiction or Reality: A Survey of the Global Evidence of Size and of its Impact from 1970 to 1995*, IMF and the University of Linz.
ERIXON (2003)	Fredrik Erixon, 'Poverty and recovery: the history of aid and development in East Africa', *Economic Affairs*, December.
EUROPE ECONOMICS (2003)	*Costs of Compliance*, June 2001, Financial Services Authority.
EUROPEAN COMMISSION (1995)	*European Observatory for SMEs*, Third Annual Report.
EUROPEAN COMMISSION (1996)	*European Observatory for SMEs*, Fourth Annual Report.
EUROPEAN COMMISSION (1997)	*European Observatory for SMEs*, Fifth Annual Report.
EUROPEAN COMMISSION (2002a)	*Observatory for European SMEs* 2002/1, 'Highlights from the 2001 Survey'.
EUROPEAN COMMISSION (2002b)	*Observatory for European SMEs* 2002/2, 'SMEs in Europe'.
EUROPEAN COMMISSION (2002c)	*SMEs in Europe, Including a First Glance at EU Candidate Countries*, Enterprise Publications, Observatory for European SMEs 2002/2.
EUROPEAN COMMISSION (2000d)	*Business Impact Assessment Pilot Project, Final Report*, mimeo, Enterprise Directorate.
EVANS (2001)	Chris Evans, 'The operating costs of taxation: a review of the research', *Economic Affairs*, 21(2), June.
EVANS *et al.* (2001)	Chris Evans, Jeff Pope and John Hasseldine, *Tax Compliance Costs: A Festschrift for Cedric Sandford*, Prospect Media.

EVCA (2000)	European Private Equity and Venture Capital Association, *Corporate Venturing: European Activity Report 2000.*
EVCA (2002)	European Private Equity and Venture Capital Association, *Annual Survey of Pan-European Private Equity and Venture Capital Activity.*
FAULKNER (1960)	Harold Underwood Faulkner, *American Economic History*, 8th edition, Harper & Row (1st edition 1924).
FAZZARI *et al.* (1988)	S. M. Fazzari, G. R. Hubbard and B. C. Petersen, *Financing Constraints and Corporate Investment*, Brookings Papers on Economic Activity, 1.
FLETCHER (2001)	Ian Fletcher, 'A small business perspective on regulation in the UK', *Economic Affairs,* 21(2), June.
FOER (2001)	Albert A. Foer, 'Small business and anti-trust', *Small Business Economics*, February.
FOREMAN-PECK (1985)	J.S. Foreman-Peck, 'Seedcorn or chaff? new firms and industrial performance in the interwar economy', *Economic History Review*, 38 (August).
FRIEDMAN (1988)	David Friedman, *The Misunderstood Miracle: Industrial Development and Political Change in Japan*, Cornell University Press.
GALBRAITH (1967)	J. K. Galbraith, *The New Industrial State*, Hamish Hamilton.
GALLI & PELKMANS (2000)	Giampaolo Galli and Jacques Pelkmans (eds), *Regulatory Reform and Competitiveness in Europe*, I, Edward Elgar.
GAMSER (1998)	Matthew Gamser, *The Role of Councils and Other Consultative Bodies in the Formulation of SME Policy*, UK Know-How Fund/Hungary Ministry of Economy, mimeo.
GANGULY (1985)	Pom Ganguly, *UK Small Business Statistics and International Comparisons*, Harper & Row.
GIBB (1980)	Allan Gibb, *A Study of the Institutional Framework for Small Firms Development in Baden-Württemberg*, Report to the UK Department of Industry, mimeo.
GIBB (2000)	Allan A. Gibb, 'SME policy, academic research and the growth of ignorance: mythical concepts, myths, assumptions, rituals and confusions' *International Small Business Journal*, April–June.
GIBB & LI (2003)	A. A. Gibb and Jun Li, 'Organising for enterprise in China: what can we learn from the Chinese micro, small and medium enterprise development experience?', *Futures*, 35.
GIBRAT (1931)	R. Gibrat, *Les Inégalités Economiques*, Sirey.

GIFFORD (1998)	Sharon Gifford, 'Limited entrepreneurial attention and economic development', *Small Business Economics*, February.
GOMPERS & LERNER (1999)	Paul A. Gompers and Josh Lerner, *The Venture Capital Cycle*, MIT Press.
GRAY (1998)	Colin Gray, *Enterprise and Culture*, Routledge.
GRAY (2001)	Thomas A. Gray, 'Federal regulation and the American economy', *Economic Affairs*, 21(2), June.
GRAY & GAMSER (1994)	Thomas Gray and Matthew Gamser, *Building an Institutional and Policy Framework to Support Small and Medium Enterprises: Learning from Other Cultures*, USAID Implementing Policy Change Project, mimeo.
GREINER (1972)	L. Greiner, 'Evolution and revolution as organisations grow', *Harvard Business Review*, July–August.
GUDGIN *et al.* (1979)	G. Gudgin, I. Brunskill and S. Fothergill, *New Manufacturing Firms in Regional Employment Growth*, Centre for Environmental Studies Research Series, October.
GUILLEN (2001)	Mauro F. Guillén, *The Limits of Convergence: Globalization and Organizational Change in Argentina, South Korea and Spain*, Princeton University Press.
HAINZ (2003)	Christa Hainz, 'Bank competition and credit markets in the transition countries', *Journal of Comparative Economics*, June.
HARRISON (1994)	Bennett Harrison, *Lean and Mean: The Changing Landscape of Corporate Power in the Age of Flexibility*, Basic Books.
HAY & MORRIS (1984)	Donald A. Hay and Derek J. Morris, *Unquoted Companies and their Contribution to the UK Economy*, Macmillan.
HERTZ (1982)	Leah Hertz, *In Search of a Small Business Definition*, University Press of America.
HM TREASURY (2002)	HM Treasury and Small Business Service, *Cross Cutting Review of Government Services for Small Business*.
HOSELITZ (1968)	Bert F. Hoselitz (ed.), *The Role of Small Business in Economic Growth*, Menton.
HOY & STANWORTH (2003)	Frank Hoy and John Stanworth (eds), *Franchising: An International Perspective*, Routledge.
HU (1999)	Ming-Wen Hu, 'The determinants of SME market share in 1991', *Small Business Economics*, February.

HUGHES (1990)	A. Hughes, *Industrial Concentration and the Small Business Sector in the UK: The 1980s in Historical Perspective*, Working Paper, 5, SBRC, University of Cambridge, mimeo.
HUGHES & STOREY (1994)	A. Hughes and D.J. Storey (eds), *Finance and the Small Firm*, Routledge.
IBRD (1993)	World Bank, *The East Asian Miracle: Economic Growth and Public Policy*, Oxford University Press, for the World Bank.
IBRD (2001a)	Committee of Donor Agencies for Small Enterprise Development, *Business Development Services for Small Enterprises: Guiding Principles for Donor Intervention*, mimeo.
IBRD (2001b)	World Bank, *Finance for Growth: Policy Choices in a Volatile World*, Oxford University Press, for the World Bank.
IBRD (2001c)	*World Development Indicators*, World Bank.
ILO (1992)	*Employment, Incomes and Equity: A Strategy of Increasing Public Employment in Kenya*, International Labour Organisation.
IQBAL & URATA (2002)	Farrukh Iqbal and Shirjiro Urata, 'Small firm dynamism in East Asia: an introductory overview', *Small Business Economics*, February–May.
JACOBS (1961)	Jane Jacobs, *The Death and Life of Great American Cities,* Random House.
JEWKES *et al.* (1969)	J. Jewkes, D. Sawers and R. Stillerman, *The Sources of Invention*, 2nd edition, Macmillan (1st edition 1958).
JOHNSON (1909)	A.H. Johnson, *The Disappearance of the Small Landowner*, Clarendon Press.
JONES (1995)	Eric L. Jones, 'Culture and its relationship to economic change', *Journal of Institutional and Theoretical Economics*, June.
JONES (2003)	E. L. Jones, 'The revival of cultural explanation in economics', *Economic Affairs*, December.
JUDD *et al.* (1988)	Richard J. Judd, William T. Greenwood and Fred W. Becker (eds), *Small Business in a Regulated Economy*, Quorum.
KALDOR (1996)	Nicholas Kaldor, *Causes of Growth and Stagnation in the World Economy* (Carlo Filippini, Ferdinando Targetti and A. P. Thirlwell eds), Cambridge University Press.
KEEBLE *et al.* (1991)	D. Keeble, J. Bryson and P. Wood, 'Small firms, business services and regional development in the UK: some empirical findings', *Regional Studies,* 25.

KING (1996)
Kenneth King, *Jua Kali Kenya: Change and Development in an Informal Economy 1970–95*, East African Educational Publishers.

KIRBY & ROSE (1994)
M. W. Kirby and M. B. Rose (eds), *Business Enterprise in Modern Britain*, Routledge.

KIRCHHOFF (1994)
Bruce A. Kirchhoff, *Entrepreneurship and Dynamic Capitalism*, Praeger.

KITCHING & BLACKBURN (2002)
John Kitching and Robert Blackburn, *The Nature of Training and Motivation to Train in Small Firms*, Department for Education and Skills.

KON & STOREY (2003)
Y. Kon and D. J. Storey, 'A theory of discouraged borrowers', *Small Business Economics,* August.

KRUGMAN (1994)
Paul Krugman, 'The myth of Asia's miracle', *Foreign Affairs*, November–December.

KRUGMAN (1999)
Paul Krugman, *The Return of Depression Economics*, W.W. Norton.

KUNDU & KATZ (2003)
Simit K. Kundo and Jerome A. Katz, 'Born-international SMEs: bi-level impacts of resources and intentions', *Small Business Economics*, February.

KUO & LI (2003)
Hsien-Chang Kuo and Yang Li, 'A Dynamic Decision Model of SMEs FDI', *Small Business Economics*, May.

LAZONICK (1991)
William Lazonick, *Business Organisation and the Myth of the Market Economy*, Cambridge University Press.

LEACH (1992)
Peter Leach, *The Stoy Hayward Guide to the Family Business*, Kogan Page.

LEYSHON (1987)
Alan Leyshon et al, *Saturation Survey in the Greater Glasgow Area*, prepared for the Department of Employment, mimeo.

LIEDHOLM (2001)
Carl Liedholm, *Small Firm Dynamics: Evidence from Africa and Latin America*, World Bank, mimeo.

LIEDHOLM & MEAD (1993)
Carl Liedholm and Donald C. Mead, *Small Scale Industries in Developing Countries: Empirical Evidence and Policy Implications*, Michigan State University, mimeo.

LIEDHOLM & MEAD (1999)
Carl Liedholm and Donald C. Mead, *Small Enterprises and Economic Development: The Dynamics of Micro and Small Enterprises*, Routledge.

LINDELOF & LOFSTIN (2003)
Peter Lindelof and Hans Lofstin, 'Science park location and new technology-based firms in Sweden: implications for strategy and performance', *Small Business Economics*, May.

LOVE & MYLENKO (2003) — Inessa Love and Nataliya Mylenko, *Credit Reporting and Financing Constraints*, World Bank Policy Research Working Paper, 3142.

MacCULLOCH (2001) — Fiona MacCulloch, 'Government administrative burdens on SME in East Africa', *Economic Affairs*, 21(2), June.

MADDISON (1991) — Angus Maddison, *Dynamic Forces in Capitalist Development: A Long-Run Comparative View*, Oxford University Press.

MADDISON (1998) — Angus Maddison, *Chinese Economic Performance in the Long Run*, OECD Development Centre.

MADDISON (2001) — Angus Maddison, *The World Economy: A Millennial Perspective*, OECD.

MADDISON *et al.* (2002) — Angus Maddison, D. S. Prasada Rao and William F. Shepherd (eds), *The Asian Economies in the Twentieth Century*, Edward Elgar.

MAGNUSSON & OTTOSSON (2001) — Lars Magnusson and Jan Ottosson (eds), *The State: Regulation and the Economy*, Edward Elgar.

MARSHALL (1919) — Alfred Marshall, *Industry and Trade*, Macmillan.

MARSHALL (1961) — Alfred Marshall, *Principles of Economics*, Macmillan (1st edition 1890).

MARX (1867) — Karl Marx, *Capital, I*, Dent Everyman's Library (1957).

MASON & HARRISON (2000) — Colin M. Mason and Richard T. Harrison, 'The size of the informal venture capital market in the UK', *Small Business Economics*, September.

MASSEY *et al.* (1992) — D. Massey, P. Quintas and D. Wield, *High-Tech Fantasies: Science Parks in Society, Science and Space*, Routledge.

MATHIAS (1983) — Peter Mathias, *The First Industrial Nation*, 2nd edition, Routledge.

MATHIAS & DAVIS (1989) — Peter Mathias and John A. Davis, *The First Industrial Revolution*, Routledge.

MAULA & MURRAY (2000) — M. Maula and G. Murray, *Corporate Venture Capital and the Creation of US Public Companies: The Impact of Sources of Venture Capital on the Performance of Portfolio Companies*, Helsinki University of Technology, mimeo.

MAULA & MURRAY (2001) — M. Maula and G. Murray, *Corporate Venture Capital and the Exercise of the Options to Acquire*, Helsinki University of Technology, mimeo.

McNALLY (1997) — K. McNally, *Corporate Venture Capital: Bridging the Equity Gap in the Small Business Sector*, Routledge.

MEAD (1994)   Donald C. Mead, *The Contribution of Small Enterprises to Employment Growth in Southern Africa*, USAID Gemini Project, mimeo.

MEADE (1978)   *The Structure and Reform of Direct Taxation*, Report of a Committee chaired by J.E. Meade, Institute of Fiscal Studies, Allen & Unwin.

MEAGER *et al.* (2003)   Nigel Meager, Peter Bates and Marc Cowling, 'An evaluation of business start-up support for young people', *National Institute Economic Review*, 4, October.

MEYER (1992)   Carrie A. Meyer, 'A step back as donors shift institution building from the public to the "private" sector', *World Development*, August.

MITI (1991)   *Small Business in Japan,* White Paper on Small and Medium Enterprises, Small and Medium Enterprise Agency, MITI.

MITI (1995)   *Small Business in Japan*, White Paper by Small and Medium Enterprise Agency, MITI.

MOKYR (2002)   Joel Mokyr, *The Gifts of Athena: Historical Origins of the Knowledge Economy*, Princeton University Press.

MOORE & GARNSEY (1991)   I. Moore and E. Garnsey, *Funding for Innovation in Small Firms: The Role of Government*, Management Studies Research Paper, 13, University of Cambridge.

MORSEL (1987)   Henri Morsel, 'Entreprises', in *Dictionnaire d'histoire économique de 1800 a nos jours*, Hatier.

MOSKOWITZ & VISSING (2002)   Tobias J. Moskowitz and Annette Vissing, 'The returns to entrepreneurial investment: a private equity premium puzzle?', *American Economic Review*, September.

MULHERN & STEWART (2003)   Alan Mulhern and Chris Stewart, 'Long-term decline of small and medium size enterprise share', *Small Business Economics*, November.

NAO (1994)   National Audit Office, *HM Customs and Excise: Cost to Business of Complying with VAT Requirements*, HMSO.

NAO (2001)   National Audit Office, *Better Regulation: Making Good Use of Regulatory Impact Assessments*.

NELSON (1993)   Richard R. Nelson (ed.), *National Innovation Systems*, Oxford University Press.

NELSON & PACK (1997)   Richard R. Nelson and Howard Pack, *The Asian Miracle and Modern Growth Theory*, World Bank, mimeo.

NFIB (2000)   *Small Business Policy Guide*, National Federation of Independent Business.

NIESR (1989)	National Institute of Economic and Social Research, *Productivity, Education and Training: Britain and Other Countries Compared.*
NORTH (1981)	Douglass C. North, *Structure and Change in Economic History*, W.W. Norton.
NSSBF (1993)	National Survey of Small Business Finance. Federal Reserve Bank of New York.
NUGENT & YHEE (2002)	Jeffrey B. Nugent and Seung-Jae Yhee, 'Small and medium enterprises in Korea: achievements, constraints and policy issues', *Small Business Economics*, February–May.
OAKESHOTT (1962)	Michael Joseph Oakeshott, *Rationalism in Politics and Other Essays*, Methuen, new and expanded edition, Liberty Fund (1991).
OAKEY (1994)	Ray Oakey (ed.), *New Technology Based Firms in the 1990s*, Paul Chapman.
OAKEY (1995)	Ray Oakey, *High-Technology New Firms*, Paul Chapman.
ODAKA & SAWAI (1999)	Konosuke Odaka and Minoru Sawai (eds), *Small Firms, Large Concerns*, Oxford University Press.
OECD (1999)	*Strategic Business Services.*
OECD (2000)	*Employment Outlook*, June.
OFT (2003)	Office of Fair Trading, *The Regulation of Licensed Taxi and PHV Services in the UK.*
OLSON (1982)	Mancur Olson, *The Rise and Decline of Nations: Economic Growth, Stagflation and Social Rigidities*, Yale University Press.
PARKER (1996)	Joan C. Parker, *Micro and Small Scale Enterprises in Zambia: Results of the 1996 National Survey*, Development Alternatives Inc./Bannock Consulting, for Overseas Development Administration (ODA), mimeo.
PARRIS (1968)	Addison W. Parris, *The Small Business Administration*, Praeger.
PATTON *et al.* (2000)	Dean Patton, Sue Marlow and Paul Hannon, 'The relationship between training and small firm performance: research frameworks and lost quests', *International Small Business Journal*, October–December.
PEACOCK (1978)	Alan Peacock, 'Do we need to reform direct taxes?', *Lloyds Bank Review*, 5(1).
PEACOCK *et al.* (1984)	Alan Peacock (ed.), *The Regulation Game*, Basil Blackwell.
PENROSE (1959)	Edith T. Penrose, *The Theory of the Growth of the Firm*, Basil Blackwell.
PIORE & SABEL (1984)	Michael J. Piore and Charles F. Sabel, *The Second Industrial Divide: Possibilities for Prosperity*, Basic Books.

POLANYI (2001)   Karl Polanyi, *The Great Transformation*, 2nd
                        Beacon Paperback edition (1st edition 1994).

PRAIS (1976)   S. J. Prais, *The Evolution of Giant Firms in
                        Britain*, Cambridge University Press.

PRATTEN (1971)   C. F. Pratten, *Economies of Scale in
                        Manufacturing Industry*, Cambridge University
                        Press.

PRINGLE (1994)   Robert Pringle, *Invisible Earnings by Small
                        Firms*, Graham Bannock & Partners for British
                        Overseas Trade Board.

RICKETTS (2002)   Martin Ricketts, *The Economics of Business
                        Enterprise*, Edward Elgar.

RILEY (1995)   Charles A. Riley, II, *Small Business, Big Politics,*
                        Petersons/Pacesetter Books.

ROBBINS *et al.* (2000) D. Keith Robbins, Louis J. Pantuosco, Darrell F.
                        Parker and Barbara K. Fuller, 'An empirical
                        assessment of the contribution of small business
                        employment to US state economic
                        performance', *Small Business Economics*.

ROBINSON (1933)   Joan Robinson, *The Economics of Imperfect
                        Competition*, Macmillan.

ROBSON (1996)   M. T. Robson, Macro-economic factors in the
                        birth and death of UK firms: evidence from
                        quarterly VAT registrations, *The Manchester
                        School of Economic and Social Studies*, 64(2).

ROBSON & BENNETT   Paul J. A. Robson and Robert J. Bennett, 'SME
(2000a)   growth: the relationship with business advice and
                        external collaboration', *Small Business
                        Economics,* November.

ROBSON & BENNETT   Paul J. A. Robson and Robert J. Bennett, 'SME
(2000b)   growth: the relationship with business advice and
                        external collaboration', *Small Business
                        Economics,* November.

ROMER (1986)   P. Romer, 'Increasing returns and long run
                        growth', *Journal of Political Economy*, 94(5).

ROPER (1999)   Stephen Roper, 'Under-reporting of R&D in
                        small firms: the impact on international R&D
                        comparisons', *Small Business Economics*, March.

SABEL & ZEITLIN (1997) Charles F. Sabel and Jonathan Zeitlin (eds),
                        *World of Possibilities: Flexibility and Mass
                        Production in Western Industrialisation*,
                        Cambridge University Press.

SAMUELSON &   Paul A. Samuelson and William D. Nordhaus,
NORDHAUS (2001)   *Economics*, 17th edition, McGraw-Hill.

SANDFORD (1984)   Cedric Sandford, *Economics of Public Finance*,
                        Pergamon.

SANDFORD (1995)   Cedric Sandford (ed.), *Tax Compliance Costs:
                        Measurement and Policy*, Fiscal Publications.

SANDFORD *et al.* (1981)   Cedric Sandford, Michael Godwin, Peter Hardwick and Ian Butterworth, *Costs and Benefits of VAT*, Heinemann.

SANDFORD *et al.* (1989)   Cedric Sandford, Michael Godwin and Peter Hardwick, *Administrative and Compliance Costs of Taxation*, Fiscal Publications.

SBA (1987)   *The State of Small Business*, US Government Printing Office.

SBA (1994)   *The State of Small Business*, US Government Printing Office.

SBA (2001)   *The State of Small Business*, US Government Printing Office.

SBC (2003)   *Measuring Training in Small Firms: The Small Business Council's Perspective.*

SBS (2003)   *The Small Business Service: Annual Report and Accounts 2002–03*, DTI.

SCHERER (1970)   F. M. Scherer, *Industrial Market Structure and Economic Performance*, Rand McNally.

SCHIFFER & WEDER (2001)   Mirjam Schiffer and Beatrice Weder, *Firm Size and the Business Environment: Worldwide Survey Results*, International Finance Corporation Discussion Paper, 43.

SCHMALENSEE & WILLIG (1989)   Richard Schmalensee and Robert Willig (eds), *Handbook of Industrial Organisation*, North-Holland.

SCHUMACHER (1973)   E.T. Schumacher, *Small is Beautiful*, Blond Briggs.

SCHUMPETER (1934)   Joseph A. Schumpeter, *The Theory of Economic Development: An Enquiry into Profits, Capital, Credit, Interest and the Business Cycle* (translated 1959), Harvard.

SCHUMPETER (1943)   J. A. Schumpeter, *Capitalism, Socialism and Democracy*, George Allen & Unwin (1954).

SCITOVSKY (1952)   Tibor Scitovsky, *Welfare and Competition,* Allen & Unwin.

SEGENBERGER *et al.* (1990)   W. Segenberger, G. W. Loveman and M. J. Piore, *The Re-Emergence of Small Enterprises: Industrial Restructuring in Industrialised Countries*, International Institute for Labour Studies.

SERVAN-SCHREIBER (1968)   J. J. Servan-Schreiber, *The American Challenge* (first published as *Le Défi Americaine*, 1967).

SEXTON & LANDSTROM (1999)   D. Sexton and H. Landstrom (eds), *Handbook of Entrepreneurship*, Blackwell.

SKIM (1984)   SKIM Industrial Market Research, *International Small Business Survey*, Rotterdam.

SLADE (1998)   Margaret Slade, 'Beer and the tie: did divestiture of brewer-owned public houses lead to higher beer prices?', *Economic Journal,* May.

SMETS & DOMBRECHT (2001)   Jan Smets and Michel Dombrecht, *How to Promote Economic Growth in the Euro Area*, Edward Elgar.

SMITH (1776)   Adam Smith, *An Inquiry into the Nature and Causes of the Wealth of Nations*, Modern Library, Random House (1937).

STANWORTH & CURRAN (1973)   M. J. K. Stanworth and J. Curran, *Management Motivation in the Smaller Business*, Gower Press.

STANWORTH & GRAY (1991)   John Stanworth and Colin Gray (eds), *Bolton 20 Years On: The Small Firm in the 1990s*, Paul Chapman.

STEINDL (1945)   J. Steindl, *Small and Big Business*, Basil Blackwell.

STIGLER (1950)   George J. Stigler, 'Monopoly and oligopoly by merger', *American Economic Review*, May.

STIGLITZ & WEISS (1981)   J. Stiglitz and A. Weiss, 'Credit rationing in markets with imperfect information', *American Economic Review*, 71.

STOREY (1994)   D.J. Storey, *Understanding the Small Business Sector*, Routledge.

STOREY (2000)   D.J. Storey (ed.), *Small Business: Critical Perspectives on Business and Management, II*, Routledge.

STOREY & WESTHEAD (1966)   D.J. Storey and P. Westhead, 'Management training and small firm performance: why is the link so weak?' *International Small Business Journal*, July–September.

STOREY *et al.* (1987)   David Storey, Kevin Keasey, Robert Watson and Pooran Wynarczyk, *The Performance of Small Firms: Profits, Jobs and Failures*, Croom Helm.

SYKES (2002)   Andrew Sykes, 'Delivering the benefits', *The Financial Regulator,* March.

TAMBUNAN (2000)   Tulus Taki Hamonangan Tambunan, *Development of Small Scale Industries during the New Order Government in Indonesia*, Ashgate.

TERAOKA (1996)   Hiroshi Teraoka, *Economic Development and Innovation: An Introduction to the History of Small and Medium-sized Enterprises and Public Policy for SME Development in Japan*, Osaka International Center of the Japan International Co-operation Agency.

THOMAS (1992)   J. J. Thomas, *Informal Economic Activity*, Harvester Wheatsheaf.

WANG & YAO (2002)   Yueping Wang and Yang Yao, 'Market reforms, technological capabilities and the performance of small enterprises in China', *Small Business Economics,* February–May.

WARNER (2003)   Malcolm Warner (ed.), *The Future of Chinese Management*, Frank Cass.

WATKINS *et al.* (1982)   David Watkins, John Stanworth and Ava Westrip (eds), *Stimulating Small Firms*, Gower.

WILSON (1979)   Wilson Committee, *Interim Report on the Financing of Small Firms*, HMSO.

WOOD (1994)   W. C. Wood, 'Primary benefits, secondary benefits and the evaluation of small business assistance programs', *Journal of Small Business Management*, July.

WORLD BANK (1994)   *Adjustment in Africa.*

WORLD BANK (2003)   *Doing Business, 2004.*

WREN & STOREY (2002)   C. Wren and D. J. Storey, 'Evaluating the effect of soft support upon small business performance', *Oxford Economic Papers*, 54.

Index

Note: the letter 'n' following a page numbers indicates a note.